Metropolitan College of NY
Library - 7th Floor
60 West Street
New York, NY 10006

Sex Offenders, Stigma, and Social Control

CRITICAL ISSUES IN CRIME AND SOCIETY

Raymond J. Michalowski, Series Editor

Critical Issues in Crime and Society is oriented toward critical analysis of contemporary problems in crime and justice. The series is open to a broad range of topics including specific types of crime, wrongful behavior by economically or politically powerful actors, controversies over justice system practices, and issues related to the intersection of identity, crime, and justice. It is committed to offering thoughtful works that will be accessible to scholars and professional criminologists, general readers, and students.

For a list of titles in the series, see the last page of the book.

Sex Offenders, Stigma, and Social Control

DIANA RICKARD

RUTGERS UNIVERSITY PRESS
New Brunswick, New Jersey, and London

LIBRARY OF CONGRESS CATALOGING-IN-PUBLICATION DATA

Names: Rickard, Diana, 1961–
Title: Sex offenders, stigma, and social control / Diana Rickard.
Description: New Brunswick, New Jersey : Rutgers University
   Press, [2016] | Series: Critical Issues in crime and society |
   Includes bibliographical references and index.
Identifiers: LCCN 2015037349 | ISBN 9780813578293 (hardcover : alk. paper)
   | ISBN 9780813578309 (pbk. : alk. paper) | ISBN 9780813578316
   (e-book (epub)) | ISBN 9780813578323 (e-book (web pdf))
Subjects: LCSH: Sex offenders—United States—Social conditions. |
Sex offenders—Rehabilitation—United States. | Probation—United States. |
Stigma (Social psychology)—United States. | Marginality, Social—United States.
Classification: LCC HV6592 .R53 2016 | DDC 364.15/30973—dc23
LC record available at http://lccn.loc.gov/2015037349

A British Cataloging-in-Publication record for this book is
available from the British Library.

Copyright © 2016 by Diana Rickard
All rights reserved

No part of this book may be reproduced or utilized in any form or by any means, electronic or mechanical, or by any information storage and retrieval system, without written permission from the publisher. Please contact Rutgers University Press, 106 Somerset Street, New Brunswick, NJ 08901. The only exception to this prohibition is "fair use" as defined by U.S. copyright law.

Visit our website: http://rutgerspress.rutgers.edu

Manufactured in the United States of America

CONTENTS

	Acknowledgments	*vii*
1	*Toward a Sociology of Sexual Offense*	1
2	*Constructing the Offense*	20
3	*Community Bonds*	65
4	*Severed Bonds*	88
5	*Strategies to Reestablish Social Bonds*	133
6	*Personal Stories and Public Policy*	163
	Appendix	175
	Bibliography	179
	Index	187

Acknowledgments

For their intellectual guidance, insight, and support of this project I would like to thank Rebecca Tiger, Karen Starr, Lynn Chancer, Bill Kornblum, Karen Terry, Michael Jacobson, and Barbara Katz Rothman.

Sex Offenders, Stigma, and Social Control

CHAPTER 1

Toward a Sociology of Sexual Offense

SEX OFFENDER POLICIES: A SOCIOPOLITICAL CONTEXT

CURRENT SEX OFFENDER POLICIES are an important aspect of what critical criminologists have identified as the "new penology"—a new era of punishment characterized by the decline of the rehabilitative ideal, the reemergence of expressive and retributive justice practices, an expansion of punitive methods of social control, and the management of ever larger segments of the population by the social control apparatus (Feeley & Simon, 1992; Garland, 2001a; Simon, 2000; Zimring, 2001).

The sex offender legislation that began in the 1990s evolved in the midst of the nation's exploding incarceration rate. Since the 1970s the US rate of imprisonment has been steadily increasing and is now eight times higher than during that decade. No other country imprisons as high a percentage of its population (Jacobson, 2005, p. 5). During the last quarter of the twentieth century crime emerged as a central feature of electoral politics, both nationally and locally (Beckett, 1997; Simon, 2000), and the United States has witnessed a transformation of criminal justice practices that include the blurring of the line between inside and outside of the system through an expansion of punitive methods of social control into the community (Feeley & Simon, 1992; Wacquant, 2001). This "carceral state" is characterized by a form of governance where "surveillance becomes routine, and a crime-centered approach shapes the activities of functionaries working in offices unrelated to the penitentiary" (Lancaster, 2011, p. 141). With a continually increasing proportion of the population "being directly managed by the criminal justice system" (Simon, 2000) in their lives outside of an institution (on probation and/or parole and/or subject to registration/notification policies), the noninstitutional world for many begins to take on characteristics of the "total institution" (Goffman, 1990).

The new penology coexists within a climate of populist punitiveness that emphasizes zero-sum rhetoric and expressive and retributive forms of punishment (ibid.). In this framework, punishment practices are less driven by the practical need to manage classes of deviants, and more driven by the emotional need to express communities' moral outrage. Megan's Law "is premised on the futility" of attempting to treat sex offenders. It employs a symbolic "cordon sanitaire" (Young, 1999) and marks the offender as an outsider in a way that creates a "negative symbolic capital that cannot be shed and will therefore weigh on its bearer for life" (Wacquant, 2001, p. 100).

The new sex offender policies can be seen as part of a larger sociopolitical movement toward "governance through crime" (Simon, 2000; Zimring, 2001, p. 146) that includes the transformation of punishment practices (Simon, 2000). Like crime in general, child sexual abuse has been described as a "valence issue" (Beckett, 1996) in that there is no pro-crime or pro–sex offender lobby. There is no space in public discourse for alternative perspectives. The movement toward governing through crime is accompanied by new forms of political subjectivity. The new rhetoric of criminal issues in general and the sex offender rhetoric in particular locate all salient forms of threat in the deviant individual, and obscure other forms of social, cultural, and political conflict and victimization (Janus, 2006, p. 22). The new era of "punitive justice" mobilizes "anger, resentment or vindictiveness, in contrast to preventative, reformative, or restorative ideals" (Lancaster, 2011, p. 147). Expressing exasperation with the state's ability to prevent serious violent crimes in high-profile cases, Megan's Law places increasing numbers of community-dwelling people under greater civil control, monitored by the state and living under conditions that mark them as a dangerous outsider. Many convicted sex offenders have become "life without form and value, stripped of political and legal rights accorded to the normal citizen" (Spencer, 2009, p. 220).

An in-depth look at the lives of several typical convicted sex offenders—those whose victims were minors and who thus bear the added stigma of "child molester"—allows us to see how larger structural conditions bear down on lived experience, and how this in turn relates to identity maintenance and deviance. The analysis presented here explores the new subjectivity that has emerged as part of this political landscape. The narratives of the men depict crimes that are representative of the larger population of convicted offenders—these are not the dramatically heinous crimes that receive so much media attention.

A Brief Introduction to Study Participants

I felt like maybe ... I'm not even human any more.... I didn't want to go look for a job, I didn't want to leave the house. I just wanted to stay in one place. From there I couldn't wait to get home, like a storm was coming. I couldn't wait to get in the house, lock the door, dim the lights, and just, I felt safe.

Reggie looked down at the table in front of us as he described the feelings of shame and paranoia that overcame him after his arrest. Over the course of two in-depth interviews he discussed his social and professional isolation, and his sense of being marked and stigmatized as an outsider. Because of his criminal conviction, Reggie would have extreme difficulty ever finding legitimate work. In addition to the loss of his means of income and professional status, Reggie also struggled with an internalized sense of profound difference from those around him, doubting that he was "even human anymore." He stated that for two years his self-esteem was so low and his sense of shame so great that he was literally unable to walk around in public with his head held up.

Reggie's offense was different from many other crimes and carried with it the stigma of monstrousness. He was convicted for a sexual offense. A forty-year-old African American man, Reggie had been carrying on a flirtation with a fifteen-year-old girl in his neighborhood, asserting that he had been pursued by her. One day they ended up briefly "fooling around" (kissing and petting with clothes on) before he ended the interaction, saying it was "wrong" because of her age and his marital status. A fight with the girl's father ensued, and when the police were called Reggie was arrested for forcible touching of a minor. He spent ten days in jail, was sentenced to six years on probation, and was required to register with law enforcement as a sex offender for twenty years. He met weekly with his probation officer, who subjected Reggie to random home visits. He was also not allowed to have any pornographic material in his apartment or on his computer.

Reggie was one of six convicted sex offenders I interviewed, hoping to understand the effects of stigma related to criminal justice policies on this growing population. Others in the sample included Terry and Karl, a gay white man in his mid-thirties who worked in the arts. He described an escalating flirtation between himself and a fourteen-year-old openly gay boy. At one point when they were alone together they became intimate and Karl performed oral sex on him. When this information spread to the school's principal, Karl was immediately dismissed from his job as a teacher. He spent a night in jail, was sentenced to six years of probation, and had to register for twenty years. Because he had a complex professional life that required traveling for projects, the conditions of his probation were a continual source of tension for Karl. His experiences with registration were fraught with conflict, exacerbated by the fact that he lived and worked in separate states. He was not allowed to leave the city without permission unless the travel was work-related. He was not allowed to be in any professional relationship or be alone with a person under the age of eighteen.

Reggie and Karl were arrested for first-time offenses, and for incidents that could be classified as statutory—in that the victims were reportedly consenting participants in the interaction (the issues surrounding minors and consent will be more fully explored in Chapter 6). Unlike them, Terry, a white man in his early fifties, had a long history of sexual offending: flashing, public masturbation, frottage (rubbing up against people for sexual gratification), and groping strangers. Terry had thirteen criminal convictions for sex offenses, but stated that "they say that for every arrest there are about a hundred other incidents," indicating that he engaged in these behaviors far more frequently than reflected in his official record (he was asked not to discuss unlawful behavior not already on record). His victims were females between twelve and forty years old. He asserted that he had gotten away with "slaps on the wrist" in the past because the offenses were not taken very seriously. His most recent act, groping the breasts of a twelve-year-old girl, was caught on a video surveillance monitor and released to the local news stations and papers. Because the victim was a minor and the case received so much publicity, the authorities took this last conviction more seriously. When the news spread to his community he was immediately dismissed from his job, excommunicated from his church, and kicked off his sports teams. He was forced to wear a GPS monitoring device and placed under house arrest. He had not yet been sentenced for this last offense at the time of my interview with him.

In addition to these three men, I interviewed an intrafamilial offender, whose victim was his thirteen-year-old stepdaughter, an Internet-based offender who made a date with someone claiming to be a fourteen-year-old girl (and who turned out to be a law enforcement agent), and another statutory offender, a man who had a brief affair with a sixteen-year-old stripper he met at a bachelor party. The term "sex offender" refers to a broad legal category covering a range of offenses from "rape, sexual assault, child molestation, lewd and lascivious acts upon a child, public nudity or exhibitionism, or the possession of certain types of pornography" (Scott & del Busto, 2009). The types of sex offenders in this sample are consistent with the population other researchers have studied. For instance, in one study the sample of twenty-nine interview respondents included 41 percent who were on probation for offenses against minors and an additional 17 percent for "statutory" charges (Meloy, 2006, pp. 73–74). Of this sample, 25 percent included men with "convictions for 'hands off' offenses such as possession of child pornography, public indecency, and Internet solicitation of a minor" (ibid., pp. 73–74). The offenses presented in this larger sample are similar to those reported by the men I interviewed. As in my study, the Meloy research did not include a serial pedophile or someone convicted of the types of brutally violent acts that loom large in public perceptions about sex crimes. Violent offenders and those who commit forcible penetration are more likely to be behind bars. This study examines community-dwelling men who have offended against minors. It is particularly focused on the issues of residing within the community while bearing the stigma of having offended against a minor. This study provides a unique opportunity to consider this form of deviance from the perspective of offenders. The stories of a few men, closely analyzed from a sociological perspective, can offer a deeper understanding of the complex relationship between public policy and lived experience.

Sex Offenders, Stigma, and Social Control provides an analysis of the life histories of six men, exploring the impact of stigma and the ways marginalized social actors make meaning of their experiences. It grew out of a critique of current policies directed against sex offenders, particularly Megan's Law. As I began to explore these policies, my awareness of them as "symbolic gestures" (Meloy, 2006, p. 113) intended to "exclude and banish" (Simon, 2000) led me to consider the possible meanings they have for offenders themselves. Specifically, I wanted to know how individuals who have been cast as monsters and social pariahs construct their sense of self. How does being labeled in this way and controlled by these measures affect one's identity and sense of social being? What impact does it have on identity? This study examines the intersection of mass incarceration, sex offender policy, and the emergence and maintenance of the deviant self.

Policy Impacts on Offenders

Criminologists refer to some consequences of criminal convictions as "collateral" in that they are not formally intended as punishment or necessarily part of criminal statutes. These "invisible" punishments (Travis, 2002) accompany all felonies, and those convicted can lose their rights to public housing, welfare, child support, and education and their parental rights (ibid.). The extreme difficulty and sometimes impossibility of reintegrating into the community after a felony conviction has been described as a form of "civil death" (Chin, 2012), a state in which the offender exists with a degraded social status. Exclusion from civil society can include consequences of social control similar to those described by Goffman in his work on "total institutions" (*Asylums* will be more fully discussed in Chapter 4) (Goffman, 1990). The conditions of felons in the United States, during mass incarceration, are increasingly becoming a crisis of democracy and citizenship. As felons, sex offenders are subject to these sanctions in addition to those imposed on them as sex offenders.

Marking the sex offender as outsider, policies and public opinion can be seen as reflecting a general societal view that this population is considered the most deviant of deviants. In total, sanctions against sex offenders represent "degradation ceremonies" taking place within the courts and the media that ritualize "the destruction of the person denounced," transforming identities through "the destruction of one social object and the constitution of another" (Garfinkel, 1956, p. 421). The new social identity is that of an outcast.

The ways in which this new outcast is affected by social control policies have been studied by numerous researchers. In a survey study of the impact of Megan's Law on 239 sex offenders, negative consequences included "job loss, threats and harassment, property damage, and suffering of household members. A minority of sex offenders reported housing disruption or physical violence following community notification. The majority experienced psychosocial distress such as depression, shame and hopelessness" (Levenson et al., 2007, p. 587). A study of the collateral consequences of current policies found that the most common difficulties involved employment (Tewksbury & Lees, 2006). Other research has shown that offenders report lower levels of self-esteem because of their label (Meloy, 2006, p. 89) and increased feelings of alienation and isolation (ibid., p. 108). These studies have also identified relationship difficulties, stigmatization, acute feelings of vulnerability, and instances of harassment, with approximately half of the respondents reporting verbal harassment (Tewksbury & Lees, 2006). Furthermore, "a smattering of vigilante cases have occurred across the country" with research suggesting that about one-quarter of offenders report being the victim of some sort of vigilante justice (Bedarf, 1995), and approximately 40 percent *worry* about being the victim of harassment (Meloy, 2006)—indicating that the threat has an effect on offenders' inner worlds. A recent double murder of a sex offender and his partner in South Carolina underscores the serious potential for violent retaliation faced by these men (Blinder, 2013). Today's convicted sex offenders living in the community face a number of serious barriers to reintegration as a result of community notification practices. The social consequences of these policies are exacerbated by residency restriction laws that push offenders toward marginal communities such as the "shantytown" under the Julia Tuttle Causeway in Miami (Skipp & Campo-Flores, 2009) and that could prevent an offender from moving in with a supportive family member (Zilney & Zilney, 2009, p. 131). Families have had to relocate because of these restrictions (ibid.). Critiques of the policies and their consequences are addressed in this analysis of the stories of six men, providing individual perspectives on the ways people are impacted and how they grapple with the changes to their lives. *Sex Offenders, Stigma, and Social Control* looks at the stories of individuals grappling with these issues and offers a sociological perspective on their experiences that provides a deeper look into these critiques.

THE SOCIAL CONSTRUCTION OF SEX OFFENDERS: A MORAL PANIC PERSPECTIVE

Current sex offender policies—the punitive measures that became cemented in the 1990s—have been described by Philip Jenkins as one of several waves of "moral panics" around child molesters (1998). This phenomenon can be defined "as any mass movement that emerges in response to a false, exaggerated, or ill-defined moral threat to society and proposes to address this threat through punitive measures: tougher enforcement, 'zero tolerance,' new laws, communal vigilance, violent purges" (Lancaster, 2011, p. 23). These dynamics describe the legislation cycles around sex offenses, which have been marked by swift public responses to atypical high-profile sex crimes.

In *Moral Panic: Changing Concepts of the Child Molester in Modern America* (1998), Jenkins argues that the United States has witnessed several distinct waves of "panic" around sex crimes, each encompassing a proliferation of fictional media depicting horrible sex crimes (the television crime drama *Law & Order: SVU* being just one contemporary example) as well as heightened public concern generated and represented by sensational news media stories. Addressing contemporary legislation, Jenkins identifies the rise of the child protection movement from the late 1970s to the mid-1980s as a significant precursor. This movement generated fears about children's well-being that culminated in a panic regarding child pornography, Internet stalking, child care abuse, and ritual abuse. This era laid the foundation for the panic of the 1990s surrounding sex offenders. National concern about child sexual abuse grew out of growing worries with child abuse in general. Sexual abuse of children was easily enfolded into a morality issue for conservative politicians taking family values stances against pornography (ibid., p. 121). As the feminist movement mobilized, it brought national attention to rape, framing the crime as a pervasive issue in patriarchal culture. It raised awareness of women's harassment and victimization and ushered in the establishment of national rape shield laws (ibid., p. 125). Child sexual abuse then gained momentum as a social problem in the media and was often referred to as an "epidemic" (ibid., p. 138). Moving away from the incestuous perpetrator who was the focus of many feminist critiques, the media eventually refocused on the threats posed by the stranger, who was once again portrayed as a compulsive predator (ibid., p. 189).

The 1990s heralded a number of legislative initiatives pertaining to sex offenders in the community that can be seen as attempts to make visible their "otherness." In addition to stricter monitoring of offenders on probation and parole, these initiatives are particularly distinctive in that they mandate monitoring beyond the length of the criminal sentence in the form of registration and community notification.

CURRENT SEX OFFENDER POLICIES

The first action in the spate of legislation passed during the 1990s was in Washington State in 1990 and affected all sex offenders, regardless of whether they are on probation or parole, or whether they have completed their criminal sentences. The Washington Community Protection Act was a legislative initiative created in response to the depraved sexual assaults, mutilations, and murders of young boys committed by repeat offender Earl Shriner (Janus, 2006, p. 14; Jenkins, 1998, p. 183; Terry, 2006, p. 183; Zilney & Zilney, 2009, p. 84). Although Shriner had verbalized his plans to commit atrocious crimes upon his release from a decadelong prison sentence, the community had no way to contain or manage him or to protect themselves. The Community Protection Act contains provisions for law enforcement agencies to provide information about released sexual offenders to members of the community, punishing them "as much for their predicted future dangerousness as for the specific act that brought them into contact with the criminal justice system" (Jenkins, 1998, p. 191). Within five years similar laws were adopted in five states and were under consideration in forty others.

In 1994 the federal government passed the Jacob Wetterling Act within the Violent Crime Control and Enforcement Act. This legislation established funds for states to maintain a registry of individuals convicted of sex crimes against children and was passed in response to the kidnapping of a twelve-year-old boy by a released sex offender (Jenkins, 1998; KlaasKids, 2009; Petrosino & Petrosino, 1999; Terry, 2006, p. 184; Zilney & Zilney, 2009, p. 85). Although they vary from state to state, registration laws require offenders to provide identifying information to law enforcement agencies. This typically includes their name, address, photographs, fingerprints, and their criminal record (Center for Sex Offender Management). The purpose of sex offender registration is to facilitate law enforcement's investigation of new sex crimes (ibid.). In 1996, President Bill Clinton amended the popular 1994 Crime Bill and mandated all states to establish registries "or risk losing federal funding for state and local law enforcement" (Jones, 1999; Terry, 2006, p. 184). Thus Clinton countered accusations that he was soft on "traditional morality and family values" (Jenkins, 1998, p. 198). In 1997 a national database and monitoring system was established. The wave of legislation continued into the new century, and as recently as 2006 President Bush signed the Adam Walsh Child Protection and Safety Act, which "requires the US Justice

Department to create a publicly accessible Internet-based national sex offender database that allows users to specify a search radius across state lines" (KlaasKids, 2009).

The hallmark of these initiatives that marked a cultural milestone was New Jersey's Megan's Law, passed quickly in response to the brutal rape and murder of seven-year-old Megan Kanka at the hands of released sex offender Jesse Timmendequas (Jenkins, 1998, p. 138; Terry, 2006, p. 35; Zilney & Zilney, 2009, p. 86). The outcry following the case was enormous, and New Jersey legislators introduced a series of bills within months of the murder, "rushing to vote without first holding customary hearings or even working out some details" (Jenkins, 1998, p. 138). Modeled after the Washington State law, this statute mandated registration of released offenders. Yet its significance lies in the fact that Megan's Law highlighted community notification—the distribution of information contained in the registries to the community about released offenders (Tewksbury & Lees, 2006, p. 311). With the passing of this law, community notification "quickly acquired the status of a national movement" and within two years was passed in thirty-five states (Jenkins, 1998, p. 138). Currently all states have a version of Megan's Law.

The implementation of Megan's Law varies from state to state. Differences include the length of registration, methods of notification, and methods of risk assessment (Finn, 1997; Terry, 2006, p. 189). The policy relies on a "containment mode" that maximizes institutional jurisprudence and coordination between agencies (Leon, 2011, p. 114). In general, upon release into the community the offender is assigned a risk level (or tier) based on various assessment measures. Levels include low, moderate, and high risk to the community and determine the extent to which the offender will be monitored. Significantly, there is no "zero risk"—that is, in spite of official statistics indicating that most sex offenders have a relatively low likelihood of committing another sex offense, *all* sex offenders are defined in terms of posing some form of risk to the community.

Community notification can include maintaining a publicly accessible Internet database of information about the offender, providing information to callers of a toll-free number, and sending announcements and flyers to various agencies, community groups, and schools (Jenkins, 1998, p. 138; Terry, 2006, p. 192; Zilney & Zilney, 2009, p. 118). In Ohio a bill was introduced (but defeated) mandating that sex offenders be issued different colored license plates ("Laws, Acts, and Legislation 128th General

Assembly of the State of Ohio"; Zilney & Zilney, 2009, p. 120). Furthermore, "a judge can even request that the offender wear a 'distinctive garb' that will readily identify him as a sex offender (Cooper, 1998), in the manner of the yellow star or hat donned by Jews in the principalities of Medieval Europe and Hitler's Germany" (Wacquant, 2001, p. 20). In addition, there are highway billboard signs in some states announcing information about local sex offenders, and in some others the offender's driver's license contains a special designation (Meloy, 2006, p. 38). In effect, Megan's Law imposes a civil sentence on offenders that is served in conjunction with the term of their criminal sentence and for many years following the completion of their criminal sentence (ten years to life).

Thus sex offenders are assigned a "specially degraded legal status that allows the state to treat them in ways that no other person can be treated. Sexual predators are relegated, as it were, to a 'reduced-rights zone'" (Janus, 2006, p. 5). This has been likened to a "camp" where sex offenders live within the community but are subject to a range of civil sanctions that are so excluding as to create a virtually cordoned off area (Spencer, 2009). Although contested by some legal scholars and the occasional journalist (Terry, 2006, p. 201), community notification has been widely popular among all demographic segments and both major political parties. However, these policies have not been based on empirical research or known facts about sex offenders. As one researcher observed, "American policy toward sex offenders is more extreme in its dependence on stereotypes, more resistant to empirical evidence, and less sympathetic to scientific perspectives" (Zimring, 2004, p. xiii).

Media Amplification

As a powerful vehicle for framing, reproducing, and disseminating issues, the media have played a key role in cementing the general public's notion of the child molester. The media represent the primary and most influential source of information about sex offenders. As one researcher observes, "Media representations of sex crime give the public important cues about how they should perceive the nature and extent of sex crime, how they should think and feel about it, how they should respond to it, and the measures that might be taken to reduce risk" (Mcalinden, 2006, p. 199).

The conception of the child molester as a dangerous, compulsive, and incurable predator is leveraged by politicians in support of child protection policies that are rarely contested. For instance, when California Governor Pete Wilson signed the state's chemical castration bill in 1996, he claimed that child molesters "have a drive to do what they do. As long as they have that drive, they'll keep doing it—unless we do something first.... Three out of four will commit a new offense or parole violation in two years" (quoted in Kincaid, 1998, p. 98). The idea that the sex offender is compulsive and incorrigible is also reinforced in popular movies and TV dramas. A self-assured psychiatrist on *Law & Order: Special Victims Unit* declares that child molesters' desire cannot be "cured," but, at best, through aversion therapy, may be controlled. An investigative reporting program, *To Catch a Predator*, was popular for its technique of luring potential sex offenders to presumed victims, only to be captured and arrested, though it has been criticized for blurring the lines between journalism and law enforcement and for appealing to the baser instincts of the public (Kohm, 2009; Lancaster, 2011, p. 146). Celebrities, who tend to influence public opinion, have also spoken out against child molesters in terms that emphasize their inhumanity and monstrousness. "Dennis Miller, billing himself as an intellectual [said] ... 'if you ever get to a place in your life where you want to fuck or murder a kid, forget prison—just kill yourself, take one for the team'" (Kincaid, 1998, p. 75). This inflammatory rhetoric supports the "naming and shaming campaigns" directed at sex offenders and evidenced in current policies (Mcalinden, 2006, p. 198).

The passionate fears of the public are based on little empirical evidence, and misleading statistics are often used in the service of presenting this horrific view of the sex offender. Whether reflecting or shaping public concern, the construction of the child molester put forth by news and entertainment media complements and supports policies that seek to punish, manage, restrict, and label sex offenders.

Recidivism

Contemporary media portray the sex offender as "inherently recidivist, beyond the capacity for rehabilitation ... incurable, so depraved" (Spencer, 2009, p. 225). Yet how dangerous are sex offenders? The media reflect a consensus that sex offenders have particularly high rates of recidivism (Jenkins, 1998; Radford, 2006; Sample & Bray, 2003; Simon, 1998; Zilney & Zilney, 2009; Zimring, 1996, 2001). The offender is portrayed as a serial abuser, a compulsive pedophile, a stranger to his victim, and a sadist or murderer (Meloy, 2006, p. 7). This image is used by politicians, interests groups, and news media to rally support for harsher punishment practices (Janus, 2006; Jenkins, 1998; Lotke, 1997; Radford, 2006; Simon, 2000). Janus describes the general public's image of the "worst of the worst": "They often seem to lack the essential empathy and conscience that mark human beings. They are 'monsters' and 'beasts.' . . . We have come to think of these men as archetypical sex offenders and have shaped our public policy responses as if all sex offenders fit this mold" (p. 2). Arguing that the public believes in a fantastical image of the archetypal sex offender, Janus posits that this image obfuscates the more commonplace instances of sexual assault, which occurs between family members and acquaintances.

In contrast to this image, official statistics and professional research consistently provide information about sex offenders that is starkly at odds with the dominant stereotype. The majority of children who are molested are victimized by someone they know, as are adult victims (Meloy, 2006, p. 5); few child molesters actually fit the criteria for "pedophilia" (i.e., they are not predominately sexually attracted to children and generally prefer adult sexual partners) (Finkelhor, 1984; Groth & Birnbaum, 1979; Pryor, 1996). Murder and brutal force are extremely rare (Jenkins, 1998; Simon, 2000; Snyder, 2003; Zimring, 2001).

Most significantly, research consistently demonstrates that sex offenders do not have particularly high rates of recidivism. Although legislators and news media have claimed extreme rates as high as 95 percent (Jenkins, 1998; Kincaid, 1998; Lotke, 1997) criminologists have argued that such claims are overreported and usually "simply false" (Zimring, cited in Lotke, 1997). In fact, sex offenders are less likely to reoffend than any other type of criminal, with the exception of murderers (Sample & Bray, 2003, p. 72). Significantly, virtually every class of offenders has a higher rate of recidivism than sex offenders. The Bureau of Justice Statistics reports that as few 5 percent (Snyder, 2003) commit other sex crimes within five years. Other studies report that 4.5 percent (Meloy, 2005), 12.7 percent (Furby, Weinrott, & Blackshaw, 1989), 12 percent (Meloy, 2006, p. 62), and 13.4 percent (Hanson, 1996, 2003) of *untreated* sex offenders recidivate. The Center for Sex Offender Management reports that "the data tells us that between 12% and 24% . . . are known to have repeated their crimes" (Center for Sex Offender Management). Zilney and Zilney report recidivism rates from 5 to 24 percent (2009, p. 114).

While perpetrators of awful crimes do exist, and a subset of these men do have a likelihood of repeating offenses, the vast majority of sex offenders are not arrested for another sex crime.

Sex Offenders, Stigma, and Social Control

This study offers a micro-sociological contribution to the moral panic perspective by illuminating those who are vilified. Examining the impact of policies on the offenders themselves, it invokes an implicit and explicit critique of existing criminal justice policies. The narratives presented here highlight the ways that sex offender policy in particular and the broader social problem of mass incarceration and the new penology impact individuals. The challenges these men face, the specific ways they have been marked as outcasts, and the ways they make meaning out of these experiences all contribute to a nuanced understanding of the effects of the penological turn, and also contribute to a critique of this crisis. This is in part accomplished by providing an opportunity to hear otherwise silenced voices, and the in-depth examination of these narratives is made possible by focusing on the stories of a few men.

The inquiry conducted in this book emerges from the sociology of deviance—a broad theoretical framework that seeks to understand the meaning of labeling processes that define and negotiate social transgressions and individual differences. Unlike psychology and criminal justice discourses, as well as some sociological perspectives, this perspective generally does not address why individuals deviate, but rather asks what our rituals of punishment mean for the social group, and explores how social processes are implicated in the trajectory of deviant "careers." The sociology of deviance highlights that social actors—not natural laws or biology—define appropriate sexual conduct, cast sexual activity with children as immoral and unacceptable, and develop and enforce severe negative social sanctions against such behaviors. Framing the offender as a "natural" deviant neglects the social processes involved in defining deviant behavior and constructing deviant selfhood. Although the medical and psychological professions articulate the heterogeneous character of the population of sex offenders, their discourses continue to reify sex offenders *as such*. That is, they ascribe what Howard Becker (1997) has termed a "master status" on the offender, an identity that subsumes all other identities and social roles. This helps us see the ways in which the deviant is defined in full by his or her behavior, and that this social definition, or labeling process, has a powerful impact on the individual.

Erving Goffman's work has been critical in understanding social identity and deviance. Social life for all individuals involves extensive work in controlling and presenting to others of information pertaining to self. In *Stigma: Notes on the Management of Spoiled Identity* (1963), he explores the particular problems that impression management holds for deviant individuals. Goffman defines stigma as a "shameful difference" associated with an individual that separates him or her from the norm, disqualifying the individual from full social acceptance. The stigmatized individual often holds the same beliefs about identity and social norms as mainstream society, and must develop ways of accommodating to the stigma in light of shared social values. Sex offenders have had their identity "spoiled" by their label, and, because of current policies, these convictions have far-reaching consequences.

Convicted sex offenders bear a social stigma that can "discredit" their social identity, and Goffman's definition of spoiled identity clearly applies to them: "it has the effect of cutting him off from society and from himself so that he stands a discredited person facing an unaccepting world" (ibid., p. 19). Current policies seek to make the stigma as visible as possible, and to make discrediting information widely available. Community notification and registration may make impression management highly problematic for the sex offender. Unlike many stigmatized individuals, sex offenders have little capacity for collective action because they are near universally reviled. Internalizing mainstream beliefs about them, sex offenders may distance themselves from their label and others carrying the same stigma. Goffman's work provides a key framework and vocabulary for understanding how stigma is lived in daily life, and how individuals manage "contaminated" aspects of their social identity (ibid., p. 9).

The Study

I chose to examine the issue of sex offenders and identity through narrative analysis. This technique offers a window into how individuals make meaning out of their experiences, manage their stigma, and present a viable—not monstrous—social self to themselves and others. Self-stories, accounts, and personal narratives are part of the presentation of self. The words people use to articulate their identity, behaviors, motives, and interpretations can help us understand the construction of certain aspects of social life.

This study explores the way convicted sex offenders—men who have been labeled and whose social identity has been "spoiled"—construct and present their selves. I collected a small sample of life histories of people convicted of an offense against a minor. I chose this population because I believed they would be vulnerable to the negative connotations surrounding the term "child molester." Using open-ended in-depth interviewing methods, I sought to provide an opportunity for these stigmatized men to construct a narrative of self that would make visible the ways in which their social identity is lived, internalized, and resisted. A total of six men participated in two separate ninety-minute interviews each. Please see the appendix for a more detailed discussion of the research process.

My sociological perspective on sex offenders allowed me to remain open-minded about the men I interviewed. As readers of their narratives we must consider the role of the situation in producing the texts. I am a woman outside the criminal justice system, and not a clear authority figure in their lives. The role gender played in our discussions is unclear. Perhaps the men were more "polite" with me, or less inclined to provide graphic sexual accounts. On the other hand, they might have felt more comfortable discussing sensitive issues if they saw women as more "nurturing." It is important to bracket these narratives as texts produced within the very specific circumstance of our interviews. Furthermore, the men who agreed to be interviewed may have had a particular need to share their stories, and entered the situation motivated to provide a particular narrative account of their actions.

The use of case studies in the social sciences is problematic in numerous ways and raises problems of truth, objectivity, and the relationship between researcher and subject (Denzin, 1990). The cases presented here rely solely on the text produced in two interview sessions, and the generalizability of the analysis is in some ways uncertain. It is important to recognize these cases as textual productions, not testaments of actual facts. The data are the narratives, not the narrators. Yet these personal accounts, analyzed in detail, support and enrich a body of data that point to the negative impacts of civil sanctions against sex offenders in the community, and offer valuable insight into how policy affects the development of deviant selfhood. In this way, these narratives employ the sociology of deviance and labeling theory to those people specifically targeted by the punitive turn. Some sociologists have contributed valuable insights on sex offenders from a symbolic interactionist perspective (Pryor, 1996; Schultz, 2005), but like Diana Scully's important study of convicted rapists, these works focus on motives and do not offer an in-depth understanding of how sex offenders live with stigma.

In the next chapter I introduce the participants of the study, men in their mid-thirties to early fifties who live in New York State. I describe their backgrounds and present an in-depth analysis of the ways in which they constructed their offenses. Here we see these men make meaning out of the events in their lives that led to their label, and the stories they generated are discussed in terms of both unique and shared themes. I explore implications surrounding the fact that many of the participants sexualized their victims, while few invoked the concept of abuse. Some presented their sexual offenses as events over which they had little control because of a sexual momentum in the relationship. One subject relied on constructs of compulsive illness to explain his behavior.

In presenting these narratives, I too am constructing a story, based on my reading of their texts and emphasizing themes that emerged from them. For the most part I explain their stories as attempts to construct their actions as understandable and human, articulating a social self that is worthy of inclusion. Others might read the same texts and find different meanings. For instance, some might read these voices as defensive or inherently dishonest. However, all accounts of deviance contain self-serving elements. What is important here is that the ways these men do so can be seen as attempts to reclaim their basic humanity. As discussed, while none of these men are serial pedophiles, the crimes they committed are representative of the convictions of most community-dwelling offenders under criminal justice supervision. While these men reported disturbing incidents, they stand in contrast to other heinous and sometimes violent crimes that do in fact occur. However these are not the transgressions for which most offenders are subject to registration/ notification policies.

Chapter 3 explores the quality of the social bonds these men experienced prior to their convictions. The general public may have the view that sex offenders are odd people who already live on the margins of society. But in this chapter we see the extent to which all participants were entwined within a social fabric. It describes their various social relationships and activities throughout their lives. In this chapter we see the matrix of their social identities and begin to understand the contexts in which they performed their social selves. For many of the men I interviewed, work emerged as a highly significant forum for expressing social identity. This chapter establishes the social standing and social context of each man and discusses which of these bonds remained intact *after* they were convicted of their sex offenses. Significantly, bonds with immediate family were the strongest.

In Chapter 4 I detail the extent to which the bonds with the community had been severed for each offender. I describe the degree to which each man was officially punished by the criminal justice systems (such as length of prison sentences, probation period, and registration requirements), and the extensive range of restrictions imposed on them. This chapter details the nature of civil death they experienced. The constraints on their civil liberties dictated the quality and rhythm of their day-to-day life in ways that emphasized their dependence on the state. Every participant found himself at least partially unemployed or unemployable because of his conviction; many lost an important social identity, and all were in downwardly mobile financial positions. One had a very different history of deviant behavior than the others, and the ways in which his community bonds were severed are discussed here in detail.

Community notification policies specifically address the identity of offenders, and a few of the men felt that their status as sex offenders could jeopardize their standing in the community. One sex offender had experienced harassment by those he referred to as "the angry villagers." Perhaps most significant, in this chapter I explore the internalization of the offenders' sense of banishment, looking at the ways in which their conviction affected their sense of social self. The specific conditions of probation and parole, and the statutes specifically affecting sex offenders, inserted the system of social control into the lives of all of these men in such a way that their daily routines and sense of autonomy were compromised. Thus their status as outsider was continually reinforced. They lived with an internal sense of isolation wherein rejection and harassment constantly loomed as possibilities.

All of the men were subject to a range of restrictions on their lives that imperiled their connection to their community. In Chapter 5 I investigate the ways in which they coped with the strains created by their "civil death" (Chin, 2012) and stigma. This chapter explores how men most vilified in our society construct themselves. We learn how they create ways of distancing themselves from their label and of rejecting its implications. For the most part they did not see themselves as monsters who should be excommunicated. Instead they employed a variety of strategies to assert their social worthiness. These included espousing mainstream attitudes toward sex offenders as a dangerous "other" and invoking a hierarchy of harm from which they could distance their own actions. Significantly, they constructed the idea of an authentic or "real" self that they contrasted with this idea of the dangerous outsider. As insiders with special knowledge of how the system works, these men were able to critique policies; they reaffirmed the need for the policies to control some offenders, but contrasted themselves with these. In this way they reasserted their deserving ties to the community and the social world that had rejected them, constructing selves worthy of belonging.

In the final chapter I address some questions raised by this study, including the way we define "victim" and "offender." I explore the counternarratives implied in the participants' texts, looking at possible alternate readings and addressing concerns regarding the effects on those they offended against. I examine current critiques of Megan's Law and the implications of the social isolation imposed by current policies, noting that researchers have posited that increased social alienation can play a role in offenders' likelihood of recidivism. Marking individuals as outsiders may lower their stakes in conformity and create extreme stress that might lead to antisocial and inappropriate ways of releasing tension and seeking intimacy, such as sexual offending. I offer some public policy recommendations based on the experiences of the men as well as the findings of other researchers. I consider the future of sexual offending legislation and offer hope that whatever direction policy takes, the perspectives of those most affected by criminal and civil sanctions can be heard within these debates.

Chapter 2

Constructing the Offense

DURING THEIR INTERVIEWS ALL of the offenders provided an extensive description of the offense for which they were convicted. They employed motifs that contributed to their overall presentation of self and that illuminated ways in which they relate to their official label. To make sense of the content of their interviews, I chose to look at them as "stories." As Norman Denzin writes, stories are narratives that are told in structured sequence, and he argues, "We can study experience only through its representations, through the way stories are told" (Denzin, 2001, p. 59).

This project is intended to analyze the texts as instances of the production of meaning by highly stigmatized members of society. As such, it is not intended to scrutinize truth statements—no fact-checking was involved. However, reviewing the extensive amount of text they produced offering their construction of their offense, I found myself at times reading with a counternarrative in mind. I became aware that I was searching for a specific truth, as if underneath the narrative lay "what really happened." In processing the texts I was silently positing an actual truth lying underneath the narrative account, one that I believed to perhaps be obfuscated by their constructions. In other words, at times I caught myself not quite buying into certain aspects of their stories and allowed my own interpretation of their texts to intrude on my reading.

This tension between possible versions of truth, particularly regarding stigmatized behavior or wrongdoing, has been the subject of sociological discourse at least since Sykes and Matza presented their concept of "techniques of neutralizations"—ways wrongdoers neutralize potential experiences of guilt associated with rule violation through reliance on one or more of the techniques the authors identify as justifications that seem valid to the deviant (1957, p. 666). These five include "denial of responsibility" and "denial of victim." The narratives presented in this chapter at times contain statements and versions of events that can be seen as examples of these neutralizations. Such instances are addressed, but the intent of this analysis is not to illustrate these concepts as much as to illuminate ways in which meaning is made. Techniques of neutralization have been criticized for assuming that the wrongdoer shares broader mainstream values about the behavior in questions (Christensen, 2010, p. 570), and for reinforcing the inherently deviant quality of those acts. The analysis presented here is not intended in this way. That is, I avoid making assumptions about the moral allegiances of the offenders at the time of their offense and instead examine their stories as narrative versions of each speaker's truths.

Yet, stories exist within a cultural context of many stories. For any one version of events, several alternative perspectives exist. These may or may not be made explicit by storytellers themselves. But in differing ways narratives speak to their counternarratives. That is, in constructing their account of their offense, the offenders produced texts that are in dialogue with the cultural context in which they exist. Assumptions, stereotypes, and listeners' common sense are all implicated in these narratives, and in some ways these men were defending themselves against these. They were engaged in making meaning within a context of meanings. And I, as listener and reader, heard and read their texts through other meaning packages. For these reasons, the analysis of their constructions of the offense has a dialogical quality that seems to me unavoidable.

The sociological literature on accounts offers some insight into this phenomenon. An account "is a statement made by a social actor to explain unanticipated or untoward behavior" (Scott & Lyman, 1968, p. 46). Here the emphasis is less on neutralizing guilt and more on making behavior understandable to another social actor. Accounts are "social explanations of events" (Orbuch, 1997, p. 456). They place unacceptable behaviors within an existing social context of meanings and allow individuals to gain or regain some esteem and construct a story that establishes order while allowing them to exert control over the meaning of events (ibid., p. 459). Mills's concept of "vocabularies of motives" posits all accounts as socially situated, stating that they "have no value apart from the delimited societal situations for which they are appropriate vocabularies" (1940, p. 913). In the case of this analysis, I look at their narratives as attempts to make meaning within the broader landscape of available vocabularies or motifs. This is based on the premise that speakers and storytellers "draw on the practical ideologies available in their language community in order to render their social action intelligible" (Lea & Auburn, 2001, p. 13). While each of the narratives presented in this chapter is unique to the individual offender, all six can be seen as attempts by participants to make their actions understandable. I present these constructions as self-stories and highlight themes and motifs rather than emphasizing the use of specific neutralizations. These stories are intended to demonstrate the narrator's humanity and worthiness of social inclusion. A number of the elements of these constructions will be revisited in Chapter 5, where I explore offenders' strategies for repairing damaged social bonds.

Raoul, an Intrafamilial Offender

Raoul was a Latino male in his late forties. He asserted that he was well liked by most people and expressed a tolerance and understanding of others' behavior that led me to believe that he was in fact easy to get along with. At the same time, during parts of the conversation he became worked up, anger registering in his voice and body. I involuntarily flinched a number of times in reaction to this strong display of emotion. Raoul made a lot of eye contact and spoke quickly. His narrative was cluttered, rushed, and filled with detail.

Raoul grew up in the outer boroughs of the city with a physically abusive father and depressed mother. He spent much of his youth doing drugs and getting into trouble and was a juvenile offender. He worked at a number of odd jobs throughout his twenties and thirties.

Raoul had been with his wife for twelve years when she began cheating on him. He was incensed by her infidelity and out of anger committed his sexual offense against her thirteen-year-old daughter (his stepdaughter). While the mother was out one morning with her new boyfriend, Raoul went into the girl's room while she slept, pulled down her underpants, and took a Polaroid of her genitals. Raoul was sentenced to fifteen years in prison for sexual assault of a minor. While incarcerated he fought for a sentence reduction and was released after nine years.

During his time in prison Raoul "found God." He described hitting rock bottom and realizing that God would take care of him. When I met with him he was deeply involved in church and his religious views had been a highly significant resource as he faced life challenges and worked on coming to terms with what he viewed was an unjust prison sentence.

Raoul created an extensive and involved narrative of his offense. When he first entered the interview he seemed eager to jump right into the story, and immediately disclosed his official charge and listed some of the contributing factors behind what he did. It seemed highly important for Raoul that his listener understand that the offense was rooted in a long-standing relationship with his wife, and he insisted that the complexities of this relationship were essential to understanding. He spoke with urgency and excitement, and at times mounting indignation and anger.

Raoul could not describe the offense itself without going back twelve years to the beginning of his relationship with his wife. In fact, when asked what was happening at the time of the incident, he quickly reverted to the circumstances when they first met. He offered these details with little prodding and described the offense in what was essentially one long, uninterrupted monologue. When I would make comments encouraging him to focus on the event itself, he expressed frustration with being interrupted and insisted that these details and history were integral to the account of the morning he took the photographs.

The motifs Raoul employed all centered around a sense that he had lost control of his personal life, that he no longer had authority vis-à-vis his wife or the women in his household. He described the years leading up to the event as characterized by "drinking and drugging," which contributed to the "stinking thinking" that enabled him to offend against his stepdaughter.

At the beginning of the first interview he made it clear that he was comfortable discussing his label and his offense.

> My life is an open book. I don't object to saying anything. I got charged with a lewd act on a child. She was my stepdaughter. She was thirteen. I took two photographs of her. There's a story. Me and her mother were pretty much doing a lot of drugs and we [moved] to try and change our lifestyle and better ourselves but after arriving over there the economy was different and a lot of things started to snowball and I ended up meeting some people with drugs and I started doing things I wasn't supposed to be doing.

Indicating that he was at ease talking about his status as a sex offender, in bare language he presented his offense. Talking quickly, with a sense of rattling off explanations that he had gone over many times before, he presented the circumstances surrounding the act. These included the economy, his social life and his friends' actions, and his drug use. Relying on the language of the official charge, he presented himself in terms of the label imposed on him, bestowing authority on the label and granting it reality: "Well I got charged with a lewd act on a child, using a child in sexual performance and possession of child pornography." Describing what he did to his stepdaughter, Raoul said, "I took the photographs, uh, close-ups of, uh, you know, her genital areas. . . . It was a Saturday morning and I went into her room and I nudged her and I told her listen, you want some breakfast, and she just kept like nudging [me]. . . . She had shorts on; I took the shorts off." He spoke awkwardly and was quick to turn attention to the relationship between himself and his wife: "I need to first clarify something. My [wife] used to be my neighbor and when I met her she had three kids. And I lived with her for twelve years and in the process we had two, which you know made it five. The victim . . . when I first came into her life she was [nearly] two years old."

When asked to discuss what he actually did to the girl when she was thirteen, he again anxiously reiterated that one needed to understand the background and context. This seemed significant to me because he was continually asserting that the event could not be seen as isolated, but instead as part of a complex and unfolding social situation. For instance, his family had moved to a town where a relative lived, and the relative ended up moving in with him. These details were presented as key to understanding the nature of the household he was living in. He explained, "It's a combination of things that led to that. It's not something that I just woke up one morning and acted out. No. It was her brother bringing stress to us, because he was staying with us; he was bossing my kids." The brother-in-law's presence in the household disrupted the equilibrium and undermined his authority over the children. This played an important role in his state of mind and contributed to the sense that he was losing control. Detailing the interactions with his brother-in-law as well as the stories related to his wife's infidelity was critical to understanding his mounting anger. His voice became indignant as he explained the months during which he gradually became aware of her "sleeping with this guy" (a coworker), and the events that were part of this gradual awareness were crucial to explaining his increasing frustration and lack of control over the woman in his life. Raoul offered an overview of the offense:

> I'm not trying to minimize, because I know I was wrong. It was my state of mind at the moment, an escalation of bad choices, bad

decisions, my lifestyle that I was living. It was a combination of a lot of things that led to that. Otherwise under other circumstances I would have never. I should have just left. I should have just left. I wanted to leave and I didn't leave and being in the house it just kept eating me up that this woman had me babysitting her kids, our kids, while she was going out to work and getting screwed. And then she's telling her daughter that I'm watching, "that's not your father." You know, so I don't know why I decided to do that. It was something that I just did, because I knew that would hurt her.

Here he framed his action as an "escalation" of choices and decisions, casting himself as a responsible agent who "decided" to retaliate against his wife. He asked rhetorically, "Why did I choose a sex offense? Why did I choose to take . . . ? At that time when I did it, I was on drugs. . . . I was watching pornography, I was doing drugs, my wife was cheating on me, it was like a combination of things." He spoke as if he had listed these before, counting off the contributing factors in a rote way. No one element alone explained what happened. Yet in spite of these issues, he still framed his offense as a choice that he made. He again used the verb "decide" to explain the action that he took to retaliate: "She had me babysitting, you know, her daughter, and she was screwing around with somebody, and I just out of the hurt and betrayal and anger I decided to do something, you know?" The "decision" was made as an effect of his mounting frustration with the loss of his authority in the house and the insult of his wife's infidelity. He expressed a need to act, to regain control over the situation, to show his power.

Explaining why he specifically chose a sexual violation of the stepdaughter as a means of retaliation, he said, "My oldest stepdaughter and my oldest stepson, according to [my wife], they were molested when they were kids by their father. And that was the reason she left the kids' father. Okay now, she always stressed that to me, when we met, I asked her what happened to the kids father, and you know she told me he molested the two oldest ones, not the little one, and that she couldn't live with him. So I pretty much knew that that was a real sensitive spot for her." He presented his reason for taking the photographs as a calculated attempt to find a way that he knew would hurt her mother. He expressed his offense as an opportunity to show his own power and do something that he knew would be significantly painful to her. He deliberately chose something that "was a real sensitive spot." To drive the point home, he made sure that she found the photos: "And I took the pictures and I put them in a card. And I was going to give them to her mom . . . I left them in the room."

Although he presented his action as a conscious decision and choice that he made, he did not justify it as rational.

> But just her telling me that she's not my daughter, kind of like put me in my rebellious state, and stinking thinking. I was saying, well she ain't my daughter. She just kept saying it, and she said it one time too many. But when I came to my senses I said man, she's not my daughter, but she's my daughter's sister, and my son's sister. So, which one is it?
>
> I guess that's just my stinking thinking, you know that's not sensible. That's stinking thinking. That's not thinking. Meaning not thinking logical.

Here he presented two different versions of his cognitive process. On one hand he based his action on his wife's consistent iteration that the stepdaughter was not truly his daughter. He employed this idea in the service of his retaliation—the wife was presented as partially to blame for making this assertion. However, he simultaneously attributed this to faulty reasoning, or "stinking thinking" that included distorting the familial relations that they shared and acting thoughtlessly.

When Raoul explained that his victim was a baby when he met her, he linked himself to a child-rearing function and his familial relationship to her. In fact, he entered his wife's household and assumed the role of "man of the house," with his relationship to the victim being essentially parental. He stated, "So I pretty much raised her . . . I always provided." He constructed her as a baby whom he nurtured through to her adolescence, someone for whom he played a significant role as caregiver and financial provider.

Throughout the narrative of his offense he highlighted the fact that this paternal relationship to his stepchildren was undermined by his wife once she began cheating on him. He explained how his wife provoked him by emphasizing that the victim was not his daughter: "What happened was my wife . . . we were doing drugs and she started screwing around with someone in her job and she started telling her daughter, my stepdaughter, that she didn't have to listen to me, that I wasn't her father. You know, sort of like to get back at me." He directly linked his wife's telling the daughter that she didn't have to listen to him to the infidelity. Her "screwing around with someone" was experienced as an insult, and added to this was the loss of his authority in relation to his stepdaughter. He had lost both roles. He brought up this fact up at ten different points in the narrative, emphasizing that his wife kept reiterating this fact. He experienced this as her baiting him, and expressed great indignation and anger at this tactic: "Now my daughter, the victim in my case, her mother kept telling her that I wasn't her father. And that hurt me, and she was doing it out of spite. 'That's not your father . . . you don't have to listen to him. If you want permission you can ask me, I'm your mother.' And I'm saying to myself, you got a lot of nerve man, after I raised her, and when she needs something, it's 'ask your father.'" He iterated again that he "raised her," and indicated a hypocrisy and lack of justice in his wife's behavior, which displayed disregard and disrespect for the years he had spent parenting her children: "She kept telling my stepdaughter I wasn't her father and I used to say to myself this woman got a lot of balls, you know. She's out there, sleeping with some other guy, she's got me babysitting her daughter. 'Cause it got to a point where she kept saying it so much that I said, okay she's not my daughter." In his construction of the offense, his wife's emphasis on the fact that his stepdaughter was not his biological daughter was presented as the final straw. Eventually the insult became unbearable, and he conceded, with hostile resentment, that he did not have a familial relationship with the girl. In his logic, this made her less off-limits than if she were thought of as his daughter, and weakened the idea of incest in his offense: "After I took those pictures and the mother saw them, she was like, how could you do this to your daughter? Ha ha! Oh, but what were you saying before? What were you saying before? That's not your daughter, you remember? Now I took pictures and now you're telling me what? How could you do this to your daughter? Right. Now you're going to burn me to the third degree and put me on the cross?" He presented his offense as revenge against not only his wife cheating on him, but also her undermining his familial relationship with the victim.

In constructing his victim, Raoul invoked adolescent sexuality and presented the girl as a sexual and provocative character. By so doing, he offered a sort of defense, or mitigating circumstances to his behavior, explaining to some extent why he offended sexually against her. Raoul painted a picture of a household filled with sexually active teens, indicating that he was stimulated by them and had begun to see people of this age range as sexual beings. He stated that the teens in the house dressed provocatively, emphasizing their sexuality. As he argued that not all minors are innocent and that many are sexually active, he began to construct the victim as having sexual agency: "They used to come to the house a lot and I was around a lot of teenagers, you know, a lot of kids, a lot of teenagers, young teenagers; mothers with no fathers who maybe just had like flings or little relationships that didn't work out, but they still happened to bear children. So I was around a lot of teenage girls and my girl wasn't giving me, wasn't showing the right example." He put forth the idea that even young teenagers may be sexually mature and that the teenagers in his life were already parents. He cast the victim as a sexual subject and reiterated this idea several times before introducing an event that he described as key in seeing his stepdaughter as a sexual subject. "My stepdaughter had a friend that was a little older than her, and she was sexually active. She had a boyfriend that was like twenty-two years old; she was only sixteen. And one day my daughter showed me a picture of her mooning the camera. She said, 'Dad, look at this!' And I said, 'Who is this?' 'That's [the friend]' and I knew right then when she showed me the picture I should have stopped her. But my mentality was already being transformed, like this wasn't my daughter." He moved from generalizing about the sexuality of teens to describing an awareness of a specific young girl's body. That it was brought to his attention by his stepdaughter led him to associate the image with her. He was already seeing her as less off-limits, not as his daughter, but as a viable subject sexually available to him. This photo and the fact that it was brought to his attention by his stepdaughter were presented as pivotal in the story of the sexual offense: "So one thing led to another with the pictures. I believe that my victim actually planted that little seed when she exposed those pictures to me, mooning, her friend mooning. Up till that day I really never thought about taking photographs of my stepdaughter. I never did." He argued that the thought of sexually offending against her germinated with her showing him the pictures. In this way she was an active subject who exhibited agency and played a role in the events that unfolded.

In addition to constructing the display of the picture as a catalyst to the offense, Raoul also presented the stepdaughter as acting toward him in seductive ways: "You know for a short period of time I started to think that maybe she even liked me, more than just her father. . . . She would come with me a lot of times, like she would come with me to the store and I would maybe do something I wasn't supposed to, drink or something and she would just like, act like she was older. Like some young girls act like they are older, dress older, and that gave me like an indication." He built a story of their relationship that moved away from the father-daughter theme; she was the one who instigated the transformation of the dynamic. She began to form the beginnings of an adult relationship with him. He again constructed the victim as a sexual subject who played an initial role in transforming the way he saw her. He described her behaviors as initiating the breaking of boundaries in their relationship. At the same time, Raoul recognized that he knew that the line he crossed represented a serious violation: "I took the pictures. But I knew when I was taking the pictures, actually when I was taking them my heart was pounding 'cause I knew it was wrong." Describing his pounding heart, Raoul was physically aware of crossing a line and committing a serious wrong. In spite of all his justifications, when it came down to committing the offense, he recalled that at the moment he knew he shouldn't be doing it.

Raoul often invoked his role as father, husband, partner, and provider more than any other social role in constructing his offense. These roles were a great source of pride for him: "But when I became a father I felt proud, because I did it, I had a son, with my wife and I was living with her and I was working and supporting them so it was a big, important day, and I felt like I got recognition from my family members and friends and I was doing the right thing. I became a man. I wasn't drugging or nothing I was just living a family life." He created a gestalt where becoming a father, being a husband, and supporting his wife constituted manhood and therefore stability of self. Social respectability ("recognition") was granted to him by virtue of performing these roles. "Doing the right thing"—successfully embodying the roles—was contrasted with the drugging he associated with chaos and the "stinking thinking" that contributed to his offense.

He described the events precipitating his offense as a wearing away of his conventional male social role, one that for him was expressed through relationships with women. Without a woman functioning as a wife, he was no longer husband. The girl whom he had raised was seen no longer as "his" but rather simply as the daughter of the woman with whom he no longer had a manhood-reinforcing relationship. The meaning of his offense was filtered through his understanding of his kinship ties, particularly those that reinforced his masculine social identity. Significantly, when he acknowledged the affective and social relationship he had with his stepdaughter, he admitted that he "went beyond the boundaries of a parent," placing the nature of what he did on a continuum of kinship: "I mean I did violate her, but, taking pictures of her private parts it's a violation, okay? Especially a major one for parents or a person trusted in an authoritative position." This was the only instance where he mentioned a violation in and of itself, and immediately acknowledged that the harm was more consequential because the violation was committed by someone in a caretaking position, perhaps a way of expressing "denial of injury" (Sykes & Matza, 1957, p. 667).

The rich narrative detail of Raoul's story can be seen as building the grounds for a socially empathic reading of his story. Going back years in time so that the listener could understand why he felt so angry, Raoul positioned his offense within a context in which his anger could be understood. In this way, he aligned himself with shared social values, particularly those that uphold fidelity and negatively sanction infidelity. Constructing his victim as biologically unrelated to him, he implicitly invoked the incest taboo and presented evidence that he didn't violate this important law. Raoul embedded his offense within a complex romantic history spanning more than twelve years. It seemed urgently important that the listener/reader understand the causes of his anger, because it is through this understanding that his actions might seem less monstrous. Critical to this effort was his appeal to the shared values that sanctify marriage. The injustice of being cuckolded and shut out from his role as caregiver to his stepchildren needed to be communicated to his listener, in order that he, at least in part, be seen as someone who was wronged, and not solely as the wrongdoer.

Tim, an Internet Offender

Tim was a white male in his late thirties. He had an open, somewhat blank face, and gave me an initial sense of affability. But as we spoke he made little eye contact and often his lips were pursed in anger.

The openness of his face began to seem defiant. He was difficult to engage in dialogue, often answering questions with a simple "yes" or "no." He shrugged his shoulders often, indicating a lack of interest in or irritation with the questions. I didn't feel comfortable probing him and was concerned that if I pushed further I would seem intrusive or argumentative. In addition, I was afraid that he would become more openly hostile.

Tim grew up in a close-knit working-class neighborhood in the outer boroughs of the city and was raised by his mother, who had died ten years earlier. Tim's brother became a police officer ("I know [my mother] raised him to be excellent"). Tim was from a large extended family with "over three hundred cousins" and was in close contact with an aunt who often helped out while he was growing up.

Tim reported having had an intense romantic relationship when he was in high school and was married to another woman for less than a year in his early twenties. He briefly dated a woman ten years older than him. But largely there had been few significant romantic relationships in his life. He stated that he currently was unable to date for financial reasons.

He worked for years in a local service industry where he had a lot of interaction with customers over the phone. He enjoyed the social contact the job provided. He had to leave this employment because of a medical issue. At that time he was told he could not take on stressful work and was currently living on disability. The monthly check barely covered his bills, and his life was highly restricted because of his limited means. The most salient aspect of his narrative was his dire financial situation, a subject to which he repeatedly returned, often with marked bitterness in his voice.

Before his medical event Tim had become involved with a girl online who eventually told him she was fourteen. By that time verbal intimacy had developed and the dialogue had become sexually explicit. He continued the dialogue and eventually arranged to meet her to give her a DVD. This girl, however, was not an actual person; Tim was the target of a "what they call sting operation." He was arrested and sentenced to five years on probation and lifetime registration. The Internet sex sting, through monitoring chat rooms and other types of sites, is in fact a common law enforcement practice (Wright, 2009, p. 118). Issues have been raised regarding the emphasis on thoughts or intent in contrast to action, assuming the potential offender would have followed through and thus potentially arresting innocent people (ibid., p. 119).

Tim was not inclined to produce a rich narrative of self. Reticent in the interview, he rarely showed an expressive impulse or any enthusiasm for the endeavor, and offered anecdotes or more detailed stories only a few times—usually in the heat of anger and indignation. For the most part, eliciting this narrative required a fair amount of prodding. At a number of key points he contradicted himself. I did not feel comfortable asking him to explore these tensions and or making them visible during the interviews, as I was intimidated by what I perceived to be hostility and defiance in his tone of voice.

Unlike Raoul, Tim did not generate a long or complex construction of his offense. He told a simple story of being tricked, casting himself as naïvely falling for a trap. Consistent elements included the construction of himself as a passive target, one who did not bear significant responsibility for the events, as he acted under false pretenses. The story he told resonated with an overall motif of powerlessness that characterized his narrative in general. This can be seen, of course, as "denial of responsibility" (Sykes & Matza, 1957, p. 667), but here it seems that Tim's sense of powerlessness resonates with an overall presentation of self as victimized.

Tim was charged with making a date with someone he met online who described herself as fourteen. He was arrested when he arrived at what he thought would be her home: the person with whom he had been "chatting" was what he described as a "federal agent." Tim was formally charged with "attempted dissemination of adult material to a minor," in addition to another charge he could not recall: "I'm not sure of the other charge. I forgot the other charge. I have it at home. I have it written at home. I forget it. I don't memorize it. I try to just put it out of my life right now because I'm trying to get my life back to a normal situation. Even at this time it's still difficult." His refusal to "memorize" the official charge indicated a resistance to the labeling process and suggested that the charge in and of itself had little meaning for him, or rather that he resisted ascribing any potential meanings. Tim did not identify himself with the formal legal definitions of his situation. They represented something that had been imposed on him by the social control apparatus but were incompatible with his presentation of self. Even as he was being interviewed as a sex offender he saw this label as irrelevant. His resistance was active ("I don't memorize it. I try to just put it out of my life") and had the effect of demeaning or undermining the labeling process—he barely recognized, let alone internalized, the official definition of the situation.

This subtle technique of expressing disdain contributed to the overall sense he presented of not having actually done anything wrong: "I never met her. It was all a sting operation. There was no victim involved." Without a "victim involved," Tim could not be said to have harmed anyone. He set himself up as both a victim of a large operation and someone who was arrested in spite of the fact that he had not in fact done anything to an actual minor

In telling his story, Tim presented the person on the other end of the dialogue as an active player in their relationship. He presented her as having had an important role in planning their meeting: "I attempted to meet the person to drop off some films, rated PG films on DVD that she had requested." He described the planned encounter as at least in part a response to her request. The meeting was presented as having been set up by her. Positioning himself as responding to what she wanted, he simultaneously cast her as calling the shots and himself as fulfilling her demands. He was not presenting himself as a predatory agent manifesting willful intent, as much as a somewhat passive participant in a situation over which he had little control.

It is significant that he initially described the planned meeting as purely social. That is, he did not refer to it as a date and emphasized that the main purpose of the meeting was to drop off these presumably nonsexual movies (which he described as "rated PG"): "No sex was supposed to have taken place, no nothing was to have taken place, just to drop off the films for her to watch." He not only framed the encounter as devoid of romantic intent, but presented it as if he were primarily performing a delivery service. In fact, he used the phrase "to drop off" twice. However, it is worth noting that this relationship was formed on a dating website for single people: "It was like, single in [the city] or something. Any age group goes in there." In addition, as will be discussed shortly, Tim's conversation with the person became quite sexually explicit before they arranged to meet.

Tim emphasized that they were engaged in a dialogue for a number of weeks before she stated her age. In fact, he several times reiterated that he did not think she was a teenager during the first few weeks of their dialogues.

Well talking to the girl, I didn't know that she was underage in the beginning. I thought she was just your average female that was around my age or close to it. I didn't think she was that young.

She told me her height, her weight, her hair color. She never told me her age. Till a month after the conversation.

But I didn't know [she was young] at first. It took about a month after I was in conversations with her to tell me her age.

It seemed important to Tim that his listener understand that when he initially engaged this person in online conversation, he assumed she was an adult. He was constructing a story of the building of a relationship between himself and an "average female" that was not based on an age difference. Rather it was presented as an attempt to establish a normal adult social connection. He was also here emphasizing that the dialogue progressed for a month before her age was stated, indicating that over a significant length of time a relationship developed that was premised on one set of assumptions.

He did say that the conversations began to get sexual. Tim emphasized that the explicit conversations occurred only after a social rapport, based on a topic of mutual interest, had been established: "The conversations we had were talking about films and the music industry. And you know, current events that were happening on that particular day.... Nothing out of the ordinary. I mean it started becoming more sexually involved like three weeks later." He stated that at this point he still had not been told her age: "We didn't start talking explicitly until the second week. Or third week after we started talking. And I didn't find out her age until a week after that. Which was like almost a whole month into the conversation." Reiterating how many weeks into their relationship they were before the conversations became explicit, he reinforced his contention that it began as purely social, not lascivious, and that their relationship was based on a nonsexual connection. That this point was important to him suggests that he may have wanted to privilege the nonsexual element of their communication as less deviant, perhaps, or at least as more legitimate, than a sexual dialogue. In so doing, he cast himself as devoid of sexual intent, and subtly reinforced the idea that the meeting between them was to have been innocent.

Tim spoke with an animated feeling of indignation when he described how long they were in communication before he was told that she was fourteen. He was clearly upset that he was allowed to speak with her for so long without being told her age. He felt that allowing the communication to go on for so long was unfair and that he should have been told sooner. Implied in this was the idea that had he known earlier, he would not have continued the conversation or arranged to meet her.

Furthermore, he argued that what happened to him was legally unsound: "I was trying to find out from my lawyers, this is what they call a sting operation. Whatever they call that, entrapment. And he goes no, because you initiated the contact. I said yeah, but they didn't tell me the age until after a month. I mean there's got to be some kind of law with that. And he goes no. And he says you initiated the contact, there's nothing you can do." Again referring to the offense as a "sting operation," he invoked the idea of conspiracy—many agents with power ganging up on the powerless guy. "Entrapment," although a legal term, implicated the agents of social control as predatory and Tim as innocent victim, unwittingly led into a trap. He was not responsible for having fallen for the bait. Once again emphasizing that it was a month into the relationship before he was told, he indicated that this length of time contributes to the seeming dishonesty and illegitimacy of the state actors' actions.

The intensity of the sexual conversations increased over time: "We started talking about going out on a date. And then she started telling me, you know, what would you do on a date, and it went from one thing to another extreme. So it just kept on increasing . . . [it got] very explicit." At this point the nature of the conversations went down a less innocent road, and he presented her as initiating the sexual tone. It was during the "sexually involved" exchanges that the person stated she was a minor. Tim asserted that he should have stopped the conversations at that point, and had trouble explaining why he did not: "I don't know what possessed me to actually continue to talking to her after I found out her age. I should have stopped it. For some reason it didn't click in my mind to stop. And I just continued talking. I couldn't stop." He could not identify his own intentions or motives. Rather, the fact that he continued was presented as a mystery. He was not presenting himself as an active agent, but as someone on auto pilot. At the same time, he was grasping for a reason for his continued contact with the person, articulating a belief that he should have stopped. In so doing he postulated the wrongfulness of his actions: "A stop sign should have went up. Stop talking to her. Don't talk to her; she's fourteen, turn away." Thus, just being told her age should have been enough; continued sexual dialogue with someone that age is wrong. He explained why it was wrong solely in terms of her age: "Because, you know. She's a kid. She's not an adult. She's not at the age of consent. To have an adult conversation." He offered the idea that she lacked legitimacy as a social actor, or that she was not an equal social actor because of her age, and invoked a legalistic argument for why sexual communication with her constituted wrongdoing ("the age of consent").

In addition, Tim made it clear that he was not in fact attracted to teenagers and had always dated adult women: "In fact just prior to talking to her I just came back from . . . meeting a thirty-eight-year-old woman. At that time I was thirty-six, so she was two years older. And she was in the military. . . . My ex-wife was twelve years older than me. I was twenty-nine, she was forty-one." Clearly stating that his propensity is for older women or age-mates, he indicated that he would not have sought out a teenager. He implicitly differentiated himself from the child molester or pedophile and asserted his normal sexuality.

Although he said he did not know why he continued to talk to her, he did offer some theories. He argued that his positive personality traits played a role in preventing him from ending the communications: "And I just continued talking. I couldn't stop. Like I said, I'm a people person, I could talk to anybody. I'm so easy. My brother says I'm too gullible. He says you've always been open and honest and you've always given to people and never taken from people. And he said it right. I'm a giving person. And that's what I am I give people everything I am, I let them take advantage of me." He implied that it was his genuine feeling for people that led him to continue the dialogue, identifying himself with such pro-social traits as "open," "honest," and "giving." These positive characteristics made him more vulnerable and were implicated in his being an easy target for a "sting operation." In particular, he emphasized his "gullibility," using the word three times in explaining why he continued to talk to the person: "I'm still trying to figure it out. I mean I say gullible. That's what I am. I'm gullible. I'm easy. I'm an easy target." Positing himself as easily taken advantage of by dishonest people in positions of power, he sidestepped the fact that he indeed knew he was talking to a minor and instead emphasized that he was set up. He constructed himself as a naïve and trusting victim of active agents of social control.

Tim also offered an additional theory of his continued engagement with the person, proposing that the sexual element of the exchanges exerted a powerful effect on him: "I saw no indication that this person was a minor. Until she told me her age. And at that point I had already gone beyond the line of talking about sex. I was too far gone already." At the point at which she disclosed her age, Tim was deeply involved in a sexually explicit online relationship with her. Saying that he was "too far gone," he implied that he was no longer in control of the situation and constructed his sexuality as overwhelmingly powerful, so much so that he could no longer make choices about his actions or control the course of events.

Tim told his story with a mounting sense of righteous anger at the extent to which he was wronged by the system. In his case there was "no actual victim." Literally no one was harmed (a strong instance of "denial of injury"). Nor did he bear responsibility for the wrong for which he was accused—he was "set up" (denial of responsibility) (Sykes & Matza, 1957, p. 667). He participated in a social dialogue with someone he assumed to be a peer, and when the communications became sexual he still thought he was talking to someone his age. He repeatedly emphasized that she disclosed her age very late into their relationship. He held this fact up as vindicating him and presented himself as a nice guy whose gullibility led him into a trap.

Aaron, a Statutory Offender

Aaron was a fifty-year-old African American man with an energetic and social demeanor. He seemed to enjoy talking, good-naturedly laughed at some of his recent difficulties, and generally presented as self-confident and genial. The interview progressed easily, and there was no discomfort in the situation.

Aaron grew up in the outer boroughs of the city. He was one of five children, all of whom were raised by their single mother. Both his parents were deceased, and he and his siblings remained close. As a teenager and young man Aaron was "not focused" and was not oriented toward school. He used drugs recreationally and occasionally sold marijuana. He was arrested in his early twenties for possession and sentenced to probation.

This experience was "a wake-up call" for him. He had a supportive probation officer who encouraged him to return to school and pursue a career. He began working in human services and had been in that field ever since. He found the work very rewarding both personally and financially. When he was arrested he was a program manager for a large unit.

At the time of the interview Aaron was in the process of divorcing his wife of eighteen years. He reflected that he had trouble in long-term relationships finding a balance between "autonomy and dependence." He had two children with her and one grown child from a previous relationship, and he was immensely proud of all of them.

Aaron was convicted for consensual sex with a minor. That he didn't know "the young lady's" age at the time was repeatedly emphasized. He was eager to tell the story of his offense, which he presented as a "special situation"—involving presumably unique circumstances that distinguished him from what others might think of when they think of "sex offenders." Aaron met the girl at a bachelor's party. She was one of the striptease dancers that were hired as entertainment for the event. He felt an instant connection between them: "And [the girls] were there, doing their thing, and this young lady came out and we—she—when she came and she danced and stuff like that, our eyes just like met. There was just something there." Aaron constructed the girl as different from the other dancers and began a conversation with her based on this perceived difference: "I said, 'You don't really seem like you're comfortable doing this.' And she said, 'You can tell?' and she said, 'This is not—this is like my first or second time doing this.' And me, I said, 'Let's exchange numbers.'" When she called him they began a casual relationship, talking on the phone occasionally, and they eventually met for a sexual encounter. The relationship was casual, and Aaron said they met only "one time, maybe two times" before he broke it off. A few months later the police came to his office and arrested him for having sex with a minor. His lawyer told him that the girl's mother had called the police after reading her daughter's diary.

Married at the time of the offense (although separated by the time he was arrested), Aaron asserted that the relationship with the girl represented something he was looking for outside of his troubled marriage. He met her at a time when his marriage was dissolving, and by the time they had their first encounter he was separated: "My wife and I were beginning to see differently about the direction where we were going.

[There were changes at work] so there were a lot of demands on me.... I began to participate in extramarital things, like staying in the gym longer, going to the pool hall, playing cards, avoiding things. And then I met this young lady, this girl, at a friend's bachelor's party." He constructed his motive for engaging in an affair outside of his marriage with problems between him and his wife as well as other demands. He largely thought of the liaison in terms of the fact that it was extramarital, rather than in terms of the girl's age. Their relationship did not appear to be particularly compelling or significant: "It wasn't like dating, anything like that. I had thought it was a developing friendship, you know. We'll call on the phone, things like that. And it would only be brief conversations . . . not about nothing important, not about what are your career goals and things like that. We just talked about small stuff." In this way the relationship represented little more than a diversion for him; the meaning had more to do with what was lacking in his life rather than what was present between him and the girl. It probably would not have been significant had he not been arrested.

However, in his narrative, Aaron asserted two different versions of how the affair ended. Although when they met the girl told him she was nineteen, at one point Aaron stated that after they slept together he had an indication of her age. She had been impressed by the fact that Aaron was relatively well traveled, and he suggested to her that she get a passport: "And I think that's when I became aware of how old she really was. Because when I was helping her to do her passport, I saw her ID, and I said wait a minute, that's not the same [as the one she had shown me]. . . . Once I realized how young she was, that she was younger than she said she was, I said, this is a potential for disaster." Aaron stated that that's when he "began to pull back," but that he had already had a sexual encounter with her at that time. Later he also said, "Once I realized that the person was younger, I removed myself." In this version of events, Aaron ended the affair because he knew she was a minor.

Yet, in another version, he offered a different explanation of his decision to stop seeing the girl. He explained that it ended because he needed to address the sources of stress in his life. "I was having some stressful things going on with my wife and things like that. And fooling around with that young lady really wasn't helping me to address the underlying issues with my wife. I didn't need to continue to pursue something over here when I knew that I was married. So I told her after the first or second time, I told her, you know, 'I think you're a nice person, blah blah blah, but I can't continue to do this, and I don't want to do this.'" He then asserted that when the police came he had no idea that she was a minor until they told him so.

Reading these two opposing versions, there is a tendency to hear the first one, wherein he described a specific scene where he discovered her age, as more "truthful." In addition to its greater specificity, it casts a shadow on his innocence. Although even here he insisted that when he had sex with her he was unaware that she was not an adult, he might have viewed the fact that he discovered her age before the police came as in some way discrediting. Aaron constructed his narrative around the theme of his innocence, and accordingly the narrative thread hinged on his ignorance of the girl's actual age. Admitting that he knew her age—even if not until after the sexual contact occurred—would make the story of his innocence seem less unequivocal. His position as misguided and naïve would be compromised, and his narrative would be less clear cut and straightforward.

Aaron constructed an adult/child dichotomy through which he organized his experience. His perception of her was visually informed, and he stated a number of times that she "looked older, was physically well-developed" and that furthermore his friends had all made the same assumption that he had. As a stripper at a party, she presented herself as an actor within a sexually charged situation. That is, she presented herself as a fully sexual adult, and in this context it may have been reasonable to assume that she was of the legal age of consent. Aaron asserted that her behavior was that of an adult woman: "She was acting accordingly because she was placed in an adult role. . . . Mentally she was savvy enough. I guess if you're in that profession that you got to become savvy to communicate and learn the lingo I guess." Acting in an adult context and playing an adult role, she was perceived as an adult. Her behavior communicated that she was sexually knowledgeable and not an innocent child. Further contributing to Aaron's perception of the teenager as an adult woman was the fact that the night he met her his friend had engaged in sexual activity with her: "The person who was at the bachelor's party, when they found out about the charge, they said, 'Shit, I can also be in trouble.' Because they, at the bachelor's party, they were doing, you know, whatever they were doing." That his peers interacted with her sexually and also presumed that she was an adult may have buttressed Aaron's belief that she was of legal age.

The construction of his innocence was particularly enhanced by his assertion that not only had he and his friends made assumptions about her age, but she had actively misrepresented herself. Like Tim's, Aaron's narrative contains a sense of having been tricked. Aaron asserted that the girl produced ID that attested to the fact that she was nineteen: "She told me she was nineteen. And that's like the average age that those girls are going in and doing the dances. She said nineteen and she showed me the ID. And what was funny was that a friend that was at the bachelor's party had even said, 'Wow, she fooled you, she fooled me. She fooled the crap out of me.'" In this way Aaron presented himself as having been deceived. He acted toward her based on the information she had given him. This narrative cast her as deliberately misleading and "fooling" Aaron and his friends. Her active agency in self-representation gave her control of the definition of the situation, and this fact was significant to Aaron in qualifying the official definition of her as the "victim": "There's always a 'victim,' as they want to put it. It's the person you offended against. But in my situation that person was a willing participant. Consenting. Minus the degree that the person was younger than she alluded to be, alleged to be. So that person has to bear some of the brunt." He constructed her as having a pivotal role in the unfolding of events to such a degree that it mitigated the extent of his wrongdoing. She was described as having responsibility for what happened between them. Aaron's narrative played against the unspoken concept of a "real" victim. It also implicitly contrasted with an offense, unlike his own, that does not involve what he termed "mitigating circumstances." Her agency was presented as defining the nature of the relationship between them. She was constructed as "willing" in such a way that Aaron was almost constructed as unwilling. That is, Aaron did not willingly engage in sexual activity with a minor. His will was seen as negated by her dishonesty and misrepresentation of who she really was. In addition to his above statements about having "removed" himself from the situation once he knew the truth, Aaron was adamant about the fact that he never would have been involved with her had he known from the beginning. He asserted that it was "wrong" to have sex with a sixteen-year-old, "because that person is in a development stage. Again, when I was telling you about the lingo that they use, if she had been honest and told me that. . . . But if any time in the conversation she would have said that she was younger than what she said she was, I would have left the room. I would have left the room." What happened between Aaron and the girl was seen as based on a lie that she told. His narrative posits another hypothetical version of events wherein if he had the information about her age, he would have flatly disengaged.

Aaron's story is constructed in such a way that he was not responsible for the events that took place because he did not have enough knowledge of the situation. He constructed his motives for engaging with the girl as being based in problems in his marriage, as opposed to a desire for sex with a minor—which may have implicated a more deviant identity. He had intended to have an affair with a "young lady" but was intentionally mislead into having sex with a "child."

Reggie, a Statutory Offender

The case of Reggie, a forty-year-old African American man who had lived in the same New York City neighborhood his entire life, was briefly introduced in the previous chapter. He presented as mild and polite, telling his story with simple humility. A feeling of sadness pervaded his narrative, and I had tremendous sympathy for his situation. He spoke with an overarching sense of unadorned and unmitigated guilt.

Reggie grew up in a small household that included himself, his older sister, and his mother. His sister was twelve years older than him and helped raise him. The three remained close, seeing and speaking to each other frequently. They still lived within blocks of each other.

After graduating from high school Reggie spent a number of years working odd jobs in food services and retail management. He did not find these pursuits particularly satisfying and was pleased when a friend helped him find a job as manager of a service department in a corporation. He found the fast-paced, deadline-driven work challenging, and appreciated the salary and benefits. Unfortunately, he was laid off for budgetary reasons and had not since found another job.

Reggie had been living with his wife for fifteen years at the time of his arrest. They had two children together, and he had another child from a previous relationship. Although he described some difficulties and distance between him and his wife, he felt they had a strong relationship, as evidenced by the fact that she stood by him after his arrest.

Reggie presented his narrative straightforwardly and simply stated and reiterated his own wrongdoing. He did not overtly utilize any of the techniques of neutralization, which further contributed to the general sense of humility. He was charged with "sex abuse forcible touching of a minor" and throughout his narrative emphasized that he was not only the adult capable of acting in a responsible manner toward a young person, but also the one with power in the situation.

Reggie explained in a direct manner the circumstances of his relationship with the girl against whom he offended. He had known her for a brief period of time during her early childhood through her father, and they met each other again many years later. When Reggie then encountered her, he knew she was a teenager ("I knew she was sixteen, seventeen, or eighteen. I knew she was around there"), but was not sure of her exact age. When they met, in her father's presence, "right there, there was an attraction." Emphasizing that because he was married, Reggie said that he felt that "it shouldn't have been there." He explained that the relationship developed with her calling him occasionally and him enjoying the attention, until one day they met in his apartment:

> But there was an attraction there and you know it led to her coming to my home one morning. We were kissing, fondling, but I stopped. For me, stopping, I think she felt that I may tell. So when I went into the living room to call her father, to call her father to come pick her up, she had called him also. And he was like, "Oh, you're feeling on my daughter!" And I was like, "listen...." The next thing you know, he came to the house, we had a big falling out in the house the led out of our household to the street and the police came. He told the police, "he was touching my daughter," and I was arrested then.

In describing the incident, Reggie emphatically and clearly judged his own behavior as "wrong," and stated that he was aware of it as such at the time: "I knew from the point when I spoke to her on the phone and she said she was on her way, I knew it was wrong." He even made a slight attempt to prevent her from coming over: "I knew it was wrong to the point that when I called her back to tell her don't come, she was already on her way to my household. Still in the back of my mind, I'll like, 'stop it.' To the point that she got to the household I knew, 'stop it.'" There was little equivocation in Reggie's narrative, just a pervading sense that he was responsible for his actions and that they were "wrong." Reggie didn't act on his instincts to "stop it" immediately, and explained that they began to engage in physical contact: "We started kissing, fondling. Stop. To the point that I wasn't going to go. I didn't have her expose her body or have intercourse with her. But I was like, this just isn't right. I blurted out, under my breath, 'I have to call your father.'" Reggie ended the contact himself and did not allow it to progress beyond fondling.

Her call to her father was an example of how Reggie conceptualized his "victim" as a "child" and acted accordingly. In fact, he constructed the girl's reaction to him making the call her father as childishly defensive. "So if she felt that I was going to call him and put it on her, and she may even be in trouble.... So she calls herself from the cell phone before I got to my house phone.... What she did, it was basically what any child would do, honestly. If they're doing something wrong and they feel they are going to get in trouble, they're going to tell on their friend first. You know, 'Mommy, Daddy, she did or he did such and such; he broke the cup.'" Likening her to a child, he placed himself as the person with power in the situation and removed responsibility for the consequences from her shoulders. He saw her actions as consistent with those of a minor, someone who needs protection and cannot be expected to necessarily behave appropriately or in her own interests, and there was an element of self-recrimination in his describing her actions as childlike. However, in contrast to his construction of her as a child, Reggie also asserted that the girl was physically mature and that in one sense he did not see her as a minor: "She didn't look like an average sixteen-year-old. Dress-wise, you know. The way her body was formed; even the way she kept her hair, even the way she spoke—was a little older. Not making an excuse for what I did, you know." As Aaron had done, Reggie responded sexually to the girl as he would to an attractive, adult female and stated that her presentation of self encouraged that perception of her. On the other hand, he quickly added that he did not think it was an excuse for his behavior, and throughout his construction of the offense he emphasized that he maintained power in the situation.

Reggie argued that were he to proclaim his "innocence" he would be showing disregard for his "victim"—a word that he learned to endorse in his treatment setting. He elaborated on the ways she was in fact a victim and how he had control of the situation: "She wasn't of age to make that adult decision about what she wanted to do. She basically was being manipulated. You know, I knew exactly what to say to her, to impress her, to turn her on. So I knew the manipulation factor. Like for instance if I were telling her 'if you don't come over I'm not going to speak to [you],' that would be more overwhelming to her than her telling me that. If she told me that, I would be like, so?" Reggie felt he had power over the girl for a number of reasons: he was less invested in the relationship and could walk away at any point and could get her to do his bidding were he to threaten to cut her off (a threat he never actually made; he had been speaking hypothetically). In addition to asserting that her biological age made her unable to legally consent to sexual activity, he asserted that he was the more knowledgeable party, the one who could "manipulate" the other toward his own ends. This ability to manipulate was key to the way he understood his wrongdoing. Reggie further explained this power dynamic: "It was basically a thought pattern.... Basically any child younger than me, you can manipulate. Even to a point where we do it as parents. You know, 'if you go to bed on time, do your homework, take your bath—you'll get a cookie.' You know, we're manipulating our child to go to bed. Because they're looking for, can I have my cookie. As they get older you can use any kind of manipulation. You can tell a young girl, come see me and I'll take you shopping. A lot of girls are hot on, I'll get a new outfit, I'll get new sneakers, get my hair done. So it's just manipulation." In his narrative he constructed the girl several times as a child with childlike thought processes and motivations, who was easily vulnerable to a more knowledgeable person with more social power and independence, as well as greater access to resources. He presented himself as having the means to easily impress and control her, and his sense of his own culpability was inextricably tied to this construction of the adult/child dynamic. Soon after he was arrested he felt anger at the girl, but he quickly recognized his own role in the situation and unequivocally linked it to the fact of their respective ages: "At first I blamed her. I didn't have the right thinking and ... I blamed her. Because she would call me; she would text me.... But then it's like, I'm the one to blame. I was the adult in the entire situation. I knew, stop it right there."

Reggie contrasted the way the girl perceived him with the disaffection that had developed between himself and his wife at the time of the offense. The extramarital nature of the offense also contributed to his articulation of the wrongful nature of his actions: "Being married I'm supposed to have blinders. I know there are women out there, but my wife is supposed to be the one and only, and I knew that what I was doing, what it was leading up to was wrong." Both the victim's age and the fact that he was pursuing a romantic/sexual relationship outside of his marriage were factors in his culpability. He explained that the attraction itself, however, was in some ways related to her youth. "She had that attraction. I guess as men we look for that look of a woman or a female being in total awe of us. Anything I did, if I worked out in the house it was amazing. Any joke I told her was funny, everything I did was like [Reggie] can always do it better. So inside it gradually made me feel like, wow. Sometime me and my wife will just pass by each other going to work, give each other a kiss on the cheek. There was nothing wrong with my relationship, but the greedy part of me wanted more." Reggie articulated the idea that he seemed more powerful and "amazing" in her eyes because she was so young and inexperienced. Average activities and words, to which his wife had grown accustomed, seemed new to her and fueled the attraction between them. Here he also implicitly acknowledged a power differential between them that did not exist between him and his wife, with whom he was on equal footing, at least in terms of age and experience.

Although framing the offense largely and unequivocally in terms of his own wrongdoing, Reggie also described it as a lapse, or a "mistake," and repeatedly emphasized that it did not represent an ongoing pattern of behavior, or what he termed a "problem": "It was a mistake I made. It was a mistake. . . . But it wasn't a problem. Like, I've never been in a chat room. I don't log on to my computer and look for children's porn or anything with a young child in it. . . . My wife is only a year younger than me. So there's never been a thing with me with younger women. I've always dated older women, actually." Asserting that he never actively sought out younger people as sexual partners, Reggie constructed his situation as a mistake that was not indicative of his sexual identity. The aberration stood in contrast to his romantic history. Like Aaron and Tim, he presented a self that was not primarily attracted to children or young girls. Although he did not use the fact that it was a mistake to mitigate his wrongdoing or as an "excuse," it was important to him that he distinguish what he did from an ongoing problem, one that might imply true deviance.

Karl, a Statutory Offender

In the previous chapter we were introduced to Karl, a genial white man in his early thirties. Exceptionally articulate and verbally skilled, he generated a self-reflective and analytic narrative. For many years he had been involved with self-improvement programs and was influenced by the language and ideas of contemporary psychotherapy. Because of his verbal facility, he managed to say more than any other participant in the same amount of time.

Karl grew up in a middle-class southern family who were very active in their church. He described himself as having been deeply religious. He loved everything about church and participated enthusiastically in many programs. In his early twenties Karl began a long coming-out process, wherein he struggled to accept his homosexuality and manage the contradictions between his religious beliefs and his sexuality. Karl had not had a long-term relationship with either a man or a woman, although he had had a number of short-term relationships.

Karl was an artistic professional with a master's degree in education. He traveled for professional reasons a great deal. In addition, he held two steady part-time jobs: one as a high school arts teacher, the other as an assistant to an artist. He lost the former job because he engaged in sexual conduct with a student. Karl described an escalating flirtation between himself and a fourteen-year-old openly gay boy. At one point when they were alone together they became intimate and Karl performed oral sex on him. When this information spread to the school's principal, Karl was immediately dismissed.

Karl's construction of the offense itself was entwined with the story of the developing relationship between himself and the student. He characterized himself as pursued by the student, whom he never referred to as a victim, and constructed their interactions as analogous to adult dating rituals. His narrative was interspersed with relative definitions of appropriate behavior and the fluidity of right and wrong, and the exploration of these meanings are part of his construction of the offense as well.

Chaos versus control was a major theme. He often described vacillating between periods of indulgence and abstinence, either from promiscuous sex or drugs. In addition, he described periods in which he traveled for work as times when things turned to chaos. When asked to describe his offense, he immediately detailed a particularly hectic traveling schedule. As with Raoul's story, Karl's back story of the offense took up many pages of transcript. He asserted that while traveling he would become emotionally less stable than usual. The difficulty he described experiencing at the time was expressed not only as a backdrop to the offense, but as establishing his state of mind. With "everything" "up in the air" he found he was not happy and indulging in a period of drinking. Traveling was directly tied to his offense. Using the phrase "up in the air"—which he repeated several times—he depicted his life as having little grounding around the time of the offense. The meaningful connection between traveling and his offense was based on the fact that traveling had an impact on his decision-making capabilities. "My life was kind of all up in the air at that point. I didn't have a real sense of grounding as well. Again. Yet again in my life, I went through, [traveling] and knowing that [it] was real difficult for me because I didn't have that sense of feeling connected and I would get a little lost and caught up in things when I was traveling . . . and not being in one place and having that consistent more settled vibe where I can feel where my life is calmer and like I'm not as easily influenced by, like in those situations I would have tended to drink more, to have sex more." He described losing his identity in the process of traveling. Without this "grounding" he was "lost"—lacked a stable sense of self and was "easily influenced" by "situations." As we will see, portraying the offense as a situation (rather than a series of actions) was integral to Karl's construction of the incident. In the situation, his sense of self was undermined. He was acting not at full capacity but as someone whose mental state was compromised by the circumstances in which he found himself.

Karl portrayed the student as very aware of his own sexuality, and as someone who enjoyed sexually displaying his body: "He dressed in a way like you could see if he was wearing underwear or not wearing underwear, and he was a kid who would get in trouble sometimes, you know. They were like, look, the principal even called him in once to say, look, you have to wear underwear, because he wore low rise and you know that would show, and he was into wearing the G-string." Karl brought attention to the fact that the student's sexual way of dressing was noticed by other school authorities. This indicated that others in addition to Karl recognized the student's deliberate presentation of a sexual self. Karl presented the student as socially precocious as well: "He was already sneaking out to bars with friends and going to drink in clubs and he was fourteen, with other kids as well. And so there was this sense that he was already in. . . . He wasn't the innocent sheltered fourteen-year-old."

Here he twice mentioned that the student was fourteen, but distinguished him in type from others that age. He placed him with the students who were beginning to embark on adult activities and who were further along on the transition to adulthood than others. Not "innocent," the student was cast as sexually and socially knowledgeable.

Karl developed a narrative of a courtship drama wherein a relationship gradually builds. The student was placed in the assertive and seductive role of the initiator, and was described as someone with a strong personality who stood out from the crowd: "[He was] really outgoing. Cute guy. Super talented. I mean really friendly. He would come by. He'd come by my room before I was his teacher, like all the time. But in a very seductive kind of way. He wasn't just coming by and being, I mean there are little kids that are just coming by and being friendly. This was very different. It was very flirty and very—it was a lot." The student was cast in the active role, seeking Karl out in a way that he distinguished from the friendliness of other students. The student came by Karl's office somewhat excessively and wasn't only seductive but was "very seductive." The repeated use of the word "very" as well as "a lot" presented the student as not only exceptionally talented but also exceptionally assertive of his own sexuality. Karl recalled a number of times when this "out gay student" would drop by his office, emphasizing the agency of the student in the development of the relationship. Also, in saying that the student was openly gay, perhaps Karl was implicitly resisting the stereotype of a predatory homosexual adult who "corrupts" young boys.

Portraying the student as flirtatious, Karl acknowledged that a certain degree of flirting is common in school settings and distinguished this student's behavior from more benign or innocent forms of flirtation: "I've had kids flirt with me before, I've had kids, that's just something that I've had to deal with. I mean that a lot of teachers just have to deal with, but this had different kind of intent. In the beginning not necessarily so much, but it was later on, realizing that it was a kid that was flirting, but much more aggressive with the way they were flirting . . . than other kids had been in the past." To Karl it seemed significant that the student was the one who escalated the flirtation to physical contact. Karl arranged private lessons with this student in his home, although this was not allowed by the school: "Once when we were going into my apartment. It'd be flirtatious, I'd be [working], and he's looking over my shoulder . . . , and he's rubbing up against me behind me . . . ; and he's standing behind me looking over my shoulder. And I knew it was happening." The student made "the first move"—initiating physical contact between them. Karl portrayed himself as passively allowing this to happen. Using the phrase "it was happening," Karl constructed this event as taking place somewhat apart from his own agency. Knowing "it" was "happening" suggested that Karl allowed it to happen, but, employing passive construction, Karl grammatically absented himself from the event. He further asserted that the situation between them would not have happened if the student had not taken the lead. Like Tim, Karl placed himself in a passive position, indicating a "denial of responsibility": "I wouldn't have known how to make that happen because I'm not usually the aggressive one in that way." Karl presented himself as the more naïve of the two, more helpless and less sexually or romantically knowledgeable, not knowing "how to make that happen." Furthermore, placing himself as not "aggressive," he, by implication, once again cast the student as the aggressor and himself as the passive recipient of sexual advances.

Again Karl differentiated this boy from others his age who may have been more "innocent." Karl further argued that more knowledgeable students are less likely to be harmed by sexual encounters with adults.

> There's this part of me that would like to know that he's okay and that what happened between us didn't really screw him up for the rest of our lives. I have a feeling that it didn't because there is this part of me that thinks there was a lot of stuff already going on that allowed him to already be in a position where he was able to come on to me that strongly anyway. Not saying to discount at all my role in this. But at the same time, thirteen-year-olds, thirteen-, fourteen-, fifteen-year-olds who are coming on to people who are in their thirties who are their teachers have probably already had things happen to them that allow them to do that.

Karl questioned the nature of what is and is not appropriate, and not seeing these things as absolutes. The construction of the student's personality hinged on positioning him as the sexual aggressor. This student was again cast as a type whose own background "allowed him to already be in a position" where sexual encounters would not have a negative impact. At the same time, Karl expressed the idea that perhaps this student was not simply socially mature, but in some ways already damaged: "I would think your average well-balanced thirteen-year-old would not be coming on to a thirty-year-old teacher.... I think there were probably some socially maladaptive behaviors ... that were already in play before this happened." The sexual interaction with Karl was perceived as part of the student's ongoing pattern of "socially maladaptive behaviors." This way, even if he did develop problems later on, it would be an indication of the fact that he was already "screwed up," not a result of the incident with Karl, but a continuation of problems "already in play." Here we see an instance of "denial of injury." Characterizing the boy as already "damaged," Karl gave no indication of the possibility that he might have been taking advantage of a troubled young person.

Consistent with his construction of the student as the aggressor in their relationship was Karl's construction of himself as passive and lacking agency in the course of events leading up to and including the offense: "I was never presented with this opportunity or this situation before because people were just flirtatious, and that was it. They didn't pursue to the degree that he pursued this." The "situation" Karl described was the overtly sexual flirtation of the student. Karl was the "pursued"— the passive and by implication vulnerable person who was manipulated by someone who persistently sought him out. Explaining the development of the relationship, Karl stated that the "situation" changed once the student was in one of his classes: "Then when I became the teacher it sort of escalated a little bit." The situation was presented as something that had a life and momentum of its own. "It" escalated. Karl continued to explain that the student was the one who asked for private lessons. Although this may have been an opportunity for Karl to have instituted a boundary, he once again constructed himself as passive and gave the student the authority to make the decision.

> He wanted to take private lessons. And he was like, do you teach private lessons and I did ... I taught other students [from the school] privately as well.

> Because once we had one there he was like, oh we can have a lesson there again.... It was like, whatever, as long as you're okay with that it's fine with me.

At this point Karl constructed the issue around the fact that he taught other students privately. He could have refused to tutor the student, but this alternative was absent in his narrative.

Although the lessons usually took place in a studio, circumstances led to them meeting in Karl's apartment: "There was a time when the studio wasn't available and I was like we could either not have a lesson today or if you want to come to my place we can do the lesson there and he's like I don't know if we should, and I was like, if you don't know if we should, then we shouldn't and if it's okay, it's okay, I said it's up to you." Here he left another decision in the hands of the student. When the student expressed doubt, Karl insisted that it was the student's decision, again deflecting an opportunity to take control of the situation.

When describing more physical contact that occurred between him and the student, he also presented an incident where they kissed as something that "happened," seemingly uninitiated by either actor: "There was once when we were going into my apartment in the entryway that we kissed once. . . . I had thought about it but . . . it's like, how do you? I wouldn't have known how to make that happen, because I'm not usually the aggressive one in that way. This only happened because we were that, I mean it was that, you're this close to each other and it was easy to kind of just do it."

Finally, when looking back on the act of oral sex for which he was arrested, Karl said, "It was a pretty stupid decision. I didn't really ever think of it as a decision ever. It's not like I said, okay, I'm going to do this. It's just something I kind of got caught up in. Obviously everything is a choice to some degree, but I didn't feel like I was necessarily making a choice with the process." Although first describing the act as a "stupid decision"—that is, a matter that was in his hands to be decided—he immediately qualified his statement. He insisted he made no conscious choice to engage the student sexually. Instead he "kind of got caught up" in it. It was "just something," meaning between the agency of the student and the power of the situation, Karl's actions were all passive. On the other hand, he again articulated the idea that "everything is a choice"—although his use of "obviously" served to minimize that statement, as if it was so utterly obvious as to be unimportant. In the less obvious sense, which he seemed to privilege, he was not engaged in making choices.

When describing his relationship with the student, Karl expressed a sense that he enjoyed the attention of the student. Although he could have refused to tutor the student, he acknowledged that he enjoyed the nonprofessional element of their relationship. That Karl found the flattery gratifying was presented as an underlying motive for the new development in the relationship. While Karl was traveling the student would send him instant messages on the computer: "At the time I thought it was sweet and you know it made me feel good. I enjoyed it. I enjoyed the way it made me feel." The flirtation and the communications outside of school were not acknowledged as boundary-threatening, but seen in terms of his pleasurable experience of them.

Karl constructed the development of his relationship with the student as analogous to the development of a romantic relationship between adults. He reiterated this analogy at several points in his narrative, presenting the relationship as essentially normative: "And I would flirt back. I mean, I would totally flirt back, and it was this just kind of playful exchange that I would have had with an adult that would be okay." Statements such as these emphasized that there was nothing deviant about the interaction per se. Rather, the deviance was a technicality, a function of their respective roles and the age difference. Discussing the instant messages, Karl explained, "He would send me an instant message on the computer. . . . And it was always late at night before he was going to bed, and it was always like, hi or sweet dreams, or whatever. But from a freshman in high school to your thirty-year-old teacher, I look at it that way and yeah, well, like yeah, not necessarily a good idea." These online communications had an intimate quality, and suggested a burgeoning romantic relationship patterned by standard courtship rituals between age-mates. He described the excitement he felt as the relationship developed: "To me it was obvious what he was doing. But at the same time I liked it. Because at that point, then all of a sudden, I knew. It was almost like we were dating in a big sense of it. Because he would send me the messages on the computer and we would chat. . . . It was very much to me the way it would feel if he were twenty-eight and we were dating . . . in many ways I saw it like this adult almost dating thing." He experienced the communications not as an inappropriate boundary between teacher and student or thirty-year-old and fourteen-year-old, but rather as the progression of an adult "dating thing." Although Karl reported recognizing aspects of it as inappropriate, he also explained that his pleasure in the situation motivated him to continue: "It all felt very sincere and very heart felt. None of it felt, it didn't have that feeling of wow, this is totally crazy and inappropriate and I need to reach out and stop this. It was like, yeah I know this isn't something that should really be happening but it feels really great so why not kind of a thing."

Consistent with his presentation of the relationship as similar to an adult dating "thing," Karl emphasized the fact that the offense itself was consensual. This framing of the event was critical to Karl, so much so that he would have gone to trial rather than admit to a nonconsensual offense.

> [It was a] B misdemeanor: sexual misconduct, I think.... Even in the confession I was saying it, and [my lawyer] was like, you agree that this and this and this and that it was nonconsensual. And that's when I talked to my lawyer and we went up to her. Because [the student] never said that I forced him to do anything. He always said it was something he agreed to and that he sought after.... When they were saying in the record that it wasn't consensual, I said, you know, I'm not going to say that. Because it was consensual. Because there are police records that say that it was consensual. And I understood it was because the age of consent is whatever here; eighteen or seventeen. And he wasn't that age. And I said that it needs to be phrased somehow that he did consent but because he was a minor.

This was a legal battle for the definition of the situation wherein Karl would not be constructed as forcing himself on anyone. On the contrary he sought legal recognition of his version of the situation wherein he was engaged in a mutual relationship. Karl dismissed the legality of the age of consent as "whatever" and privileged the romantic nature of his connection with the student.

Throughout Karl's narrative was an exploration of the nature of right and wrong, legitimate and illegitimate, appropriate and inappropriate. These words did not have absolute meanings for him and were defined in terms of contexts, motives, and characteristics of actors. One way that Karl constructed the nature of the offense was by contextualizing its "wrongness" in terms of harm to the person cast as the victim. As we have seen, Karl constructed the student as unlikely to have been damaged by the experience because of his precocity, prior experiences, and preexisting socially maladaptive behaviors. In addition, Karl presented the cases of people who had experiences in their youth that they looked back on as harmless. "I have several other teacher colleagues that I remember them telling me when they were in high school they had an affair with a coach. And they had this whole relationship, and they were involved all throughout when they were in high school together. So there were these little messages I was getting from people I knew and respected that was like, well it happened with me and I thought it was great and it didn't scar me for life and it was that wonderful experience. And part of me maybe felt it wasn't that really bad." These "wonderful" experiences were presented as possibly analogous to his student's. He presented these as "little messages" that mitigated the sense of wrongdoing on his part. Examples of nonharmful relationships between adults and minors reassured Karl that he had not done anything "really bad" to the student.

In expressing why the relationship is considered wrong, Karl maintained that the mainstream sanction against adult-minor or teacher-student relations is somewhat arbitrary. "So it was, you know, it was more because society says it shouldn't be happening that it shouldn't be happening. Not because we didn't want it to be happening. . . . I wasn't even thinking of it in terms of, wow, you could go to jail. Ooh your teaching career, this shouldn't be happening. It was just that it was just more societal stuff in the way it would be viewed. That it was inappropriate because of our age difference and because of me being his teacher." Karl identified the status of their roles and ages as the factors that are considered inappropriate, but presented these as things that "society" ordains as wrong. He contrasted this view with what he and the student wanted "to be happening," suggesting this may have been a more legitimate, or at least an alternative, way of viewing the situation. Karl did not see himself through the lens of society, but maintained his own definition of the situation.

On the other hand, in spite of the fact that he argued against society's set of values regarding the legitimacy of social actors' desires, his discussion of what happened immediately following the sexual offense proper articulated a clear sense of wrongdoing: "After it happened it was . . . more of a, wow this probably shouldn't have happened than it was with the kiss . . . And I remember telling him, we really can't say anything about this to anybody. And he was like, no. He agreed. And there was that part of me that, as soon as he left . . . I had that feeling like, this was really stupid, because I knew it was something I needed him not to say anything about." Karl described an immediate and visceral sense of guilt, as well as fear of social recriminations. He presented the situation as something both parties felt needed to be kept a secret. Here he described it as something that "shouldn't have happened" and direly inappropriate. Although before he stated that he hadn't been thinking of the relationship in terms of consequences affecting his career or bringing jail time, here his fear seemed to concern such social consequences.

Karl linked his offense with overall patterns he identified as consistent throughout the course of his adult life. Primarily, he identified periods of chaos associated with traveling as undermining his decision-making abilities and promoting poor choices. Although he constructed the offense in this context as a "stupid mistake," he qualified this assertion by stating he did not feel he was making choices. More important, the entire construction of the offense cast him in a passive role within a situation that seemed to take on a life of its own. Karl mitigated his responsibility by differentiating between mature and immature young people, questioning the nature of what is appropriate and exploring the extent to which anyone was actually damaged by his actions. In addition, he disavowed his own agency by constructing the student whom he offended against as an active seducer. These elements came together in the telling of the story where he participated with a quasi-equal in a romantic relationship analogous to adult courtship dramas. The overall picture he painted was that in which he was caught up in events that were beyond his control.

Terry, a Serial Offender

Unlike the other men in the study, Terry was a serial offender. His case was also briefly presented in the previous chapter. He was a mild-mannered white man in his early fifties. He seemed polite and reserved, although I also got the sense he wanted to please or be a good interview subject. He tended not to make eye contact when he spoke and seemed to choose his words very carefully. In fact, he took pains to correct himself if he thought he didn't have exactly the right word. In spite of this concern he contradicted himself several times.

Terry had always lived in upper-middle-class suburbs. He characterized his family life as pleasant and traditional. He was "a star athlete" and excelled in academics. In his early twenties he attended a technical college where he dated a woman for three years. It was a celibate relationship; neither believed in premarital sex. Eventually he asked her to marry him, but she declined his proposal. He had dated on and off but hadn't had any significant relationships since college.

He entered the financial industry after college and had been working at local institutions his entire adult life. He had lived in the same community for years and participated actively in church organizations and sports teams.

Terry had a history of public masturbation and frottage (rubbing up against people) that began when he was in high school. He had been convicted thirteen times, although he stated, "There had been other instances. They say that for every arrest there are about a hundred other incidents." His victims were between twelve and forty years old. He asserted that he had gotten away with "slaps on the wrist" because the offenses were not taken that seriously and because he was a seemingly responsible member of the community. He was able to keep the majority of these arrests a secret, and his lawyers negotiated a schedule of serving jail time on weekends and during vacations so as not to disrupt his professional life.

Terry began sexually offending as a teenager and described this behavior as "completely separate" from what he saw as his "normal" life. His most recent act was caught on a video surveillance monitor and released to the local news stations and papers. He was immediately dismissed from his job, excommunicated from his church, and kicked off his community sports team. All his professional contacts were severed and his relations with family members were tested.

Unlike the other participants I interviewed, Terry described a series of offenses and a long pattern of behavior. Thus he was creating meaning not for one incident, but for an aspect of his self. Although the narrative of his offense spanned and was entwined with his construction of his overall life history, he repeatedly maintained that offending was completely separate from the rest of his life.

Terry explained what he did as "all similar offenses, either public masturbation or molesting a woman. They were things that were thought out." These actions were planned, and he deliberately chose "crowded places" such as "shopping malls" and large stores. The first time Terry was caught was in a department store, where security was already aware of him. "I was at a department store at a mall and, um, brushed up against a woman's rear end . . . intentionally. . . . I was in the store and, um, let's see, they told the customers to be aware of pick pockets, and as I was leaving the store security came up to me and detained me until the police got there. And the police arrested me. . . . They went back into the store and pulled the woman aside and asked her if she'd come down to security with them. . . . She was approached because they were watching [me] on security cameras." Terry did not present of himself as a victim of security or law enforcement efforts, and rather seemed to accept that his behaviors were those for which security exists. In this way, he tacitly accepted the view of himself as a public menace (and, as will be discussed in Chapter 5, considered himself someone for whom sex offender policies should exist). He was a surveilled individual who deliberately and furtively attempted to perpetrate illicit acts. He said he was afraid of the consequences of his actions, imagining severe sanctions. However, the charges were eventually reduced to a "public nuisance type thing."

Terry's most recent arrest was for "grabbing the breast of an underage female in a shopping mall." This time, he noted the zealousness of officials: "My most recent offense, the detective really wanted to find out who committed it so he put pictures of the surveillance video out into the media and the schools and law enforcement areas.... I was visible. So of course after I was arrested the TV stations did a follow-up and put my mug shot up and you know, explained my crimes."

Terry was marked as an outsider and threat to the community. Exposure of personal problems was an ongoing theme in his narrative, and early in life he sought out therapy as a way of keeping "skeletons in the closet"; for this reason in particular it was likely that exposure to the community was especially traumatic for him. The very first time Terry committed an offense he was caught, and he described this exposure as playing a significant role in the development of his sexual offending pattern.

> The first incident of a sex offense [was] when I was in high school. I was in a classroom and for days or so I had been, let's see, I had been hanging over my desk with my hand and brushing the girl's rear end in front of me with the back of my hand and she got tired of it I guess and turned around and said what the hell are you doing and uh, the class erupted in laughter and the teacher turned around, and you know, brushed it under, kept on with the lesson.
>
> At the time I did not think of it as significant. I was certainly embarrassed by it. But I didn't realize really how important it was. It changed my whole personality. I was no longer sociable . . . because the hurt would be there if I made a mistake socially. The embarrassment gave me a feeling of uh, a very terrible feeling of embarrassment, and I didn't want to be awkward on social occasions and feel that again.... There were no other social consequences. It was in my head more, and it was very traumatic for me

The "terrible feeling of embarrassment" made a lasting impact on Terry: "I would have never felt the embarrassment and gone further down the road [if she hadn't responded]. You know, lashed out. No . . . I'm sure [it would have been a one time thing]." It is worth noting that he identified his pattern of sexual offending with his response to social circumstances, rather than to biological impulses that he later referenced. He argued instead that if the girl hadn't turned around and the class hadn't laughed, he would not have offended again. Thus he offered an explanatory package that privileged psychological maladaptation, rather than a medical model, which he also later espoused.

In addition, Terry identified this girl with the types of women he chose to offend against throughout his life, and asserted that this incident led to his preference for offending against "extremely feminine" women: "And it probably got me disliking women to some extent because I was so embarrassed. . . . I do think, getting back to high school, the woman, the first one I offended against, was one of the most popular women in school and one of the most feminine women in school. And I feel like maybe it's a I'll show you attitude that I'm using these other women who are similar types as an I'll show you." Terry continued to offend against women who seemed similar to this girl from high school. His feelings about her exposing him to ridicule were linked with negative feelings toward women in general. He presented his offending as hostility toward women that was rooted in his resentment of his high school peers' reaction to him. He stated that he was "using" the women he offended against to make up for the original scenario. Again, here he located the source of his offending with a psychological reaction to circumstances, rather than a biological illness.

Articulating his social normality, Terry described traditional male identities. His narrative interwove concepts of masculinity and femininity with conflicts about sexual desire. He emphasized his engagement with sports as a youth when describing what he viewed as his typical upbringing. In fact, he saw his life course as particularly male-identified, contrasting his skills in math and science with the humanities and literature. In making this contrast he pointed to the fact that pursuing these "male" interests limited his association with women.

The words "masculine" and "feminine" cropped up frequently. When pressed, he could not unpack them well, suggesting that they had deeply rooted hegemonic meanings that exceeded his capacity to define them.

For instance, in addressing what "feminine" meant, he answered, "primping all the time, that sort of thing" and masculine was "not primping all the time." Femininity was linked with appearance, presentation, and display. He frequently referred to women as being either feminine or masculine, one or the other. Interestingly, he used those two terms only in reference to women. Feminine characteristics were positive, seen, and marked. Masculine characteristics were neutral, the absence of feminine markers.

Terry said he had social problems with women who do not play stereotypical roles (i.e., who present as more "masculine"), particularly with what he described as "authoritative women" in the workplace. Yet he asserted that at the same time that he was romantically attracted to more "masculine" women. The women he offended against, on the other hand, were described as extremely "feminine"—although he claimed he was not attracted to them sexually. In isolating his sexual deviance from his "normal life," it seemed important for Terry to make it clear that the women he offended against were distinct in type from those with whom he socialized: "The women I've been involved with are less feminine even though they're extremely good looking women. There's no chance for a real relationship, there was no threat." The contradiction here, between romantic (yet not particularly sexual) relationships with masculine women and sexual misconduct directed against women he was not attracted to, can be interpreted in a number of ways, indicating conflicts about sexuality and romantic relationships. He did not think that sex is necessarily an important part of a serious relationship; a strong relationship was "where you fulfill each other, where you're able to work together and smooth out the bad points, the rough edges of your partner. Comrades. Best friends. It doesn't have to be sexual."

Terry had sought psychological help since he was a young man, and stated that the root of his troubles with "depression" lay in his offending. He had considered it a problem that could be solved through intellectual and emotional understanding. However he eventually came to believe that his problem with offending required more specialized mental health professionals: "Therapy went very, very well for my emotional moods, but there aren't many therapists out there who know much about sex offenses. And they really did not help me with my sex offenses at all, until my most recent psychiatrist within the last couple of years. . . . He was an expert on sex offenses, the history of sex offenders. How to combine medication and tools for preventing further sex offenses." Terry asserted that his specific problem with sex offending required someone particularly knowledgeable. He cast himself as a special subject, in need of expert help. He actively sought out those who could help him refrain from committing further offenses. But doing so required a specific combination of treatments administered by elite personnel.

Terry first began to conceive of his sexual offending as related to an illness when he was in treatment as part of probation: "[It] is really just a learning center. Every once in a while the offenders had to talk but mainly it was just a learning where you went up to the blackboard and that sort of thing. And he told us about the cycle of offending and compared it to gambling and alcoholism, and said often times sex offenders before they start offending have a problem with alcoholism and when they counter the alcoholism they move to sex offending. When they conquer sex offending they move to gambling or something like that." Conceptualizing the offending as a form of addiction, Terry aligned his behavior within a particular type of illness paradigm that encompassed an array of problematic social behaviors. Terry continued to explain, "It's something that gives you a very sense of a high when you do it. The um, the, danger of getting caught, that sort of thing, and it gives you a flow of adrenalin. So it's kind of addictive in that sense. So it's one of those addictive kind of illnesses." Illness was related to a feeling associated with the behavior—the fear of getting caught, perhaps the thrill of getting away with something—and with the inability to resist the "high." Thus, Terry cast himself as lacking a certain degree of control over his behavior, and in that way a certain degree of agency. He grouped himself with others who lack control, although the problematic behaviors he listed were not as highly stigmatized as sex offending. In this way, he put his actions on a continuum for which there was an understandable and common root. Aligning himself with people who struggle with addiction, Terry invoked "denial of responsibility"—in this way he attempted to humanize, rather than demonize, himself.

In fact Terry had been diagnosed with obsessive compulsive disorder (OCD), which he explained "causes you to check things all the time or have obsessions, sometimes even cutting or scratching all the time. And causes you to have compulsions. And [offending] was one of the compulsions." However, Terry distinguished between the compulsive aspect of the sexual offending and other aspects: "I see [the sexual offending] as separate. The OCD did contribute to it. And I when I took medication for OCD it lessened it a little bit. But it didn't overcome it. So it's a component of it, but not the main." The sexual offending was presented as a complex illness, with addictive and compulsive components, among others. Earlier Terry had presented a psychosocial account of his offending when he identified the reaction of the girl in high school whom he offended against, and when he associated his violations against women with her. So in some ways he saw his illness as having a psychological component as well.

Perhaps the most dramatic component of Terry's illness paradigm is the overtly biological. Terry was currently taking medication to eliminate his sexual urges (colloquially referred to as "chemical castration") and reported that at several times he had asked to be surgically castrated. This suggests that Terry's feelings about his sexuality were in part directed against his biology. He identified his male biology—both penis and hormones—as a conspirator in his deviance. The penis was seen as separate from the self. The self was normal, the penis was deviant. Bringing castration—chemical or hormonal—into his narrative, Terry introduced the idea of the male sexual apparatus gone awry. The male organism had to be managed to better fit the social identity. The improperly functioning system could, through science and medicine, be successfully calibrated and brought into line with the properly functioning adult male.

However, professionals in the criminal justice system and psychiatric establishment informed Terry that physical castration would not help: "Therapists and the courts and my attorney . . . said it doesn't do anything. It doesn't take away the criminal activity. . . . I understood it and believed it. Because criminal activity, my criminal activity, wasn't completely sexual. It was a lot of addiction and compulsion and that sort of thing."

Although Terry agreed with them, citing the addictive and compulsive components of his illness as those that would not be affected by castration, he still requested the chemical castration treatment. Although he reported that the medication was quite expensive, he maintained that it was extremely helpful: "[It] makes a big difference because it gives you a break from your sexual desires. And you can look at yourself and put the tools into place to overcome it. . . . I'm very satisfied with it. Very, very much. It's the greatest thing in the world. All repeat offenders might want to consider it." By freeing him of his need to offend, Terry argued that he was able to see his behavior from a clearer point of view. At this point, he began to construct himself in terms of another kind of sickness—a sickness that has a monstrous quality that he described as "perverted and hideous," rather than the more humanizing quality of addiction as illness. In a sense he took on the gaze of the other, seeing himself as mainstream society depicts sex offenders. Through the illness paradigm he was able to take on this view of himself as deviant while overcoming the behaviors.

By referring to himself as a "true sex offender," Terry relied on a generalized body of knowledge to construct himself as a specific class of person and offender. Placing himself in this category, he expounded on the nature of true sex offenders and how they should be managed in the community. He constructed himself as lonely: "Because almost all sex offenders that I know of, myself included, um, were isolated or lonely when they committed their, it was a contributing factor in their crime." Invoking a characterization of himself as socially isolated, Terry identified this loneliness as a causal link in the offending behavior. It was a cause not just for his behavior, but for that of "almost all sex offenders."

Identifying himself as a "true sex offender," Terry created a narrative that was designed to explain a series of events and repeated behavior pattern, rather than an isolated incident or situation. Other than the description of the first incident in high school, the details of each offense lacked richness and read as reportage of bare, official facts. Instead, the complexity of Terry's narrative concerned explaining the fact that he was a sick individual, someone struggling with an illness experts have officially identified. Linking himself with his "true" label mitigated the extent of his wrongdoing by placing him in a category that links him to people who struggle with various addictions, as well as other psychiatric disorders. He described himself as taking actions to seek treatment for the problem, which he subtly constructed as something for which there may be a cure. Thus, his sick self may in fact be a transformable self. While concepts of masculinity and femininity were firmly established in the fabric of his narrative, Terry did not invoke masculinity per se to explain his sexual deviance. Gendered concepts were routinely employed to demarcate women, rather than himself. Yet he emphasized his normative social standing in terms of traditional male activities. While fulfilling some requirements of hegemonic masculinity, Terry distanced himself from his sexuality and sexual behavior by pathologizing and disavowing his genitals and hormones, and labeling his urges "perverted." The ways in which Terry both embraced and disengaged with his deviant identity are further explored in subsequent chapters.

Narrative Accounts of Sexual Offending

This project is designed to contribute to the sociological literature on deviance, particularly the symbolic interactionist strands of the field. Classic studies in this tradition have tended to champion "outsiders" (Denzin, 1992) who have often been presented as in some ways unfairly treated by society, victimized by social conventions and morality, or relatively harmless (such as the mentally ill, the homeless, prostitutes, and drug users). Sex offenders pose a particular problem for this type of analysis because their behavior is generally considered harmful to others. The purpose of this work is not to deny that such harm exists, nor to provide an etiological explanation for sexual offending. Looking at the narratives presented in this chapter we can see how the offenders themselves understand their own behavior, and how they make sense of this particular form of deviance.

As we have seen, with the exception of Terry, the offenders I interviewed did not accept an overall deviant identity. They all saw their offense as an isolated incident, a behavior that could be explained by the circumstances surrounding the event. In their explanations they did employ "techniques of neutralizations." Reggie, Aaron, Raoul, and Karl all portrayed the minor they offended against as in some ways sexually precocious, neutralizing the sense of "victim." Karl did not articulate having a victim at all. Many of these men minimized their responsibility, such as through deceit on the part of the victim or life events that rendered them incapable of reasoned decision making. However, Terry did see himself as a social deviant and could not relegate his multiple offenses to a mistake. Rather than trying to explain an incident, Terry's narrative outlined a condition or deviant career. This included recourse to a medical model of compulsion and addiction that in some ways neutralized Terry's responsibility for his actions, although this was not a dominant theme in his story.

The different presentations of sexual offending offered by the men I interviewed were part of life histories that included identity-reinforcing bonds with others. In the next chapter I explore the ways normative identity was maintained through the community relationships these men had prior to their offense.

CHAPTER 3

Community Bonds

SOCIAL STIGMA IS THAT which separates the bearer from the rest of the community. In order to understand the impact of stigma on the participants in this study, it is important to have a sense of the extent to which they maintained community bonds prior to their convictions. This chapter makes visible the social fabric in which the offenders were entwined, providing a sense of the ways they established and maintained normalcy. Each participant had been living a relatively stable life, and, with the exception of Terry, did not carry a sense of stigmatized identity. None saw themselves as what Goffman would call "discreditable"—they did not have a shameful difference they needed to conceal. Their sense of belonging to the larger group was more or less intact. All of the men had maintained, to differing degrees, social bonds through typical affiliations: church, work, family, and friends. It is important in the study of deviance to appreciate what binds members to the group as well as what severs them. Understanding how the men in this study lived prior to conviction will help illuminate that which was lost as a result of both formal public sanctions and informal social stigma. In this chapter we see that as family members learned of the men's sex offense, they retained a connection with the individual and in many cases did not alter the way that they saw him.

TERRY

Terry described himself as having been a particularly active and engaged member of his community throughout his life. He grew up in a family that attended church regularly and frequently socialized with neighbors. Raised in what he described as a typical upper-middle-class suburban neighborhood where people knew each other, he was accustomed to the overlap between social roles and social zones: for example, neighbors were active in the same PTA and church groups and socialized regularly. Since his childhood Terry had excelled in the kinds of activities stereotypically valued in mainstream American society, such as sports, extracurricular school programs, academics, and church-sponsored community service. He said he had many friends, was well liked, and, in addition to his academic achievement, was "a star" athlete, participating in sports every season.

In his adulthood, Terry's family of origin continued to play an important part in his life, offering support, companionship, and regular contact. Terry's brother and sister both lived in the same county as he did, and he would speak to them on the telephone on a weekly basis. In addition they got together periodically and had vacationed with their families. He also spoke with his father on a regular basis.

Moving only a few towns over from where he grew up, he had a deep sense of familiarity with this community in which he had resided his entire adult life. He felt as if he knew the people there, in both individual and collective senses. As he did in childhood, Terry participated in several local sports leagues and, as his parents had, attended church regularly and was active in its programs and community events. These elements are all critical in terms of "social capital" (Putnam, 2000, p. 59)—the "social networks and norms of reciprocity and trustworthiness that arise from them" (ibid., p. 19). Being embedded within the community in these ways likely provided Terry with a strong sense of belonging and enhanced a stable social identity.

Significantly, Terry's professional identity was particularly integrated into the fabric of the community. His position conferred social status upon him, and he believed he was seen as an important member of the community. In this way his job played a central role in his sense of belonging. In turn, his sense of belonging contributed to his professional status: "In fact [the place I worked] was in the town that I grew up in. That was helpful. They did that on purpose because they figured I'd know the customers and be able to spur business." His personal connection to individuals made him a desirable job candidate, someone who could enhance business. It facilitated rapport with customers and inserted both himself and the institution he worked for into the routines and structures of the community.

Terry derived personal satisfaction from this job precisely because it provided him with a social connection and role: "I really enjoyed [the work] because it was social. . . . I did have to interact with the customers a lot and there was a sense of fulfillment because you did have to help a lot." That Terry derived "a sense of fulfillment" from his work indicated he was pursuing a "career" rather than simply a "job." In other words, his work can be seen as having been critical to his identity, to who he was, rather than what he did. The distinction between performing a social role (which is an aspect of his identity) and serving a function underscores the significance of the relationship between his job and his connection to the community. He saw himself as an important part of the lives of community members, as someone who could offer help. Fulfillment came from the fact that the work was "social"—it involved working with people and reinforcing and maintaining a social identity. That Terry emphasized helping people indicated that it was important for him to see himself as playing a crucial, necessary role: people were dependent on him.

The strength of Terry's bond with his community figured significantly in his sentencing. Although he was a serial offender, for several years his high social standing influenced the way he was processed by the criminal justice system. Although he committed numerous offenses, state actors continued to see him as someone who belonged in the community. They were reluctant to cast him as a deviant who should be expelled; rather, they tried to find a way to maintain his inclusion. His social respectability derived from his active participation in a variety of highly valued social realms, which made an impression on powerful actors in the criminal justice system such as judges and prosecutors.

Describing his first arrest, Terry stated, "They kept me overnight at central holding.... I went before the judge and the judge released me on my own recognizance.... Where you just have to come back at a future date. And eventually it was resolved and reduced to a disorderly conduct charge or something like that." Terry was seen as nondangerous. State actors saw him as essentially *creditable* (Goffman, 1986, p. 4) and were willing to rely on his social standing as an indication of his trustworthiness. They viewed him in terms of his prestigious social function and reinforced that he was successfully performing his professional and social roles. They gave more credence to his credible professional role than they did to his discrediting deviant behavior. Trustworthiness was imputed to him, in spite of lawbreaking behavior. In fact, it is worth noting that middle-class people in general, and middle-class whites in particular, are "weeded" out of the criminal justice system at every key stage, including sentencing (Reiman, 2001, p. 129). In addition to being middle-class and white, Terry was so integrated into the fabric of the community that the criminal justice system resisted "othering" him.

To accommodate his standing in the community, judges worked with him over several years to keep his criminal sentences from disrupting the routines of his white-collar lifestyle and allow him to perform his creditable social role. The sentences seemed specifically designed to prevent stigmatizing him. The punishment rituals in Terry's case continued to respect and uphold his insider status, and resisted banishing and excluding him: "I was able to keep it out of the papers and just go to the courts on my days off and that sort of thing, and do the jail time when I was on vacation. I spent my vacations in jail." Apparently, state actors did not want to expose him and protected his privacy. They colluded in hiding his deviance. Allowing him to serve his jail time on scheduled vacations demonstrates a particular regard for the demands of white-collar work life, and a sympathetic understanding that having to go to jail and disclose his criminal activities would risk his job. This consideration does not reflect the typical treatment given to most people processed through the criminal justice system (ibid.) and seems designed to accommodate and reinforce Terry's nondeviant life, rather than to ascribe and enforce a deviant social status: "That time was before work or family knew anything was going on. So my attorney was able to talk the judge down to either weekends in prison or a shortened time where I can just take an extended vacation, so that's what I did. They thought I was contributing highly to society . . . I was doing good things for the community aside from my other life." Accommodating his schedule, judges and attorneys extended continued deference to what he claimed they saw as his valuable contribution to society. His strong connection to the community protected him from exposure, labeling, and the social consequences of his deviant acts. His social status within the community and his confirmed membership were recognized and affirmed by the criminal justice system through accommodating sentencing structures.

This deferential treatment may have allowed him to continue to regard himself as "normal." His active and positive contributions to the community stood in stark contrast to his continued deviant sexual behavior. His participation in highly regarded activities allowed Terry to uphold a sense of normal identity that was deeply important to him.

He continually reiterated that his sexual offending was "a completely separate life," and his narrative expressed that he cherished the esteem he held in his community. It protected him from fully internalizing a deviant identity and allowed him to maintain the dichotomy between the self he constructed as "normal" and that which he constructed as "sick." By protecting his standing in the community, the criminal justice system preserved his ability to view his offending as a separate sphere of life and to maintain an internalized connection with the community and sense of belonging—in spite of, or concurrently with, his internalized deviant identity.

Without being marked as a sex offender, Terry was able to continue to perform his social role. He kept information about his deviant activities secret from those around him: "Until it hit the papers, no one, completely no one, knew about it. . . . And uh, so you could pursue your life normally as if you were a normal person." Knowledge of his deviance was not available to those with whom he interacted, and because of this he pursued and maintained normative activities (and deviant ones as well). Because his most recent arrest was for an offense caught on surveillance video, control of information became more difficult. However, prior to that, he felt he was able to live in the community "normally"—as any other member, without a stigmatizing difference, or spoiled identity.

His family learned about his deviant behavior before the information was released to the community. Terry stated that his probation officer decided to alert people close to Terry about his sexually deviant behaviors, something that falls within law enforcement's purview as a result of community notification statutes (Meloy, 2006, p. 38). The officer called Terry's brother: "My brother called me and I wasn't home. He left a message on my answering machine. He said, 'I got a call from your probation guy and he told me what's going on,' and you know, he said he still loved me. . . . My brother's one of the people who liked to brush it under the cover, pretend there's nothing going on." In spite of the discrediting information, Terry's brother maintained a normalized view of him. Although Terry no longer had control of highly stigmatizing information, his brother did not let it influence or change his view of him. He refused to integrate the new information into the conception he had of Terry. The bond was not severed because his brother dismissed the news ("brushed it under the cover"), an avoidance tactic that Terry ascribed to the way members of his family generally handled difficult subjects. Knowledge of Terry's deviant conduct did not alter his brother's impression, and this familial bond remained intact.

While his brother "pretended there's nothing going on" and his representation of Terry was not altered in light of new information, Terry's father took it more seriously. He looked for a way to understand the news that would allow him to acknowledge it while maintaining his bond with his son. Thus, he sought an explanatory package with which to frame the new information. Terry's father offered support in the form of finding him treatment for what he constructed as an illness: "My dad acted surprised and concerned and did a lot of research and tried to get me help ... with the problems." By researching Terry's behavior, his father looked to a body of knowledge that would make the deviant behavior understandable and treatable, to professionals who possessed expert knowledge about sex offenders. Outside their immediate community he found a world where deviants were understood, controlled, and helped. In this way, his son's deviance would be manageable. He constructed Terry as sick and in need of cure. Rather than severing a bond with him he bestowed a new deviant identity on him based in illness. This paradigm casts Terry as potentially transformable—capable of reintegration into the community. Terry's father saw his son as someone with a problem that could be overcome and who could still be accepted.

Tim

Tim, who was convicted of an Internet-based offense, was raised in a traditional working-class neighborhood. His immediate family was close with their neighbors, and he had a large extended family that was constantly present in his life. One friend from school used to visit him often during a long-standing childhood illness and remained an important connection throughout Tim's life. They currently spoke on the phone every day. His friend Joe was sympathetic to Tim's financial situation and made sure to be the one to call, since Tim had a limited phone plan. Their social bond was based on shared difficulties. Like Tim, Joe also suffered a disability and they could commiserate: "He talks to me about his medical problems now. He's got a bum leg; he can't walk, so now he's homebound ... it's a forty-minute ride down the mountain by car. That's just to get down the mountain." Tim laughed affectionately as he told of Joe's struggles and acknowledged that they shared a sense of humor about each other's situations, which seemed to be an important coping resource for him.

Tim's extended family was important throughout his life, and one aunt in particular played a crucial role as he was growing up. She had consistently provided significant support to his family: "There were times when my mother didn't have enough money, for like let's say for Christmas. Plus she was out of work for a while, my aunt would help her with that . . . give her money because she didn't have enough to buy us Christmas gifts when were little kids. She always made sure Christmas was handled correctly." This aunt remained a continued source of personal support and material assistance. When Tim was between apartments because of financial difficulties, she let him stay with her for several months. She currently called him every day "to check in"—a phrase that implies familial concern about his well-being, in addition to a friendly and regular conversation.

Mediated communication is increasingly a feature of the modern world (Giddens, 1991, p. 84), and although different in quality from interacting in the same physical environment, it still offers social connection and an arena to perform social identity. Before he went on disability, Tim's job provided significant social contact. He worked long hours that were filled with interaction on the phone, and he said he particularly enjoyed it because he considered it social. Through work he got to know many people in his neighborhood. He was able to establish relationships in this context, but they were not based on face-to-face encounters.

At home Tim had regular contact with the staff at his local video store. As he was a "movie person," this interaction was important to his sense of identity. He found it enjoyable and missed being able to spend money on movies. In addition, he engaged in conversations with people on the Internet, particularly in chat rooms, where he discussed movies and developed a sense of himself as an expert, "someone who knew what they were talking about. Particularly the classics." The phone and the Internet were clearly important media through which Tim interacted with the social world and maintained his sense of connection and identity, both at work and at home.

After being convicted for his noncontact Internet-based offense, Tim's bonds with family, friends, and coworkers remained intact. Significantly, Tim's conviction did not affect his bond with his employers. Because his particular work environment was tolerant of criminal deviants, his job was secure: "People at work were understanding: Because they had some people that worked there that had felony charges on them too. For other reasons. But they were arrested and released or on probation or done with probation. Some people that worked in there have already been through the system, so my boss understood. He had people working for him that were ex-cons. So he didn't really care." This community was inclusive of people processed through the criminal justice system. It did not marginalize him through informal or formal means of exclusion (e.g., social withdrawal or termination). Because he was not the only person with a criminal record, he could maintain an identity as a normal person or "average guy," and his relationships with colleagues, employers, and customers remained intact. Until he went on disability Tim was able to maintain this important social connection.

Tim's familial and social connections also remained unaltered after he was convicted. His relationships with his best friend and aunt did not change. After he was convicted, Tim confided in only Joe and his brother, who worked in law enforcement. Tim's brother arranged for him to disclose the information to the rest of the family.

> I told two people. My brother, of course, and my friend. I'm not sure how anyone else would have taken it and then after I spoke to my brother he says we're going to have to have a family gathering and he says I want you to take each family member and tell them what happened because they already know you were arrested, but they don't know why. So he says I want them to sit down with you and you talk to them and you tell them one by one what happened to you. Just the aunts and the uncles, not the cousins. It didn't concern them. And that's what I did. They accepted it. They weren't happy about it, because they said, me of all people, I'm not that type of person.

Tim's brother acted in such a way that suggested their extended family regarded itself as a community, one in which certain information about its members needs to be known. This implies a particular style of familial network where public and private information is controlled and managed within the group. It does not seem that Tim objected to or questioned the need for disclosure and instead took the family meeting as a matter of course. When he stated that his sex offense didn't concern his cousins, he implicitly acknowledged that it did in fact concern his aunts and uncles. In this way he indicated a belief in the necessity for senior members of the family to know about the potentially discrediting information. This further indicates the extent to which he saw himself as embedded in the family network, and not as an isolated individual.

It is worth noting that it is the nature of his offense that required a formal meeting. The family already knew about the arrest. The criminal activity in and of itself was not cause for the meeting. Rather, it was designed specifically as a forum for Tim to disclose the sexual nature of the offense and that he had become a labeled sex offender. The *sex* offense was seen, at least by his brother, as particularly stigmatizing and in need of explanation. In a fashion similar to Terry's brother, Tim's family did not respond to the information by reformulating their conception of him from nondeviant to deviant, or from insider to outsider. His new status in the larger society did not affect his familial bonds. Asserting that he "is not that type of person," his family members reaffirmed their conception of him as nondeviant and worthy of inclusion. In a sense, they were able to cordon off what he did from who he was, and the new information did not discredit him.

His brother became an ally for Tim as he began to navigate the criminal justice system. Like Terry's father, Tim's brother reacted to the news by researching professional discourses, in this case the criminal justice system's treatment of sex offenders. As a member of law enforcement, Tim's brother took it upon himself to learn how sex offenders are processed, and he sought legal advice for him as well. This included entering into psychological treatment, something Tim's brother was instrumental in procuring for him: "My brother says, at that point, this is what's going to happen. They're going to ask you to go seek some professional help. So him and his wife was seeing this guy.... They asked him what happens with sex offenders." Tim's brother played the role of mediator in initiating Tim into the system and adapting to certain conditions of being a sex offender, thus participating in what Goffman refers to as the "socialization process" where the newly stigmatized individual comes to see the "consequence of possessing it" (Goffman, 1986, p. 32).

While in some ways a loner who had minimal social contact prior to his arrest, and someone whose social isolation increased following his physical disability, Tim had maintained a connection to his neighbors through the nature of his job, where he enjoyed a great deal of social interaction. He had worked in a community that could and did tolerate his criminal activity and had the support of a good friend and a network of extended family members. After going on disability the phone and Internet became a particularly important medium for his social interaction, without which he would be far more isolated.

KARL

As we have seen, Karl grew up in a small, tight-knit religious community where the church played a key role. This was a critical form of connection and identity for him. At an early age, Karl became an enthusiastic participant in church and school activities and eventually became a leader in both realms. He described himself as "an overachiever," and in fact many of his social connections throughout his life had been contingent on his accomplishments. As Karl was an artist, his professional relationships were based on participating in and winning competitions and funding opportunities. Many of his work ties were based on his talents.

The church provided him with a worldview that included a connection to God as well as to community members. It was a physical and ideological space where he developed a sense of belonging to something larger than himself. He had believed deeply in the church's teachings and took the Bible literally:

> If it says Jonah was in the belly of a whale, he was literally in the belly of the whale.

> I used to go door to door asking people if they knew Jesus is their personal lord and savior and leading them into the land of salvation so they would not burn in hell forever.

Proselytizing and holding strictly to dogma formally expressed his membership and allegiance to the church. In addition, he maintained a personal and private connection with Christianity.

> Certain songs and certain lyrics are really comforting and the lyrics that always get me the most are the . . . "I know you and I love you and I think you're wonderful and beautiful." And those were always the ones. And those are the songs that I can still sing.

> Again, I love church so much. I'll get teary. I really do. It does a lot for me. And it's been a really positive thing in my life.

Articulating the meaning the church had for him, Karl linked this institution with a primary and deeply felt sense of self. He expressed the comfort and security he received from participating in church music and made it clear that the ideas and spirit of the church resonated within him in an essential way.

Karl's coming-out process played a critical role in establishing an identity independent of the traditional beliefs of his church-oriented community. These experiences allowed him to find communities that accepted him as gay, enabling both personal autonomy and social inclusion. As an adult coming to terms with his sexuality, Karl passed through many periods of abandoning the church or feeling abandoned by it. He saw its teachings as directly opposed to what he was coming to see as his nature: "There was a lot of extreme back-and-forth in my life dealing with my sexuality versus my religion ... [which teaches] if you have those feelings and those desires then you have them, but you are not allowed to act on them because that is a sin." He explained that he could not remain in a community where homosexuality was viewed as a sin without experiencing self-hate. He resorted to periods of sexual abstinence followed by abandoning the church for periods of excess: "I was a very devout Christian, not going to do this, not going to do this, and then I'd feel like I can't contain it anymore and then I'd go back to being wild and crazy for anywhere from three to six months and then back. So it was just back and forth from one wild extreme to another." Vacillating between extremes was a feature of Karl's adult life that rendered his experience of belonging to a community as something precarious and contingent on his internal stability.

As he began to accept his gay identity, he developed a new self-esteem while exploring other belief systems: "From twenty-five on I said I'm not going to put myself in a position where I'm being told that I'm not good anymore and that's where my self-respect really started happening.... I was able to explore different spiritualities and look into Buddhism and Hinduism and all the things that offers, and find a very nurturing accepting religious beliefs that are about you and your journey and it's not you having to be on this journey that's spelled out for you." He eventually found a Christian church that honored his newly found sense of self and spirituality. In addition, he maintained professional and personal connections with specifically gay-friendly churches and religious communities. Self-acceptance was reinforced through an accepting spiritual community that tolerated differences in beliefs and upheld the value of the unique individual.

Although a limited source of belonging and community identification, Karl's professional life played an important role in his self-esteem, and his success was a source of pride. His professional connections played a key role in his life. In addition to the "intense" periods of bonding with others during artistic collaborations, Karl experienced financial and social security through his part-time teaching job. He enjoyed the structure of the work and took pride in his accomplishments as an educator: "So it was nice, especially being an elective . . . and it was important for me to be one of those teachers that people wanted to be in their class because that's how you grow your program." In addition to providing a steady paycheck and professional gratification, teaching gave him flexibility to pursue his art career. He maintained regular contact with students and colleagues, but did not have to "do all the really tiring stuff that one had to do as a full-time classroom teacher." Teaching presented another realm where he could remain connected to the community while maintaining a sense of autonomy.

Karl's other job as a personal assistant was also a very important source of connection for him. He had begun working for this artist in his home several years before the arrest, during which time he had become close with both his boss and his boss's partner. These friendships provided him with stability and moral support through the difficult time following his arrest. The man he assisted was "kind of like a father" to him, while the man's partner and Karl "became really good friends . . . we work together all the time and have our lunches together. He knows me probably better than anybody else."

This relationship was crucial when Karl was arrested for the encounter with a student at his school. They were the first people he called and helped him find a lawyer. Furthermore, they provided a sense of solace that broke his isolation during the turmoil surrounding his arrest and conviction: "He has been with me through talking about this whole thing, and since we're on similar spiritual paths I hear all his aches and pains . . . and he was able to do that through my whole process with this." Having a sounding board through his "whole process with this" was a way for Karl to offset the isolation that can befall people with a highly stigmatizing label.

This couple played a critical role reinforcing Karl's place in their community when they championed him during the crisis with "the angry villagers" (which will be discussed in greater detail in the next chapter). In the face of complaints and harassing phone calls from neighbors who discovered Karl's sex offender status, his employers asserted his right to be there and argued on his behalf. They refused to fire him and were willing to become embroiled in a community debate for his sake.

Karl's relationship with his family was reinforced through his coming-out process when he learned that they were not as dogmatic as he had thought. He had to reconstruct his notion of them at the same time that they were coming to accept his homosexuality. Because they participated in a fundamentalist religion that views homosexuality as a sin, Karl was concerned that his relationship with them would be severed when he told them about his sexuality. However, they "stepped up to the plate" when he insisted on full acceptance: "I said, I need to be able to feel normal. To feel accepted. And I'm going to bring up conversations sometimes. I don't want to get to the point where it's Christmas and I have to choose to be with my boyfriend or with my family because I can't be with both." Karl argued that he didn't want to feel any different than his heterosexual brother who could introduce his girlfriends to his family. He wanted to be able to openly discuss aspects of his social life without feeling stigmatized. This was an important step in his relationship with them, and also a moment when he realized that they weren't as traditional as he had thought: "I realized my parents and my brother were not nearly as dogmatic religious as I was. Because we went to the same church. It was odd. I don't really understand how I got my sense of religion because I was much more black and white than my parents are. My parents don't even go to church now. They had me go because that's how they thought you should raise kids. It was maybe more social. And they took what they took and then they left the rest. I did not take what I take and leave the rest." Their pragmatic view regarding their religion allowed them to reconceptualize their sense of who Karl was without having to excommunicate him. It provided a way for them to affirm family ties rather than ideological affiliations. Karl's parents valued their connection to him more than strict adherence to doctrine.

Karl stated that it was very difficult to tell his family about the arrest, and that when he first told them he lied and insisted he was innocent, that the sexual violation had not occurred. Their support was demonstrated by the fact that they provided the majority of the thirty thousand dollars he needed in legal fees. Both parents were educators, and Karl stated that this amount represented a substantial portion of their savings. He did not disclose to them that he was in fact guilty until after he was convicted and sentenced. He said at that point they were "shocked," still indicating that the information challenged their conception of him. But they stood by him and remained an important source of social support.

Karl lived in an urban environment and felt comfortable within his ethnically mixed working-class neighborhood. It is perhaps surprising that his relative anonymity gave him a sense of belonging. He contrasted his idea of working-class values with those he associated with the homogenous, upper-class suburbs where he worked. He described his neighborhood as having a

> working-class town mentality: It's probably a mentality of not being as concerned with what other people think. Just mind their own business and doing their thing and taking care of their lives. Which is what I like. . . . I'm like one of the only white guys in my neighborhood. I don't see even a lot of other people that are even like me but it's a great place to be. . . . You don't feel that sense of, "oh I don't fit in"—even though I don't necessarily fit in in that sense. . . . I feel like in [the very affluent suburbs] where it's wealthier, more Waspy, that kind of mentality. There's certainly this emphasis of like how that could be a real a stigma.

Karl's sense of connection seemed to be derived from his ability to live autonomously and free from scrutiny. Although he acknowledged ethnic differences between himself and his neighbors, he did not experience himself as an outsider. This security and sense of informal inclusion were directly contrasted with the suburban environments wherein he was harassed. Although the "wealthier, more Waspy" neighborhoods tend to be upheld as more desirable places to live, Karl constructed them as communities where membership is tenuous and there is great potential to be stigmatized. He expressed the view that belonging in a wealthier community is more contingent on maintaining status and social norms.

Reggie

Reggie's primary roles in his community were articulated through his familial relationships, and these remained intact in the aftermath of his sex offense conviction. He grew up in a lower-middle-class household in an urban neighborhood, and was raised by his mother and older sister. A very social person with many friends, Reggie described himself as seeking out company. He attributed his need to be among people to his childhood experiences:

> And also dealing with my mom and sister not being there as a child to go back to that. I always had a fear of abandonment. You know the fear of being alone. So sometime, like if I had the day off I'll get up early and just go to one of my friend's houses and watch TV or play video games till my wife got home because I just didn't want to be alone at that time. Because my mom would work, my sister's older than me, so she was at work, and I would just be left alone, and my mom was very overprotective. So sometime I couldn't even go outside. I had to be in the house by myself.

Having always lived in the same neighborhood, Reggie had a strong sense of belonging in the fabric of his community. He had known many of his neighbors his entire life and he said that walking down the street he often stopped to chat with people, many with whom he "goes way back." Reggie and his current wife used to attend church regularly. They went less often now, because they felt that this particular church community did not reflect their values. "It was more about money than about getting that empowerment feeling, you know. Getting that faith in you. It was more of a fashion show, gossip. You're supposed to go to church for a problem. If you have a problem, you go to church to speak to the pastor. You get enlightenment. And then there, you know, rumors would just spread. So after church we would know who's sleeping around, who's on the couch, who got put out, who's having a baby by this guy over here. And it just was too much, like we have to find another church." The experience Reggie had at this church reflects the fact that people in his community knew each other well and were familiar with each other's family structure and personal issues, indicating a close-knit community (although at times an uncomfortably close one).

Reggie was married to his second wife, whom he had originally started dating over twenty years ago. They married after a period of separation of several years. They had two children together, and he had another son with his first wife. He and his current wife were close and mutually supportive and shared a rich history. He was also close to his children, and he saw his two younger sons on a regular basis. They watched TV together, played video games, and talked easily: "I want to make sure they know to talk to me about the important things. That I'm here for that. And they do, most definitely." In addition, Reggie was very close to both his mother and his sister. He spoke to his sister regularly and saw her several times a month. He visited his mother a couple of times a week and talked to her on the phone every day.

Reggie's family was clearly very important to him, and the bonds he shared with them were the most important in his life. Fortunately, each member of his family was supportive of him when they learned about his conviction for the sex offense against the teenage girl. Reggie constructed his offense as a "mistake," and his family members all saw the offense in that light, accepting his definition of the situation.

When he was first arrested Reggie spent ten days in jail. During that time he was too ashamed to call his wife, and tried to put it off. Telling her was "one of the hardest things. When I first told my wife, that was hard. She wanted to come visit me when I was incarcerated . . . I refused to see her. I didn't want to see her. Just the fact of being incarcerated. We had never had that kind of relationship where I was incarcerated. I just didn't want to see her on those terms." Reggie's reluctance to see his wife while incarcerated reflected the fact that he felt differently about himself as a result of the conviction. He was ashamed and didn't want to be seen as a criminal by her. He was concerned with how he would appear in her eyes and expressed a fear that it would change their relationship.

He explained the circumstances of the incident, and in doing so had to address his infidelity: "I told her it was just basically, you know, the best way I could put it to her was like, I guess that, the guy that works on the beach with all the girls just looking at him like, ooh and ah, and that's how [this girl] was to me. Instead of keeping it at a little puppy love crush with her, I took it further. That was wrong." Upset more by the infidelity than the age of the girl, his wife did not see Reggie as sexually deviant. Eventually she gave him her full support: "She was upset at first, you know, but she said that we would work through it, and you know we have. We don't argue about it. If we have a disagreement she doesn't throw it back in my face, you know, 'what you did' type of thing. She's not cautious of anything. She has full trust. One thing was, I was honest with her. I was honest with her." The emotional support he received from his wife provided continuity and stability as he lived with the consequences of his conviction. He stated that the relationship had not changed and that he now shared his experiences with probation and the treatment program with her: "Each week I go to the program like I'm supposed to. I discuss everything in the program with her. I don't state the names, but the different stories, scenarios. So she knows what it's like for me there." Emphasizing the importance of honesty and openness, Reggie was less isolated in his experiences as a convicted sex offender and was able to communicate these experiences to the most important person in his life without risking severing that bond.

Reggie's mother and sister were "shocked" to learn about his conviction. He argued that the news was so confounding to them because they had never known him to behave inappropriately or to "go down that road." He explained that he had never been with "someone younger than me. No one. I mean not even going down to the park to play football with someone younger. I explained to my mom, explained what happened. Being we're a tight-knit family they understood. You know, as long as I told them I go through the correct channels, you know. I know I'm never going to erase this mistake, but make sure it never happens again." Reggie asserted that he needed to reassure his family that he was following the procedures associated with his probation and doing what he needed to do by attending the program (going through "the correct channels"). They accepted that he made "a mistake," and did not abandon their long-standing conception of him. The relationship and the identity he maintained with them remained intact.

When Reggie first told his seventeen- and eighteen-year-old sons about the conviction, they reacted with anger toward the victim's father: "My sons, they were protective. They wanted to go look for her, look for him, you know what I mean? And I was like, 'I was wrong. Let me explain what happened.' And they listened. They took it in. And after we finished talking they went about their business . . . it didn't change them." Reggie was able to neutralize his sons' anger by explaining his version of events as well as his own agency in the incident. Reggie did not demonize the girl or her father, but, as he did in his explanation for his wife, he focused on his own wrongdoing. Reggie made sure to use his experience and his conviction as an opportunity to educate them about the possible and severe consequences of certain transgressions.

> Every time I go to my group I basically explain to them what I'm going through so they don't go down that road . . . you know get on the computer saying the wrong thing in a chat room. That'll get you in trouble. . . . They responded. We sat there and we watched. . . . I like to have them sit there and watch *Lock Up* which comes on CNBC and shows you different jails, San Quentin, Kentucky, New York. These are places you do not want to be. Then we also watch *Dateline, To Catch a Predator*, to show them, playing online, this is what will happen. And they take it all in. The entire time they probably won't even blink, in amazement. And I say, "one slip up and that's it."

Using his experiences as an opportunity to educate his children, he took the conviction and the negative consequences and transformed them into a means of reasserting his role as father and protector of his sons. His family provided a source of support for him, and he reaffirmed his family connection by turning the offense into a learning experience for himself and his sons.

Aaron

The two most significant sources of social connection for Aaron were his family and career. He had been working in social services for over twenty years at the time he was arrested for a consensual affair with a sixteen-year-old exotic dancer. During the span of his career he had taken on increasing responsibility and felt that he was "productive" both in terms of "contributing to the community" and in terms of maintaining a material lifestyle that he enjoyed. When describing his career, Aaron exuded a sense of personal pride: "I had a caseload of fifty people. I was in charge of the unit. I was productive, I was doing the things I needed to do. I was married. I had a house, vacation twice a year." He asserted that the personal satisfaction he derived from helping others was more important that the salary. Describing the meaning his work had for him, Aaron stated,

> Just taking someone that didn't believe [they could accomplish their goals], you know, and encouraging them. . . . And just watching them blossom. Those are the greatest rewards. In the human services it was never financial. It was all about just being able to meet someone where they're at and then help them move to the next plateau in their life station. That was the biggest importance to me. And

in between, even if they've fallen, to be there to not cushion their fall, but to be there to help them get back up. To be there to help them back on the bicycle. That's the biggest reward.... I enjoyed what I did. I had a passion for what I did.

The positive impact he had on others was a source of self-esteem for him.

Aaron's career played an important role in the trajectory of his adult life, and finding "meaningful employment" helped him establish a stable, middle-class lifestyle. In his youth he had drifted between odd jobs and had been more concerned with socializing, using and dealing recreational drugs, and focusing on things to buy with his money than he was with developing career goals. This changed after an arrest for drug possession. He happened to have a supportive probation officer who "encouraged me to change, to modify my life. So I went back to school, took up a few courses." He argued that the arrest was "a wake-up call" and that his life may have been far worse had he not had the "rapport" he developed with this probation officer. He explained that the experience "straightened me out. Put me on the straight and narrow.... I'm grateful to be fifty years old. A lot of my friends who I grew up with are not here presently. When I say that I mean they're not here in a mental capacity, because they're either tripped out, or they're not here in the physical aspect because they're six feet under, or they're somewhere incarcerated for something ... so I thank that person. I thank that person for encouraging me and being supportive at the same time." Aaron also received a great deal of social benefit from work. He was deeply immersed in the culture of his job ("I was the go-to guy"), interacting with all levels of staff and outside authorities in his capacity as program manager. He developed social bonds with a number of people with whom he would go out for lunch and invite to family barbeques on weekends. He regularly worked out in the agency's gym with colleagues and acted as an informal "personal trainer" to a number of people.

Work not only was an enjoyable way to connect with the community but also provided an important distraction from marital problems that Aaron was having several months prior to his arrest. He had been with his wife for fifteen years, and when they began to have problems Aaron started spending more time at work. Throughout his adult life he was in committed, monogamous relationships, and his most recent marriage was his longest union. He described relationships in general as difficult and involving work managing the tension between "autonomy and being dependent." Yet being in a relationship was clearly a significant source of social bonding for Aaron. He had begun dating a woman soon after his separation from his wife, and this girlfriend remained supportive after his sex offense conviction. In fact, although they were not living together at the time he was arrested, she moved into his apartment while he was incarcerated to prevent him from losing his lease.

Aaron identified his children as the most important part of his life. All grown, his three children remained in frequent contact with him. They spoke regularly, and his son and his family would come over every Sunday for dinner. His children were close to each other and had retained a sense of being a family. Aaron expressed pride in the fact that they all completed college with professional degrees. Watching them grow up and seeing them "be positive and succeeding" continued to be a rewarding experience. The sex offense conviction did not change his relationship to them, and he stated that they remained "supportive and encouraging."

Aaron's siblings also provided an ongoing form of social support throughout his life. They were close as children and "looked out for each other." He reported that his siblings were more career-driven as young people, and that they each went on to college after high school. They supported him after his drug arrest in his efforts to return to school and find a career: "We remained close and supportive. Even with that first conviction. They were disappointed in me. But they didn't turn their back on me.... Even when I first got married they were happy and congratulatory of that. When I got my GED, they were happy about that." As they had been with his arrest in his youth, Aaron's siblings were supportive after learning of his sex offense conviction. They retained their image of him and assured him, "we know you are not a rapist." They did not see his identity as altered nor label him a sexual deviant; he did not lose significant family bonds as a result of his new label.

Raoul

Like Reggie and Aaron, Raoul expressed his social self most strongly through reference to his family ties. His sense of self-worth derived from these relationships. He emphasized his roles as husband and father, and in particular expressed great personal pride in his children. He distinguished his social role within a kinship system from his stigmatized label: "Before I was a sex offender I was a father, a brother, an uncle, a son."

These roles weren't compromised by his conviction for a sex offense against his thirteen-year-old stepdaughter. Raoul's family maintained their connection to him when he was arrested, as well as throughout his prison stay, and they continued to provide support: "[My family] was shocked. And they were supportive. They helped me out, we kept in touch ... from the beginning." Raoul currently lived with his mother, and expressed gratitude at being able to be with her. He described her as depressed and "negative," and while he was in prison he had prayed that he could be with her and help her: "She looks forward to me getting on her case, kind of. Because she doesn't have anybody. When I first went to my mother's apartment she was introverted, in her room, in her little routine. I kind of like snapped her out of it and gave her some life and I kind of like thank God for that because I did. That was one of my prayers."

Relationships with women, particularly the long-term relationship with his wife, formed a significant part of the entwined family network in which Raoul was situated. He maintained contact with his wife and his own children while he was in prison and after his release. He asserted that his wife deeply regretted having called the police after discovering the photos, and reiterated that she did not want to press charges against him. She had not anticipated the severe consequences of her actions, and stood by him throughout his ordeal: "She helped me out, believe it or not. [My wife] sent me letters, sent me money, brought the kids to ... the jail, so I could see them. She cried to me. To take a plea." Raoul seemed immensely proud of his continued relationship with her. The fact that she maintained contact with him helped sustain a sense of social normalcy in the face of his status as sex offender. Her support in particular seemed to help sustain his regard for himself as a husband and father. It was with great pride that he relayed that he would be seeing her in the near future: "And you know what? My victim? Her mother is coming Friday. She called me on the phone.... She wants to go to church with me, on Sunday."

Raoul grew up in an urban environment in a neighborhood where many of his peers had committed crimes and had come into contact with the formal social control apparatus: "I had a lot of friends that were delinquents ... that were high school dropouts or selling drugs, and people stealing and stuff like that." His early days in juvenile facilities and his immersion in drug treatment programs introduced him to a life organized in part by criminal justice and social service agencies. Thus, he was embedded in a community where certain forms of social deviance were more common and in some ways normalized. His lifestyle was distinct from that associated with the mainstream middle class, and he was raised as part of a community that did not necessarily see some forms of criminal behavior as abnormal or deviant per se, and there was no sense that these community bonds were in any way severed as a result of his conviction.

Raoul's relationship with God and the church provided a network of social support in addition to a spiritual connection with something larger than himself. When he was in prison he felt that he had lost everything and had "hit rock bottom": "I started to realize I was losing my family, my freedom, all the things that I had worked for. I seen everything, I was losing everything. That was like the rock bottom." That's when he "found God" and began to develop a spiritual connection with something bigger than himself through which he could cope and find meaning within his prison experience: "Finally I came to my knees and I had to cry out to God. I didn't know who God was at that time but I cried out I knew there had to be a higher power to keep me from losing my mind you know ... but God changed me while I was locked up. I was touched." His spiritual connection helped him manage life in prison and he became a "model inmate." When he was released from prison, he continued to attend church regularly, and found acceptance there in spite of his status as sex offender: "I tell people from the church [that I'm a convicted sex offender]. I had to sit down with the pastor and the deacon and I had to tell them because there's kids in the church, and I felt embarrassed. . . . [They were understanding and] love me in the church." He felt embraced and valued by the community he found at church and expressed a sense of social responsibility toward the institution, as reflected in his sharing his offense. They did not reject him and continued to be a source of support.

Social Self and Community

Listening to these stories, it becomes clear that men who are considered abhorrent outsiders because of their stigmatizing label are often in fact individuals embedded within a network of social relationships.

They perform various public and private identities and assume a number of roles that are independent of their deviant behavior. Because of the dehumanizing effects of stigma, it is important to have this opportunity to see that Tim had a close friend who provided an important connection in spite of relative isolation; that Karl, Aaron, and Terry derived enormous job satisfaction and worked in creative and professional endeavors that contributed their community; that Reggie saw himself as a family man; and that Raoul found meaning through engagement with his church. The intimate narratives of six men go a long way in individualizing and humanizing men who might otherwise be dismissed and ostracized as sex offenders.

Significantly, each of these men was able to maintain familial bonds in spite of his conviction. All the men explained this through recourse to a real self—an essential self that is good and knowable—that the family members trusted and believed in. This concept of their real self was larger and more significant than their isolated deviant sexual behavior, and the stigma attached to these behaviors did not, at least for their family members, override previous knowledge of them or become a master status. In subsequent chapters I will argue that this essential self was a foundation that allowed them to resist the complete internalization of a stigmatized identity.

CHAPTER 4

Severed Bonds

CLASSIC SOCIOLOGISTS SUCH AS Durkheim, Garfield, and Erikson have argued that as a symbolic means of reinforcing communities' boundaries and identity, rituals of punishment ascribe outsider status to the transgressor. Sex offenders on probation and parole, like many felons, find themselves living within the community at the same time that they are effectively excluded from participation in numerous social realms. Sanctions specifically against sex offenders, as well as the conditions of probation and parole, subject them to a range of social control policies that further reinforce their outsider status. As Jonathan Simon argues, the intent of these laws is explicitly to exclude and banish (Simon, 2000). As an exemplar of the new penology that emphasizes managing risks as opposed to transforming or reintegrating subjects, current sex offender policies mark these subjects as dangers to the community who must be managed as "social waste" (ibid.). These policies place offenders within the community while denying them the civil liberties that are integral to "normal" social engagement. This "civil death" handicaps their status as members of society, and their ability to conduct themselves as full citizens—legally and personally—is severely restricted. These laws can be seen as having such an "encompassing" character that they create living conditions similar to those Goffman describes as "total institutions." Although sex offenders on probation or parole, and subject to registration for years or decades after that sentence, are not living behind physical barriers in a literal sense, scholars have likened their condition to life inside a "camp" (Spencer, 2009). This is a "state of exception" where "the law protecting the sex offenders' rights is suspended and they are abandoned by the law" (Spencer, 2009, p. 229).

Constraints on their liberties directly affect offenders' relationship to the community, and so, presumably, impact the internal bond between the individual and society. The conditions imposed by the criminal justice system limited participants' physical movement and social freedoms and in so doing altered the contours of their daily lives. These routines are deeply entwined with the relationship between individuals and the social institutions that shape their identity (Giddens, 1984, p. 85). Through various restrictions, the social control apparatus continually reinforced the offenders' status as outsiders by disrupting routine activities and the normal round of social life. Furthermore, the limited employment options available to them constrained their social identity, career trajectories, income potential, and job security. Where one lives often plays a key role in one's sense of belonging, and Megan's Law relies on residence as a defining feature of community. These policies potentially expose sex offenders to their neighbors and jeopardize their privacy and ability to live as an insider with a place in the group.

This chapter is divided into five sections exploring the ways in which social bonds and normative identity were disrupted as a result of offenders' convictions. It looks at their accounts of social control and civil restrictions, employment, housing, additional consequences for Terry (the serial offender), and subjective experiences of stigma. Unlike the previous two chapters, this one is not organized around cases. Each participant's narrative is analyzed in terms of the five themes.

Social Control and Civil Restrictions

The New York State Division of Criminal Justice Services manages convicted sex offenders in the community, and state policies regarding sex offenders are detailed in the New York State Sex Offender Registration Act (SORA). New York State requires that anyone who is convicted of a sex offense register with local law enforcement. In addition, the Electronic Security and Targeting of Online Predators Act, which took effect on April 28, 2008, requires sex offenders to report all their Internet accounts, email accounts, and screen names. Although law enforcement agencies do not release information regarding offenders' Internet accounts, this information may be given (on request) to social networking websites with users under eighteen years old. A 2009 article in the *Daily News* reported that 3,500 sex offenders registered in New York State had their Facebook and Myspace accounts closed (Lovett, 2009). Those offenders classified as low risk (Level I) must register for a minimum of twenty years. Those classed as moderate to high risk must register for life. Failure to register is a felony and will result in a minimum of one year in prison. The state maintains a toll-free hotline from which the public may obtain information about offenders. Details pertaining to physical appearance, the crime committed, the terms of probation or parole, and zip codes are obtainable through this number for *all* levels of offenders. For Level III offenders, the state will also release the exact street address of the offender's residence. In addition the state maintains a website where visitors can search a database of Level II and Level III offenders by name, county, or zip code. SORA does not monitor what individuals may do with information they have obtained, although using it to harass offenders is against the law. An individual may release whatever information they receive from the toll-free number or website to whomever they wish.

Notification to schools and other organizations is left to the discretion of local law enforcement. SORA allows law enforcement to release the publicly available information to "entities with vulnerable populations related to the offense" (i.e., schools and facilities that serve children) for all levels of offenders but does not include any restrictions regarding where an offender may live. However, the terms of an individual's probation or parole may include such limits. In addition, many counties in New York State impose residency restrictions on sex offenders that bar them from living within a certain distance from schools. SORA does not limit where a sex offender may work, with one exception: sex offenders cannot work on an ice cream truck. Certain professions, however, do routinely check fingerprints and perform background checks in order to refuse employment to individuals who have committed certain types of crime. For example, convicted sex offenders are not allowed to work as teachers or school bus drivers.

In addition to those outlined by state law, the criminal justice system can impose an array of restrictions on an individual as conditions of probation or parole. These can range from curfews to prohibitions against being in certain areas such as playground, contact with specific people, interaction with persons under eighteen, and the use of alcohol. Offenders can be required to wear GPS monitors, undergo random drug screening, be denied use of computers, and have restricted mobility outside of their city.

Anthony Giddens's work addresses the problems of identity under conditions of modernity and can illuminate the ways restrictions such as those listed above may deeply affect individuals' orientation to their world. Linking micro-sociological analysis to macro-level structures through a scrutiny of day-to-day life as structured around routines, Giddens outlines a theory of identity where daily physical movement through social zones plays a key role. In order to function socially, individuals require a degree of ontological security that is related to "an autonomy of bodily control within predictable routines" (Giddens, 1984, p. 50). A significant consequence of restrictions on sex offenders is the loss of individual autonomy, which was experienced differently by different subjects depending on their probation/parole conditions and their lifestyle. These policies heavily impact the routines in which they operate and perform selfhood; they restrict movement, compromise privacy, and alter the relationship of the individual to those around him. The policies effectively take control of the management of public and private domains. In so doing they generate a specific set of routines that mark the offender as deviant. Cumulatively, they reinforce offenders' identities *as sex offenders* and undermine their ability to successfully perform nonstigmatized ones.

Raoul

Raoul, who took photographs of his stepdaughter's genitalia, served nine years of a fifteen-year prison sentence. He had to register for thirty years, attend group each day, and report to his probation officer each week. In addition, he had a nine-o'clock curfew: "I know I did wrong and I'm labeled a sex offender, I'm a bona fide sex offender. I'm on the web, you know. I have to report to probation every week. I have to register. I go to programs. You know, it's really stressful, really, you know. I did nine years in prison, followed by ten years of probation. I have to register for thirty years." Raoul indicated that the fact of being a sex offender is in and of itself a restriction that constrained his social identity. That information about him was available on the Internet was seen as a now critical aspect of his social status and identity, part of being a "bona fide" sex offender. Being "on the web" was part of the way in which he was officially labeled as someone who committed a socially unacceptable ("wrong") act.

The effects of social control were continually experienced throughout his "daily round" (Goffman, 1986, p. 8) and his weekly routine, constraining and structuring the ongoing experience of his everyday life. Having to attend hour-long group therapy on weekdays required an hour of travel each way. This considerable portion of the day affected his availability for work ("I mean, I have to be there every single day"), as well as his ability to control and structure his own time. His weekly routines revolved around his status and the conditions of probation. He could not "put the past behind" because his past action, and the attendant stigma, was reinforced and reexperienced on a daily basis. That three hours of his day (nearly half a traditional workday) were devoted to his stigmatized identity curtailed his ability to pursue nondeviant, non-state-controlled activities within the community and demarcated a set of routine practices that distinguished him from those around him.

Raoul experienced these constraints as extremely stressful and suggested that the rationale for them was not completely a matter of justice: "Public assistance, Medicaid pays for [the program]. I think it's a racket; I really do. They had me going there every day. That was stressful. Besides having to do with the probation and having a curfew, right? When I went to this program, they told me you got to come every day. How am I supposed to continue on with my life if I have to be here every day? And then probation once a week." Arguing that the frequency of his attendance in therapy is in part "a racket" for service providers to make money, he positioned himself as a pawn of the state that manages low-income individuals who enter various institutional systems. He asserted that his autonomy was compromised through mandated treatment that benefits payees of social control services. In addition, curfews represent constraints generally associated not with autonomous adults but with dependent adolescents. This is a significant imposition and intrusion into an individual's ability to control his own activities and is a daily reminder and reinforcement of the presence of formal social control.

Raoul's daily routine and ability to establish "ontological security" were so sufficiently constricted that his ability to "continue with [his] life" was undermined. Probation emerged as a mechanism through which his status as a sex offender was reinforced and his full membership in the community was compromised.

Tim

Tim was sentenced to eight years of probation for making a date with a law enforcement agent claiming to be a fourteen-year-old girl. He had to register for twenty years. In addition, he was not allowed access to a computer and was subjected to a nine-o'clock curfew for the first few months of his sentence. This restriction was eventually dropped, although he was still not allowed out on Halloween (a provision that he said he "understand[s]. I agree with that"). Tim's deep frustration with injustices in sentencing and probation requirements will be discussed in the following chapter.

Tim was required to attend his treatment program once a week. He did not mind having to attend the group, but payment for the sessions posed a tremendous hardship: "They're fifty dollars a session. I'm on twenty dollars a session because I don't have the funds. I went from ten dollars to twenty dollars so I had to cut my phone expense in half cause I have a house phone, a regular house phone. I went from the unlimited package to call by call. Next thing I know they'll be turning my electricity off 'cause I can't afford that because they'll raise me to twenty to thirty dollars to catch up to paying them." The program's cost took critically needed resources away from him. Because of his considerable financial constraints, the payments represented a significant expense that impinged on his ability to communicate with others. As discussed in the previous chapter, the telephone was Tim's most significant medium of interaction with others, and having to decrease his phone usage may have contributed to additional social isolation.

Furthermore, his frustration with the system was articulated through the fear that program costs would continue to increase, leading to further hardship and social marginalization. This indicated a significant degree of ontological *in*security. Tim expressed the idea that anything can happen in the future; the conditions of probation contributed to a sense of powerlessness over his fate. He felt that the way his life was managed by the criminal justice system stripped him of control over important aspects of his life.

Aaron

Aaron served six months in jail and was sentenced to an additional ten years of probation for his affair with a sixteen-year-old dancer. He had to register for twenty years. He saw his probation officer once a month and attended group therapy once a week.

Aaron was confused and frustrated by the way his probation was handled. In discussing the conditions of his probation, he expressed intense dismay at the fact that he had not been given proper documentation of the restrictions that applied to him. He claimed that his probation officers never gave him the papers and that the conditions kept changing.

> So it's like, okay, I just signed some conditions, but do I get a copy of it? It's like, stay out of trouble; find a job; don't use drugs. Don't— like, there are certain places that you can and can't visit. Like, I don't have any children. I have grandchildren, so I don't have any reason to be going into those schools. But again, my offense wasn't about that. So, you know, I said, "That's not applicable." At one point they said I wasn't going to be able to go to the mall. But the judge ruled, no, that's absurd. That I wasn't going to be able to use the Internet, but then he ruled that out. That you can't be within a thousand feet of a school, but then they ruled that out, and they modified it to more feet or something. . . . Again, I signed the paper, but I don't believe I was given a copy.

Expressing frustration with the way the system managed his status, Aaron was exasperated by the way constraints on his behavior were continually changed. Laughing when he told these stories, Aaron communicated dismay at the extent to which he lacked control over decisions that affected him.

Being a convicted sex offender was experienced less acutely as a loss of civil restrictions and more intensely when he described the loss of his career. He even talked about the time he spent in jail as a difficult but temporary situation, one that didn't have lasting consequences. The most serious result of his conviction was the fact that he could not return to work (which will be discussed in greater detail later in this chapter).

Reggie

Reggie served ten days in jail, was sentenced to six years of probation, and was required to register for twenty years for his encounter with a fifteen-year-old girl. While on probation he met weekly with his probation officer and attended weekly treatment groups. He was subject to random checks by his probation officer and was not allowed to have pornographic material in his apartment or on his computer. He stated that as a sex offender he was not allowed "to work anywhere where you're affiliated with children. You can't baby-sit kids. My kids can't have sleepovers if the kids are underage. You're not really even supposed to go to the park if there's like little kids in the park . . . but like certain things you just can't avoid. If it's a public park you just can't help it; if you go there to workout or to jog, and there are kids there." The seeming ubiquity of children in his neighborhood curtailed his ability to participate in recreational activities without being reminded of his status. The conditions of probation compromised his role in relations to his sons and their friends, and impinged on his ability to freely conduct himself as a parent and community member.

He argued that anything he did that was a possible violation could reinforce his sex offender status. Even when he no longer had to go to weekly sex offender treatment, he felt that the possibility of returning to them would loom over his head for the duration of his probation: "If you do something that has nothing to do with a sex offense, they could land me right back in sex offender classes. You know, if I'm speeding, which is really a violation, not a crime, which has me being a sex offender puts me right back in the sex offender classes." Reggie articulated a concern with the fact that there were graver consequences to minor—and non–sexually deviant—forms of law violation for him. There was no escaping his status as a sex offender.

Karl

Because he had a complex professional life that required traveling for art projects, the conditions of Karl's probation were a continual source of tension for him. He was sentenced to six years of probation and had to register for twenty years for having a sexual encounter with a student at the school where he taught. His experiences with registration were fraught with conflict because he lived and worked in separate states. With the exception of work, he was not allowed to leave the city without permission. He was not allowed to be in any professional relationship with a person under the age of eighteen, nor could he be alone with anyone in that age group. Karl was aware of the tentacles of social control reaching into every significant aspect of his life, intruding on his privacy in ways that marked him as an "other."

Karl experienced his probation requirements as a devastating loss of freedom: "I remember sitting in the probation office with my probation officer and the first time we were going over, look you can't travel and you can't do this, and . . . I was just crying. I was just crying. I couldn't really do anything. I was just devastated realizing all the things that were being taken away from me." The initial realization of the enormity of his situation was expressed in terms of the loss of mobility and control over his lifestyle. He was "devastated" as he felt that he was being stripped of the accoutrements of identity that are taken for granted in modern democratic societies.

Because his probation officer could drop in at any time to ensure that he had not "committed a violation" (i.e., failing to meet the conditions of his probation, but not necessarily committing a new crime), Karl felt that his life needed to always be open for inspection: "This morning my probation officer came by and knocked on my door at seven in the morning and if I had somebody there and they didn't know about it, they would be wondering why these people are knocking on my door and walking in and looking around and making sure I still live there." The distress of this unexpected morning intrusion was strongly articulated in reference to an incident which *could* happen (and less so in terms of what *did* happen). Karl expressed the impact of the inspection through a what-if scenario, imagining the difficulty of having to explain the intrusion to a potential new boyfriend. He specifically depicted someone who would not know he was a sex offender. And the source of anxiety centered around exposure and disclosure of discrediting information. Karl recognized the abnormality of having one's life inspected by agents of social control and knew that it would require special explanation. Anticipating such moments created anxiety about how he could be seen by others. As Goffman observes, possibilities of exposure make discreditable persons more "alive to the social situation": "What are unthinking routines for normals can become management problems for the discreditable. These problems cannot always be handled by past experience, since new contingencies always arise, making former concealing devices inadequate. The person with a secret failing, then, must be alive to the social situation as a scanner of possibilities, and is therefore likely to be alienated from the simpler world in which those around him apparently dwell" (Goffman, 1986, p. 88). Control of private and discrediting information was essentially taken out of Karl's hands, and he recognized the impact this could have on his personal relationships. The unannounced inspections reinforced his status as an outsider because most people do not have to endure this sort of invasion. Intimate relationships could pose a special problem because these "can necessitate time spent together, and the more time an individual spends with another the more chance the other will acquire discrediting information about him" (ibid., p. 86). For Karl, the possibility loomed large that such information would be revealed before he was ready to disclose it. The fear of exposure was felt just as vividly as the surprise of the actual inspection because exposure could stigmatize him in his personal relationships and make him vulnerable to social judgments. That he could not control situations like this meant that he could not control when to disclose his "story" to a potential partner. It could force him into greater and premature intimacy, and could possibly lead to rejection, which might contribute to a sense of social isolation.

In addition to surprise visits from probation officers, the inability to travel outside of the state was also experienced as a formidable constraint that could potentially disrupt his personal relationships: "So that's a discussion that has to happen because if I'm dating someone that lives [out of state] I have to tell them, because I can't just go [there]. They're like, 'what do you mean you can't go . . . ?' And you can only say, 'Ah I don't like going [there]' so much before they're like, 'wait.' Because I'm not that kind of guy who's like, 'I don't travel outside of [where I live].' . . . I could just withdraw and go into a shell and avoid it all until it's over." Again Karl imagined a dating scenario where he would have to explain his status. He expressed his frustration in terms of potential situations that could arise and saw the development of future relationships threatened by the conditions of his probation. Significantly, Karl described explaining his inability to travel in terms of his identity, contrasting the type of person the conditions cast him as (someone who doesn't leave the area) with the type of person he truly was. In this way, he saw the limitations as actually constraining his social personality, turning him into someone he was not. Rather than adopt a false persona of "that kind of guy," he would prefer to explain his situation to the hypothetical romantic other. The alternative is what Giddens refers to as "situational withdrawal"— "the refusal to behave as a capable agent" (Giddens, 1984, p. 156). Karl expressed this idea as going "into a shell" to "avoid it all until it's over." Refusing withdrawal, Karl attempted to assert his social relationships by adopting (or rather envisioning adopting) a forthright stance where he could present others with the discrediting information. It was preferable to assume the stigmatized identity of a labeled sex offender, rather than equivocate and assume a false identity.

Terry

With thirteen convictions for sex offenses for such behaviors as public masturbation and frottage, Terry lived under greater conditions of social control than anyone other participant. He had to register for thirty years, was on house arrest, and wore a GPS monitoring device. The extreme lack of mobility imposed on him isolated him in his home. Although here he could enjoy more freedom and comfort than if confined to prison, he nonetheless lived under conditions of punishment and isolation where the law influenced every aspect of his social existence.

Terry explained the conditions of house arrest that allowed him three hours a week outside the home: "I've been on house arrest for twenty months and I'm on house arrest indefinitely. . . . You can go to therapy at a set time. You have three hours a week outside the house where you can do errands. And for anything else you need permission. . . . Permission doesn't come along very often." House arrest kept him separate from the community and restricted him to the confines of his home. It relegated him to a private realm, denying him a public or social existence. Proscribing the specific activities for which he could leave for a few hours a week, the sanction very directly controlled the nature of his routine day-to-day life as well as his movements in the community.

These conditions further entrenched him in an identity as sex offender. The additional activities for which he could leave the house—therapy and appointments with his probation officer—pertained exclusively to this status. He was permitted to enter the community under the condition that he did so *as a sex offender*, participating in mandated activities directly linked with his management by the criminal justice system. So the majority of interactions he had were with people who knew he was a sex offender and who interacted with him according to that status. Thus, his participation in the world was limited to his participation as an individual who had committed a sex offense. His other identities were denied expression, movement, and visibility; they were denied a stage on which they could be performed.

His lack of autonomy and dependence on the state were reinforced by the fact that he needed to ask permission for any contingencies that might arise. Placed in the position of having to justify his actions, Terry had little control, and had to consider what he might want or need to do in terms of the concerns of the criminal justice system. In this way official authority took on a reality in his thoughts. While opportunities may be envisioned, they could be realized only at the state's discretion. The state became a presence in his mind, playing a critical role in his ability to imagine the future.

House arrest is a method of social control that simultaneously keeps the offender both inside and outside the community. In contrast to those incarcerated, Terry could spend his time in the home doing as he pleased. He could wake when he wanted, and eat what and when he chose. He could dress however he liked, talk on the phone whenever he liked, and enjoy access to all his belongings. Of course, house arrest would be less punishing for those whose material life is more comfortable; the consequences of this form of social control are largely affected by class. For Terry, control of his private time remained his. He could live within his home in many ways like someone whose life is not under state control. The ability to do errands allowed him a respite from isolation, a few hours when he could casually interact with members of the community as an ordinary citizen taking part in the ordinary routines of life.

Yet these "freedoms" were highly controlled, and the conditions under which Terry spent his time in his home or doing errands in the community severely restricted his ability to perform many social roles. His life in the community was distinctly that of an outsider whose day-to-day routine was circumscribed by the criminal justice system and whose routines were highly surveilled. Enforced isolation was in and of itself a "lifestyle" that differed dramatically from those of Terry's neighbors and the people with whom he interacted in the supermarket. His situation is a prime example of Spencer's argument presented at the beginning of this chapter, that today's sex offender is a "homo sacer" living in a "camp" that is diffuse throughout society and creates "an indistinction between exclusion and inclusion, resulting in an inclusive exclusion of the homo sacer" (Spencer, 2009, p. 223).

When he did leave the house for his three hours of running errands, Terry was required to wear a GPS monitoring device that allowed law enforcement to track his exact whereabouts. This is a common law enforcement practice throughout the United States (Meloy & Coleman, 2009, p. 263). This device was worn around his belt and looked to be about two inches thick and four or five inches square. It was obtrusive, and Terry believed it was deliberately intended to stigmatize him as a convicted criminal. "I've had GPS devices on for twenty months. They were different. They are getting a little better. When they first started they were the size of a cinder block you had to carry around, and then it got down to the size of a brick. And now it's down to this.... It's just another way to put a scarlet letter on you. On your chest.... They could make it the size of a cell phone if they wanted to. The cell phone size is easy. I don't know why they have to have this size for that. You know. Always the reminder there." Whether the cumbersome device was deliberately large or not, it functioned as a constant reminder of his status as sex offender, preventing him from inhabiting a normalized identity. Not only were his movements tracked by the state, but he emphasized that the mechanism of tracking, the device itself, would not let him forget his status and served to set him apart from others.

Offenders on house arrest who have jobs are allowed to go to work, but this activity is highly monitored: "If you are working you are allowed to go to and from work. As long as you take the same route every day and the same times every day. You just have to carry the GPS device and wear the bracelet." However, as will be discussed in the next section in greater detail, Terry lost his job as a result of his most recent arrest. The provision allowing him to pursue work activities was moot in this case, and there were no provisions for work-seeking activities. Thus the unemployed offender on house arrest endures greater isolation than those employed and is limited in his ability to pursue employment. In this way, the sanction inadvertently metes stronger control on those who may already be marginalized and/or isolated.

Employment

The work one performs is directly related to one's social status and class, affecting one's material conditions, consumption opportunities (increasingly significant in the expression of social identity in the modern world), and sense of security. In addition, work is often closely tied to one's identity. For many people performing one's professional role is a large part of the presentation of self. As Americans spend more hours a day at work, the workplace has emerged as a potentially significant site for community connectedness. Although Putnam argues that workplace ties tend not to be intimate or "supportive," they can still offer the opportunity for "rewarding friendships" and "a sense of community" (Putnam, 2000, p. 87). Putnam also observes that "for the one American adult in three who is not employed, workplace ties are nonexistent" (ibid.,

p. 87). Thus, even if the workplace doesn't offer as much potential for social capital as one might wish, those denied work do not even have the opportunity of establishing these kinds of connections.

Although SORA does not ban sex offenders from pursuing any particular form of employment (other than, as mentioned, operating an ice cream truck), many employers perform background checks and refuse to hire convicted felons, particularly sex offenders. This means that in pursuing work options, sex offenders must rely on either marginalized, "off-the-books" jobs or jobs they can secure through personal connections. Because of these limitations, convicted sex offenders are potentially excluded from high-status careers and high-paying jobs, putting them in a socially insecure and downwardly mobile position where the privileges and comforts of middle-class life are closed to them.

Tim

Tim had worked the same job for several years at the time of his arrest. As we have seen, he had not been overly concerned about letting his employers know about the offense and stated that the business already employed a number of former inmates and "people that had been through the system." He said that when he told them about his arrest "they didn't care." Tim was not aware of being stigmatized on the job and was in an establishment where his deviant behavior did not "other" him from the community.

However, because of a subsequent health incident, he needed to leave this job. He stated that because of the nature of the job, he could not return to it: "I couldn't go back [to that industry] because it's too much stress." While his disability limited some of the jobs that he could consider, Tim's conviction for a sex offense was even further limiting. Tim believed his health would not interfere with a number of government jobs, but recognized that as a sex offender he would never be eligible for them: "If I ever wanted to get a decent job like let's say working for the transit, or working for a city government agency, I could never get any of those jobs now, because of my offense." Tim was frustrated by his financial situation and resented that he was charged with a felony sex offense for a noncontact crime without an actual victim: "I mean, it was just a set-up." The conviction further entrenched him in the dire financial straights he found himself in by barring him from better-paying jobs with security. Dually limited by his disability and his conviction, Tim was shut out from opportunities that could alter his financial condition and help him reenter the working class.

Reggie

Reggie was unemployed at the time of his arrest. He had worked at a corporation for nearly ten years as manager of one of its service departments. He enjoyed the responsibility, the pressure of meeting deadlines, and the professional environment. He had been laid off because of cutbacks and had been unemployed for a couple of months prior to the arrest. At the time of the interview he was still receiving unemployment benefits from the state.

Living on these benefits, Reggie was in a vulnerable financial position at the time of his arrest. Although he reiterated that he was only a Level I offender, he was convicted for a minor felony for sexual contact with a minor, an offense that outlined on background checks. He stated that he could never have the type of job he had had previously because of his record. Thus, his conviction had a significant impact on his ability to find meaningful employment of the kind he was accustomed to and would have liked to pursue.

Reggie had applied for a number of jobs, and in the process the potential employers all ran background checks that disqualified him. He stated that these experiences were very "discouraging," and his words reflected a sense of frustration and futility: "Even when you apply for a job and they tell you, you have to sign this form for a background check. You don't even want to go that far with the interview because it's going to come back that I was charged with sex abuse forcible touching." Reggie suggested that it was futile to present himself to potential employers because they would not consider him once the discrediting information was known. For this reason he felt he had few realistic options.

In addition to being disqualified for jobs, Reggie had endured humiliation from interviewers in human resources who confronted him with his stigmatizing label: "I went for one interview for a temp agency, and one lady came back and she was like, 'My God, you're a rapist! You're a rapist!'" Describing this encounter, Reggie expressed outrage at the word "rapist," which he argued did not describe the situation between him and the victim (with whom he had not had intercourse). Reggie said that this experience "was terrible"; the word "leaped out" at him and made him feel "like the sticky stuff at the bottom of a barrel." Although "shocked" at the way she threw the word "rapist" at him, he stood up for himself and confronted her: "Basically what she's saying to me, it's against my rights. You're not supposed to speak to me in that manner, you know. Disqualify my application and that's it. But she personalized." The interviewer had reinforced a stigmatizing label in a way that had deeply offended him because she made assumptions about his identity. He was confronted with dealing with her as a person who was judging him, which was different from simply managing bureaucratic protocol.

As someone on probation, Reggie was eligible for a course on seeking employment designed to help people with criminal records find jobs. Although he learned a few important techniques for managing discrediting information, overall the course further contributed to a sense of futility, hopelessness, and powerlessness. In describing the course, Reggie expressed cynicism about its true purposes: "I graduated from an employment course that they sent me to, which they're supposed to help you find jobs. But it's more of they get funding for each person that signs up. After I received the certificate and I sat down with the advisor, I haven't even received a phone call in three weeks. And they're supposed to do some of the footwork and I do some of the footwork." Although Reggie had earnestly attended the course in the hopes that it would help him find work in spite of his record, he left feeling frustrated and believing that he was just someone in a system that processed him for its own aims and functioning. He was willing to put effort into job seeking but found there was no support for him in these endeavors.

Looking for the good in the situation, Reggie acknowledged that he received some practical information: "So the only thing they taught us was that if you sat down with an interviewer, to explain, if they ask you to explain your conviction, make it from a negative to a positive. Don't really go into it, just let them know I was convicted of a nonviolent, nontheft crime and during those two years I've been in the programs to better myself, and I've also helped counsel others and like that." In this way, Reggie hoped that he would be able to use some of the techniques they taught him to neutralize the stigmatizing information. He very much wanted to improve his material and social situation and was frustrated that there were few opportunities available to help him better himself. Even feeling that he had tools with which to talk about his situation should he get a job interview, Reggie continued to express frustration with the fact that since the program he hadn't "received any phone calls, any leads, anything." This contributed to a sense of despair about the future and that there was little that he could do to influence the course of events.

Aaron

As we saw in the previous chapter, Aaron's management position and work environment were deeply important to him. In addition to providing economic stability and material comfort, the job offered Aaron a sense of meaningful contribution to the world. Furthermore, he was embedded in the social fabric of the institution and had many strong bonds with colleagues. The job loss resulting from his sex offense conviction was particularly devastating to him, severing him from his own professional identity, economic standing, and social ties.

The police came to Aaron's office, handcuffed him, and escorted him from the premises. He was not concerned when they first arrived and wanted to speak to him, because he often interacted with law enforcement in a professional capacity.

> What happened was the police came to my job, and when the police came, you know, I've always interacted with the authorities, because of our caseload.... So when they showed up and said they were here to see [me], I said "yeah, that's me." I had no idea what was going on. So when we went into my office and everything, and they said they were here to arrest me on this charge, I was floored. And then [my manager] had to become aware, because it happened on the job. I said, "Well, listen, I'll go with you guys. It's not a problem, but you can't put handcuffs on me in here. Let me walk outside because it's my job." But they were not sensitive to that at all. They were not sensitive to that at all.

Aaron was dismissed, although he went to the union and tried to fight the decision. The loss of the job entailed the end of his career in human services. He asserted that the sexual nature of the charge against him disqualified him from that arena where he felt that "people, they don't want to have anything to do with me, because, now you're dealing with people." His sex offense conviction was more consequential because his job involved working from a position of authority and in a helping capacity. This frustrated him because he claimed the act he was charged with "didn't have anything to do with any client." In spite of the fact that he believed his offense was unrelated to his work situation, this door was slammed shut. Despite his twenty years of experience, Aaron found himself unable to find employment in his field because of the extent to which he had been officially discredited.

Needing a salary, Aaron applied for civil servant jobs in public administration, but, like Reggie, quickly found that any employer who performs background checks would not consider him. Aaron described applying for one position and completing several stages of the hiring process: "And they did a whole background check on me, so they knew. But when I went to the last interview—which they said to me I was clear to go to—the supervisor at that particular plant came and interviewed me and said, 'Unfortunately we cannot offer you a position at this time because you're currently on probation.'" Aaron explained that although the reason they gave was simply that he was on probation, the truth was that they did not want to hire someone with a sex offense conviction. He argued with the interviewer: "So I said, 'I don't believe it. Where's that in writing because you are currently on probation you can't have this employment?' I was upfront with them. I was truthful with them. I said, 'maybe I think this is your bias.' But he said, 'You have to leave the building.' So I couldn't complete the interview. I have some friends that work [there]. They told me just put everything upfront in your application and they won't discredit you. But at the last minute, the rug was pulled from under me." Aaron insisted that each time the background check disqualified him, the underlying reason was the "nature" of his conviction. He surmised this from the fact that employers were willing to talk to him in spite of the fact that he had a criminal conviction, and did not rule him out until specific information about the offense became available. He argued that "just the connotation of that label—the label itself has tremendous negative impact."

Aaron reviewed his situation and tried to get a sense of what his employment options were. It was important to him to find meaningful work, but as he considered the possibilities, this goal seemed more and more unlikely. He explained that each new career he considered brought up issues that made it an unpromising prospect.

> I would report to the probation officer. I would let him know about the dilemma because the big thing there is they want you to get

employment. And I said, "So this is some of the things I was going to do." I was going to go take a course in cable installation. The probation officer said, "Nah, I don't think that's a good idea for you." I said, "Why?" He says, "Oh, because you're going to be in people's homes." And, well, I'm not going to be in people's homes by myself, but he shot that down. I said, okay, fine. How about, I used to do videography work. I used to videotape weddings and bar mitzvahs, all of those things. So I said, maybe I'll go back and do some independent videography. "No, I don't recommend that because you'd be using a camera." But I had no charges on that. There's no video, no camera, no Internet. But it's like everything I was trying to do. So I was like, now let me see if I could perhaps go into some type of small business where I go into a cleaning business. "No, we wouldn't want you to do that because of the hours." But, I said, "I'm on probation, they never stipulated no curfew to me."

He was thwarted at every turn. Each idea that could relieve his financial situation and provide him with a livelihood was dismissed because of connotations associated with sex offenders. Although there was seemingly no reason why Aaron's offense should render him a danger in someone's home as a cable installer or cleaning person, the probation officer put forth a conception of him as potentially unsafe in these circumstances and treated these ideas as inconceivable. Although Aaron's offense did not involve camera equipment or pornography, and although he was not aware that his probation prohibited him from taking pictures, the idea of a job using a camera and possibly involving photographing children also raised a red flag for his probation officer. The sex offender label's connotations with pedophilia intruded on this officer's management of Aaron's case and led to him reinforcing Aaron's stigma. So this idea, which might have afforded some creative stimulation and financial relief for Aaron, was also tabled. Thus, he found himself "between a rock and a hard place" where employment options were limited for him. Unable to envision desirable work, Aaron expressed frustration regarding his current situation and some despondency regarding the future:

I told the probation officer, at my last visit, I said, "I'm [between] a rock and a hard place." He stops me, and he says "I too—a rock and a hard place. Because you, as far as employment, you're either overqualified or underqualified." Being fifty years old, having a probation officer that's much younger than me—you know what I'm saying? It is what it is. It's difficult. And not being able to provide any type of resources. Again, having a criminal conviction of this nature, being fifty years old, trying to go back into the workforce. Potential employers are looking at you, "You're fifty years old; you've got this recent conviction over you."

The loss of his career and lack of viable options at his current stage of life were particularly difficult situations to manage. Emphasizing his age, Aaron implied that these losses impacted his sense of self-worth, or rather his sense that it wasn't socially appropriate, at his age, to be unable to support himself in a meaningful way.

Aaron had formed a number of important social connections with colleagues at his former job. However, after his public arrest he found that many of these friends no longer wanted to associate with him. He stated that he didn't have to tell anyone at work what happened because everyone already knew.

> Working in the [social services] is like working in a Payton Place. I was a guy that if I was going to lunch, I would go to the [staff] and ask, "listen, you guys want anything?" I was always the one that was always participating and things like that. And after this event took place, I went back ... and I noticed how there were some people that I developed a keen friendship with that was like "I'm really sorry that this devastating stuff has been happening to you." And then there was other people who were very fair weather types. Distant. Distant. It was just different. The whole interactions was just different.... The biggest thing: the phone. It stopped ringing.

Not only did Aaron lose his salary and professional identity, but a number of the social bonds he had invested in were damaged. He had asked ten people to write character references for his trial, and a number of people refused to do so: "Then I had some people write, 'due to the nature of the charge that you're being charged with' you know what I'm saying? 'I find that inexcusable and bah, bah, bah' and 'I can't support this, dah dah dah.'" Aaron found that the nature of his offense opened him up to the judgment of peers who would not condone his actions and would not support him in his attempts to exonerate himself or mitigate his sentence.

Raoul

Raoul's life was dramatically uprooted and irrevocably altered by the nine years he served in prison. Previously he had worked in a variety of jobs, such as painting and construction. He never belonged to a union and often maintained several jobs at one time. After his release from prison he was faced with the difficult task of reentry and was pursuing a training program paid for by the state. He found the application process highly distressing because it involved explaining his criminal record to the school's admission counselors and other administrators.

> When I was trying to get into school, I had to go through three interviews, with the counselor, the president of the school, all because of this. I was like, you know, yeah I got a sex offense. I had to tell them.... They asked me what was you in prison for.... There was a big time span there that was unaccounted for.... "I was ... in the department of corrections." "For what?" "For a sex offense." "Well you know, what kind of offense?" and I tell them, "I took some photographs of my stepdaughter's vagina, uh, I got charged with a lewd act, using a child in a sexual performance, child pornography. Uh, it was a isolated incident." People don't tend to believe, though.

The three separate interviews "because of this" indicated greater scrutiny of his life by nonstate actors, and a greater level of administrative procedures with institutional gatekeepers. In detailing the dialogue that took place, Raoul offered a clearer sense of the difficulty of "that discussion" that Karl had only alluded to in his narrative. The administrators wanted to know exactly what kind of sex offense he had perpetrated, indicating that what he actually did was of consequence to them, and perhaps indicating that they did not lump together all people labeled sex offenders. In providing the information, Raoul relied on the stark official language of his formal charges, possibly an attempt to distance himself from the information in order to lessen the discomfort of having to disclose intimate details about the sexual nature of the incident. To make the actions seem more acceptable and himself as less dangerous, Raoul asserted that the offense was "an isolated incident," not part of a pattern of behavior. It was one action among all the actions of his life, something he *did*, but not who he *was*, not something indicative of his identity. This is a distinction that will reemerge in his narrative, as well as those of other participants, and its significance to social identity will be explored in the following chapter.

Karl

Like Aaron and Terry, Karl had invested years of his life cultivating a career path. He was an educator who had planned on teaching from a young age. With a master's degree in education, he had always worked with middle school children and adolescents. In addition he had always maintained leadership roles in programs at several churches. Because his offense was against a student at the school where he was teaching, he was dismissed as soon as allegations were brought to the administration's attention. Karl maintained a part-time job with an artist, and because of the strength of this personal and professional relationship, this second job remained intact. Yet, the sex offense conviction had thoroughly affected the career he had spent his life training for: "I'm in a big transition. I was a teacher before. I was an educator. So that career is kind of like no longer." Significantly, he referred to teaching in terms of being, not doing. It represented the person he was, not simply a job that he performed. He had a strong, long-nurtured connection and commitment to this identity. His deviant behavior led to the immediate severance of this tie, and the long-term consequence was that he would never be able to return to this profession. The phrasing, "that career is kind of like no longer," relied on understatement, leaving the impact of the loss to the imagination and implying a dead end. As his career trajectory was abruptly halted, he found himself not only stripped of a connection to an important aspect of his social identity, but stripped of future possibilities in this field.

In order to compensate for lost income, Karl pursued off-the-books odd jobs obtained through personal connections: "I started working ... through a referral. And I was doing a lot of waitering because I already knew these people. I didn't have to go through the whole interview, application process." Karl was fortunate in that he had an extended network of contacts on which he could rely. This made it possible for him to avoid the exposure and rejection that he feared a formal application process would entail. He would not pursue anything "that would mean a background check." However, the positions he had taken through informal networks were inferior to his job at school. They did not provide the fulfillment he found in teaching, nor did they provide the same social status. In addition, they did not pay as well, did not include benefits, and were a sporadic and unreliable source of income. In these ways, Karl had been socially demoted, moved from middle-class to working-class status, as a consequence of his sexual offending.

Avoiding official application processes was of prime importance to Karl. He saw the process as requiring a difficult conversation involving exposure and explanation: "I just didn't want to be involved in going through an application process and people finding my records and then having to have that discussion. Getting hired when you have a record of any kind isn't easy, but especially when you're a sex offender it's a totally different ball game. And they don't really care what you did. They don't care about you as a person. They just see that and that's what they see and they don't go any further." "That discussion" was a phrase that appeared several times in Karl's narrative. It implied a weary familiarity with a difficult and unpleasant chore as well as anxiety. He anticipated having to tell people about his offense and expressed frustration at having to contend with their reactions, which he presumed would be based on stereotypes about sex offenders and pedophiles. He recognized his dual stigma—as both someone with a criminal record in general and someone convicted of a sex offense in particular. This type of offense, he argued, defied explanation ("they don't really care about what you did")—that is, the stigma could not be affected by explaining mitigating circumstances. He expressed that once they heard the label, his potential audience would not be interested in details that might humanize him in their eyes. Karl believed these details would be less stigmatizing if others were aware of who he was "as a person"—if the action could be placed in a context he had power to define. However, his experience was that the label was usually seen through a lens of stereotypes and presumptuous associations. He was certain his listeners would bestow a status on him as a sex offender that would preclude and override everything else about him.

Terry

Prior to his most recent arrest, Terry had worked in the same field for over twenty years. He interacted with the public as a representative of an institution that viewed itself as integral to the neighboring suburban communities. Through his work, Terry performed a social identity that was highly significant to him, and when his offenses were broadcast he immediately lost this connection. Once his picture and the details of his crime hit local papers and TV news, every aspect of his life was affected. His employer was quick to take action: "One of my arrests was chronicled in the newspapers and [the place where I worked] decided to offer me a severance package so that I would no longer be working for them. They made me leave work immediately." Unable to control information from being publicized about him, he was suddenly transformed from a discreditable person (about whom "his differentness" is "neither known about by those present nor immediately perceivable by them") to a discredited one (about whom the stigma is "known about already or is evident on the spot") (Goffman, 1986, p. 4). He moved from being a person who was able to hide his crimes and relegate them to what he repeatedly referred to as his "double life," to one about whom stigmatizing information was generally known.

The publicity alone (without a criminal conviction) was enough to discredit him and enough for his employers to make a decision. It is possible they were concerned that his personal stigma would spread to the institution (what Goffman terms a "courtesy stigma") (ibid., p. 30). It is also possible that they based their actions on an underlying assumption about how the public would react to him—with the distrust, disgust, and fear the public has toward sex offenders. The leadership of the institution may have been worried that if they did not take action they would be seen as endorsing his behavior. Viewing themselves as playing a prominent role in the community, they might have felt a particular obligation to uphold the community's values, to preserve the collectivity's identity and boundaries.

Losing his job severed Terry from his identity as an important and upstanding member of his community, and cost him all his professional contacts. People at work had to make sense of this new, stigmatizing information: "They didn't know how to handle it. I had relationships with a lot of these people for twenty years and some weren't answering calls anymore and others were just aloof when I did contact them." Colleagues and customers who refused to speak with him, or who were "aloof" presumably altered their representation of him as he became discredited. Although he did not commit professional misconduct (nor commit acts on company time or property), he lost all professional credibility.

Terry had spent his whole adult life pursuing one career—everything he had built was now void. He was not trained for anything else: "So I had to switch careers and there weren't many careers out there that

I could do. . . . It was very difficult." With his entire professional identity discredited and his career virtually over, Terry described having few opportunities for employment outside of his specialized field. In addition, his status as sex offender made it hard to find legitimate work of comparable social status. To make ends meet, Terry was working at home at independent pursuits he managed on the computer. Because he worked for himself, he did not have to worry about disclosing his criminal record to anyone. However, he was engaged in a risky financial undertaking and was in an economically vulnerable position. Furthermore, he was professionally isolated with few opportunities to interact with others in socially meaningful ways that might reinforce a nondeviant identity from which he could derive esteem and a sense of belonging.

The Loss of Community—Additional Consequences Experienced by Terry

As previously discussed, Terry's narrative differed in a number of ways from the others presented in this study. Terry occupied a higher status and was embedded in a suburban community prior to his most recent conviction. Most important, however, unlike the others, he had a history of deviant sexual behavior and a history of arrests for sex offenses. His last offense was publicized throughout the community. The consequences of Terry's most recent arrest were more severe and extensive. Looking at some of the specific ways in which Terry's connection to the community was severed that were unique to his narrative, it becomes clear that combined these represent a near complete annihilation of community connections and opportunities to express a social self.

Although, as we saw in the previous chapter, his father and brother maintained their relationships to him once they found out about his offending behavior, almost all of Terry's other social connections were damaged by the publicized information.

Terry had been involved in church activities since he was child. This connection provided him with many social contacts with whom he shared a history. As a result of his arrest, he was excommunicated from his church: "I definitely had [gone to church regularly]. Recently when it came out in the paper, the church decided to kick me out. Yup. And I haven't found another one yet. I'm looking a little bit. But I was very regular, three or four times a month." The phrase "kicking him out" indicated total expulsion and implied a lack of negotiation. Once they had discrediting information about him, they excluded him from their community. As he stated, he had been an active member and the connection was meaningful to him, both socially and spiritually: "The church was a very, very difficult situation, because, you know I really felt that I contributed a lot. I was involved in a lot of the events and it was difficult." Terry implied that his contributions to the community were not valued once discrediting information came to light, and the difficulty he spoke of suggests that this was a painful loss.

Terry described himself as a social person. Unfortunately as a result of media exposure he lost a number of friends and informal social contacts: "Yeah, the community is difficult too. Everyone except one or two friends has disowned me from the community." Those that maintained contact altered the nature of their relationship with him and confronted him with their feelings: "When I was in the paper, my friends all just left me. I did talk to some of them that were willing to talk, and you know, they said that they were annoyed that I was let into their house. You know they let me into their house and that sort of thing." That they had feelings about letting him into their house indicates that they restructured their account of their past with him in light of the new information. That is, they revised their narrative of their relationship. What had presumably been friendly interaction in the home was seen as a potential invasion by a dangerous other. They indicated that they would not have let him in had they known about the discrediting information.

Sports had been an important part of Terry's life since childhood. Athletics are an important vehicle for social bonding and provide opportunities for developing and displaying mastery of skills as well as relieving stress. As an adult he played on several teams, all of which dropped him upon learning about his offense: "My sports groups, my pool team, my soccer team, all kicked me off the team and would have nothing to do with me." The loss of these activities and the social contact they entailed further and more completely excluded Terry from the community.

Terry's sister learned about his history of sexual offending at the same time as his brother and father. She, however, had a very different reaction than they had. Terry reported, "My sister disowned me at first." Being "disowned" implied a total severance and annulment of a connection. However, he continued to explain, "There was no particular conversation. There was just a change in attitude. We used to contact each other every day and then, you know, then contacted each other once a month.

We used to vacation together. It was kind of an aloofness the last time we vacationed together and she wouldn't let me sleep in the same area as my niece, that sort of thing." Rather than completely ending all contact with him, his sister withdrew from the relationship, establishing distance by speaking less frequently and treating him differently. Not letting him sleep near his niece indicates that she saw him as a sexually dangerous other, one who could not be trusted near children. She constructed him as deviant and changed her view of him in light of the connotations associated with his label.

His sister's attitude eventually changed. Like his father, she invoked an illness paradigm to explain his behavior and to help integrate his new label into a social identity: "That was previous to my most recent arrest and when I got arrested again it actually made her think, or believe, that it was an illness. You know. And something that maybe psychological help could overcome." Although she still kept a distance from him, invoking the medical paradigm helped her mediate and mollify the meaning of his stigma and allowed her to reconceptualize him as a potentially transformable self.

With the exception of his contacts with his immediate family, Terry was completely banished from the community and left with no intact bonds. It can be speculated that the nature of his crimes (offending against strangers), their frequency, and the publicity they received served to more firmly invoke stereotypes of sex offenders and more effectively cast Terry as a dangerous outsider. More than any participant he was treated as a full pariah with little recourse to meaningful social supports or relief from the stigmatized identity. The "normal" and "separate" life he had worked so diligently to maintain was completely destroyed.

Housing

Megan's Law emphasizes "community" notification. At the policy's core is a sense of "meaningful communities" (Simon, 1998). While residential communities, based on geographical proximity, have become less central to people's sense of identity and belonging (Wirth, 1938), the law invokes the concept of tight-knit middle-class neighborhoods built around the nuclear family and where people rely on each other and share social connections. Housing has been one of the most salient issues in public debates about sex offenders. Community members do not want offenders living with them. Community leaders petition to legislate more and more restrictive local laws about where offenders can live, such as increasing the perimeter around schools they must not invade. Residency restrictions laws are increasingly popular and exist in at least thirty states (Levenson, 2009, p. 268). Concerns about neighborhood vigilantism and harassment accompany these laws (ibid.; Meloy, 2006, p. 44).

Most of the men interviewed for this study, with the exception of Karl, did not experience any incidence of harassment or endure any sort of particular attention regarding where they lived. Although Terry, a homeowner, lost his job, was excommunicated from his church, and was thrown off his teams, he did not report any concerns expressed or actions taken by his neighbors regarding his residential situation. Raoul lived with his mother in a neighborhood where people knew him, and was part of a low-income urban community that was in part composed of people who have been processed through the criminal justice and/or the social service systems. His status as a sex offender did not raise any particular issues in the neighborhood. Reggie felt very connected to his neighborhood as he had grown up and lived in the same area his entire life. Many of his neighbors knew about the incident and his charge, and for a long time he felt a deep sense of shame and exposure in the community. However, in spite of his feeling of exposure, he did not report any conflict with neighbors. Concerns about neighbors were also absent from Aaron's narrative.

However, Megan's Law has contributed to a landscape of fear and distrust that affects many sex offenders, regardless of their actual experience. In Karl's and Tim's narratives, stories heard in their treatment groups and on the news entered their sense of who they were in the community and informed their sense of the generalized other's attitude toward sex offenders. Before discussing this aspect of anecdotal, imagined, and feared harassment, I present in detail Karl's story of "the angry villagers."

Karl

Although all the men expressed some degree of fear about being harassed by neighbors and/or thrown out of their residences, Karl was the only one who actually endured it. Karl worked in the home of a gay couple that lived in an affluent suburb. Because this was out of state, he was required to register there and comply with that state's laws regarding sex offenders. Information about him, including his picture, was posted on the Internet. A resident learned about him and informed the neighbors, who then mounted a campaign to have him fired. This event was of such significance to Karl that retelling it took up a large portion of his first interview: "They started calling the sex offender registry in [the other state] and [here], trying to find information about me, why am I here and what kind of a crime did I commit, and trying to get the details on all of that information, and because I had, it had my birthday and all that kind of information so when they call . . . they can get more information about the crime." With little effort an individual in the community was able to procure information regarding Karl's status as a sex offender, in addition to other identifying information. Karl did not know what prompted the search in the first place or who initiated it. But once the community was made aware they began to complain to his employer: "It was to the point where they were really calling *a lot* . . . it was just to the point where they were harassing [my bosses], like, 'we need to change this.' And I was like, 'but I can't change it. If I'm there the state has to know I'm there and however the state chooses to list it on their registry is however they choose to list it.'" Karl said the harassment escalated to the extent that the neighbors called police and claimed that he wasn't there when he should have been.

> But they had called the state police, maybe it was the local police. They don't give me all the details and all the information, because they don't know if I'm going to, if someone's going to go and retaliate or whatever. . . . So I get calls from the state police saying "look, you know, we were informed that you weren't working at the address where you registered, and the local police went out and you weren't there and so, you need to call us, or a warrant is going to be issued for your arrest." . . . And look they knew. It's all in the files that I'm not there every day. It's not a nine-to-five Monday through Friday kind of job. It's a come and go; it's not that structured. My probation officer knew, and she knows when I'm there and when I'm not there and that's all in the file, but the guy didn't look in the file. He just looks in the computer and sees that I'm registered that I work there, and then is like "why aren't you here?"

Karl's anger and indignation with the events was clear. Although the law allowed him to work there and his probation officer understood that it was a part-time job with unstructured hours, neighbors were still free to alert the police, who had to follow up on the complaint. Karl pointed out that although information about him was available to the public, he was not entitled to information regarding those who were harassing him. This may indicate that nonstigmatized members of the community are protected by law enforcement at the expense of the stigmatized.

Karl's probation officer referred to the situation as "the angry villagers," and "because they were really causing a lot of problems . . . it was inferred from my probation officer that I was being surveilled. I was under surveillance by the neighbors." He was fortunate in that his employers championed him in spite of this pressure from their neighbors and their landlord saying that Karl could not be on the premises: "My boss's lawyer sent them something saying 'look, you're not, this is basically not to be discussed, because on the website it says that you're not allowed to harass anyone based on any of the information found here.'" Enlisting the services of a lawyer, they made it clear to the community that they would not tolerate neighbors pushing the limits of legal behavior. They reframed the legal issue as the neighbors' behavior, not the presence of a sex offender.

In addition, Karl's employers attempted to educate the community about sex offenders in general: "[My bosses explained to the neighbors that] most of the cases of sexual activity and sexual misconduct with children are incest and pedophilia and generally happen within people of your family. With people you don't know about, it's not the people you know about that you need to be worried about. . . . It's uncle Fred and Aunt Sally within your family. But of course they don't want to hear any of that." Here the employers tried to inform them about the relative risks posed by the presence of an offender like Karl in their neighborhood and that their fears were misplaced. The neighbors, however, were not interested in this information. Karl believed it was because their concern was never really about their children: "[When] the neighbors got wind of it, they were like, 'our property values.'" Karl reiterated several times that his took place in an affluent area where people were very concerned with their community's image. Karl's sense that they were upset about his presence because of material concerns was reinforced by the fact that safety was never mentioned by any of the angry villagers: "They didn't once address concerns about their children and the safety of their children."

Karl's experience with the angry villagers was an example of how seriously Megan's Law and the registration of sex offenders are taken by some communities. Karl was fortunate to have an employer who stood up to the landlord and the neighbors. Other sex offenders may not have such a strong tie with individuals capable of advocating for them and influencing others.

The angry villagers episode led Karl to further speculate on why communities, particularly affluent suburbs, reject sex offenders: "It's a stigma of it being listed in their neighborhood, because, and it's the fact that, our children when they have play dates their parents look at the site and decide they don't want their children to come over to play because there's someone registered in the neighborhood." He argued that the offender's individual stigma can spread to the entire neighborhood, tainting it with what Goffman calls "ill-fame." He speculated that his neighbors feared that *their* neighbors would reject *them* because of Karl's stigma. He implied that members of his community might not be afraid for their children's safety. Rather, they were afraid of what their friends would think.

Karl asserted that his status as sex offender precludes him ever entering the middle-class housing market: "If I want to buy a co-op, [it's] probably not going to happen. How am I going to get approved to buy a coop when I have this kind of crime on my record? When I can't live within so many yards of a school? So many hundred yards of a school or whatever of a park. Well in this city it's really difficult to find a place to live that's not close to a park or a school." As Karl recalled the life he had previously wanted for himself, he contended with the fact that his future options were limited. The problems he faced while on probation, would continue to thwart him because (a) he had a permanent criminal record for a sex offense, (b) he was required to register for twenty years, and (c) certain municipalities bar sex offenders from living within a certain distance from schools. He recognized that he may in fact be permanently denied opportunities to achieve a privileged status because of his legal and social stigma. Even were he to achieve financial success, he argued that he would not be able to buy into the kind of community he would like to be part of.

Other offenders' experiences with landlords and neighbors contributed to Karl's sense of fear, and reinforced the negative impact of the angry villagers episodes. Group therapy provided a forum in which sex offenders heard other offenders' stories. These entered Karl's imagination and contributed to a shared landscape of experience: "Well I'm in my group therapy ... I hear stories of a lot of not so pleasant things. Where people are really harassed or where people lose their house because the landlord gets pressure from the neighbors because they're renting to a sex offender and they need to stop, and then they lose their apartment, and then they have to find a place to live." That which had happened to others in his situation was as vivid for him as his own experiences. The possibility of being forced to leave his apartment contributed to a sense of instability and ontological insecurity that pervaded his narrative. Even though Karl was for the moment in a secure living situation, accounts he heard in therapy reinforced the fact that he could not take his situation for granted. He continually experienced the possibility of social rejection, exclusion, and banishment.

Tim

Having lived in the same working-class neighborhood for a many years, Tim claimed that he had a sense of his neighbors' strong opinions regarding sex offenders: "Well, I didn't tell people in the building about the sex offense. But I had asked them how they feel about sex offenders. And I have a general sense of how they feel and that's why I've not disclosed to them that I am one." He had enough of a rapport with community members to begin a dialogue about sex offenders, and the vehement reactions he received led him to keep his status to himself. He recognized himself as discreditable, someone who would be rejected from his community if discrediting information came to their attention. Because he was listed on the state website for sex offenders, this loomed as a distinct possibility. The fact that he felt he needed to conceal his status indicated that he lived with a sense of shameful difference from those around him.

His report of his neighbors' reaction reflected a critique of the criminal justice system for being neither consistent enough nor punitive enough with sex offenders: "They figure they should be locked up for whatever the sentence was for the duration.... Some others say they should be taken out back and shot, which I don't take that, straight at the face of looking at it. People don't like the idea that sex offenders are walking free." Although he shared his neighbors' attitudes (which will be further discussed in the following chapter), the fact that such extreme, albeit hyperbolic, measures entered the discussion reflected his awareness of the seriousness of his position as a sex offender in this particular community. The extent of the community's intolerance—or at least his perception of it—and unwillingness to incorporate sex offenders within its boundaries was described as potentially violent, and indicated that his need to keep his stigma a secret was in part motivated by fear and self-protection.

Like Karl, as a member of group therapy Tim also heard stories of harassment of offenders in their neighborhoods. One story vividly stood out for him and involved an acquaintance he frequently referenced.

> We had one guy last year.... He did twelve years in jail. He's a Level III sex offender. For life he's on the registry. And early in the year, last year, all the POs, including the head honcho of the department, and the borough president, borough councilman, comes to his house with all the probation officers, line up to find out how far he is from the nearest school. Find out he's less than a certain distance from the school and so he has to move out. They forced him down south ... just because he was a Level III sex offender and he was fifteen feet less than the actual range from the school.

Another example of how the collective experience of sex offender treatment created an inner landscape of possibility of harassment and banishment, this story concerned political excess. It was an example of what Goffman terms an "atrocity tale"—stories of "extreme mistreatment by normals" (Goffman, 1986, p. 25). Here Tim described a political, public mission, a spectacle to "force" out a sex offender from the community. He emphasized the display of power, the full weight of the social control apparatus mobilizing everything it can in the purpose of expulsion. When Tim relayed this story, he seemed outraged, and emphasized that the individual in question was "a nice guy. I knew him"—expressing frustration with the injustices that pervade the system. Implied in his depiction was fear and recognition that such measures could be applied to him.

The Loss of Subjective Bonds with the Community

In narratives subjective states can be gleamed through speakers' use of speculation and imagination—in this case, an examination of what they think others think about them, and about what they fear might possibly happen. It involves a projection onto the future and onto the minds of others, and often involves the experience of shame. This section illuminates ways in which these men conceived of themselves as outsiders. Some participants were more articulate and self-reflexive than others, and the interviews with Tim were particularly difficult. At no point was I able to elicit anything about feelings or subjective states from him, and for this reason the internalization of stigma will not be discussed in his case. In addition, Aaron's narrative concerned the loss of objective connections, particularly the loss of his job, and he did not reflect on his internal states.

Terry

Terry had been managing deviant identity for much longer than the others in the study, and the strategy he developed involved the formulation of what he described as a double life. Terry had been living with a discreditable identity throughout adulthood. From the first embarrassment he experienced as a consequence of an incident in high school, he learned that he would have to keep his behavior secret from others. He was caught early on and thought he knew what to expect from others' reactions. He had thus lived with a private sense of having a hidden stigma. His narrative included aspects of having to manage discreditable information, as well as ways in which his perception of his community had changed since he was publicly exposed.

As we have seen, Terry identified the first time he was caught as shaping the way he had since seen himself socially in relation to others. He had been rubbing his hand against a girl's "rear end" during class, and she turned and said something. This was followed by collective laughter, and his response is worth quoting again: "I was certainly embarrassed by it. But I didn't realize really how important it was. It changed my whole personality. I was no longer sociable . . . because the hurt would be there if I made a mistake socially. The embarrassment gave me . . . a very terrible feeling of embarrassment, and I didn't want to be awkward on social occasions and feel that again." He identified a relationship among his action (touching the girl), the reaction to it (she announced his behavior), the subsequent public humiliation (the class's laughter), and his own inner state (embarrassment). He claimed it changed his "whole personality," and explained that by this he meant that he became more guarded out of fear of further exposure. His personality shifted to avoiding embarrassment/exposure. He later identified the laughter as taking on particular significance—that in fact the group's reaction was the only real consequence of this first sexual violation: "There were no other social consequences. It was in my head more, and it was very traumatic for me. The initial laughter. But . . . everyone still wanted to be a friend.

There were no social ramifications from it. Just in my mind." His inner state was most affected. He became transformed from someone who did not have or know that he had a stigma to someone who learned that he was discreditable. He was not fully discredited by this incident, however. It appeared that he did not earn a label from his peers as a result. But the mockery led him to reorient his sense of self in relationship to others.

Concealing his behavior from people who knew him established a dual identity, which Terry described along moral lines: "There is a duality thing. Because most sex offenders, myself included, are very moral people and very law-abiding people. So it's kind of a separate life. And people at work and people closest to you don't know anything about it." In referring to "duality" Terry delineated a split in his own identity (although he expressed that this phenomenon is common to most sex offenders who share his stigma). He asserted that sex offenders can be "moral" in most spheres of life. Because offending did not align with *this* identity, or with the assumptions one makes about "moral" and "law-abiding" people, Terry assigned the behavior to a separate identity. In this way, for him, the behavior did not undermine the sense of being moral (or normal); it did not challenge that definition of self. Rather, it indicated the existence of another self.

Maintaining his secret was crucial to the performance of his social role throughout his adulthood, and he inhabited this duality for years, maintaining a life completely separate from his sexual offending. He said that he was able to live "like a normal person," embodied in one identity, and that his behavior in the separate life did not have an impact on this separate existence even after he was arrested several times. However, current policies changed his internal orientation. "It didn't change my thoughts until I got put on the registered sex offender list. Then it changed my thoughts. You kind of walk down the street and you look around and you realize that you're not the same as the other people. It kind of isolates you. You have a skeleton in your closet that could cause you or other people pain if it's found out . . . it's out there for people to see so you never know who's going to come up to you and say, you're that sex offender . . . that lives in the neighborhood."

As he was a registered offender, information about him was potentially available to anyone who cared to search for it. Being registered meant that he had no control over the management of this information, and changed the basic relationship between his self and community. He began to see himself as "not the same as other people" precisely because he could be exposed. Others may have what he calls "skeletons in their closets," but his were presumably more damaging. He identified feeling isolated, no longer a part of that community, but outside it, someone who did not belong even as he walked down the street. He described the acute fear of being suddenly discredited in public, and the unstable and insecure sense of not knowing what could happen next, of not being able to walk down the street without fear that the rug might suddenly be pulled out from under him; in this way he was alive to his outsiderness. Significantly, he shifted voice to the second person, indicating that he was viewing himself from the outside, that he was describing someone other. When discussing being shunned or exposed, he saw himself as separate from himself. When describing his duality, Terry also shifted the narrative from his own situation to sex offenders in general and then adopted the second person. This verbal tactic invites or implicates the listener in the experience in such a way as to facilitate empathy. At the same time, it distances the speaker from the described actions by subtly veiling his presence.

In describing his sense of otherness he referred several times to "walking down the street"—as if this commonplace scenario of being anonymously among others had become potentially treacherous: "However, there's a fear of walking the streets as a sex offender. There's a fear of being found out and being kicked out of where you live. Or all your relationships, both male and female, they just don't understand it and they will discard you." Being registered meant that his entire connection to the community was even more tenuous and could easily be severed. He implied that his offense would override all other social knowledge of him, that others would not be interested in any mitigating circumstances but summarily treat him as social junk and banish him—even though all his other actions in the community have proved him worthy of inclusion. His fears of walking down the street and being suddenly exposed indicated an experience of the social bond as a fragile one, easily broken by certain information, and dependent on one's ability to keep secrets. Without the capacity to protect oneself from scrutiny and exposure, one is vulnerable to humiliation and expulsion. In addition, he emphasized that he would be shunned by both men and women—the implication being that he would be made an outcast even by people who would never be potential victims (i.e., men). In other words, Terry found it surprising and significant that he would be seen as undesirable to society as a whole, not just to potential victims of his behavior.

Raoul

Raoul felt socially and personally burdened by the label sex offender and believed that people viewed him through the lens of their stereotypes. He had clear ideas of how others would regard him if they knew about his stigma, and this was a source of embarrassment for him: "The title sex offender kind of carries a lot of weight. When you tell people, 'I'm a sex offender,' they automatically assume the worst. The label sex offender is vague.... You could have raped a three-year-old or that's a sex offense, photographs, fondling, sexual contact, using a child in a sexual way, all that falls under sex offender, lewd act, prostitution, all that. So the sex offender label is not categorized, although they do have different levels." He recognized that people make assumptions about the label and that it did not matter what he did as an individual. What mattered was that they would "assume the worst," that his own offense would be subsumed by the connotations associated with it, and that he would be lumped in with someone who committed far more heinous acts of deviance such as "raped a three-year-old."

Raoul was aware that the media play a significant role in shaping the public's perception of sex offenders: "I was reading on the Internet the other day that sex offenders are likely to offend like a 117 kids. I'm like, yeah right. That's a damn lie." He was affected by the sensationalized misinformation put forth by the media, and assumed it affected how people would view him if they had information about him. The "lies" he encountered on the Internet shaped how he saw himself in the eyes of the community.

Even among those who knew him and had accepted him, Raoul still felt the weight of the stigma: "Sometimes I deal with a little embarrassment, I get embarrassed sometimes telling people. It's not something that I go announcing.... I tell people from the church. I had to sit down with the pastor and the deacon and I had to tell them because there's kids in the church and I felt embarrassed.... They love me in the church. But still I go through embarrassment." In spite of the fact that he felt loved and accepted in this environment where he carried personal credibility that overrode his stigma, he still experienced embarrassment. It stemmed not from their actual acceptance or rejection of him, but from an internalization of how others see sex offenders. As Goffman observes, "The standards he has incorporated from the wider society equip him to be intimately alive to what others see as his failing, inevitably causing him, if only for moments, to agree that he does indeed fall short of what he really ought to be. Shame becomes a central possibility arising from the individual's perception of one of his own attributes as being a defiling thing to possess" (Goffman, 1986, p. 7). In Raoul's daily life there was a pervasive sense of being "a bona fide sex offender"—something that caused him shame and that he disclosed only when absolutely necessary, as he presumed negative judgment in the eyes of others.

Reggie

His conviction of a sex offense had a profound effect on Reggie's sense of himself, and his interior world was altered as a result of being labeled. This took the form of a pervasive sense of being exposed: "I'm a very laid-back person, but this here has made me even, has pushed me farther back, because it gives you a sense of you're labeled. You know someone doesn't know, but you feel like they do know. It puts you in a state of paranoia. As you walk down the street you feel that every person that walks past knows that I'm a sex offender. And I'm Level I, so it's not on any database or anything, but that's the feeling you have. It's just a feeling I have." Reggie described walking around feeling like people knew about his label, that his private wrongdoing was known and visible to others. In a sense, he felt that he was already discredited rather than discreditable. His acute sense of stigmatized identity shifted the way he believed others saw him. This feeling was so strong that he initially experienced a state of depression: "I didn't want to look for a job. I didn't want to leave the house. I just wanted to stay in one place. I couldn't wait to get home. Like a storm was coming, I couldn't wait to get in the house and lock the door, dim the lights, and I just felt safe like that." A previously social person, Reggie found himself shunning the company of others. He preferred to isolate himself away from the gaze of people in front of whom he carried a sense of exposure and shame. Reggie found adapting to the new label extremely difficult emotionally, and began to internalize a sense of being a dangerous other: "I guess before, I'd watch the different programs and [sex offenders] were monsters. These are definitely monsters; they shouldn't even be on this planet. That's the feeling I had watching the *Dateline* specials and the different shows. Before, the *Law & Order*, you sit back and you laugh at those things. And it's a totally different feeling when you become classified in that. You fall into depression. You have thoughts, like I never had. Sometimes it's just like, What am I living for?" Reggie expressed an inability to integrate his view of sex offenders with the fact that he had now been labeled one. He internalized his belief in their monstrousness and, unlike Terry, could not articulate a sense of self separate from that image. He had become someone who he had previously mocked and abhorred.

When he was first arrested, he felt ashamed in front of his wife, not just for the infidelity, but for the fact that he had technically been convicted of a forcible offense: "For like the first two months, I didn't even touch my wife. Because I didn't know what she was thinking. I didn't want her to think, well, am I forcing myself on her? You know, I was paranoid with anything I did." He doubted how his actions were being perceived by others, even in the privacy of his relationship with his own wife. After being convicted, he internalized the associated label and again began to doubt himself and his motives.

> Being labeled, a lot of times they label you something. If someone calls you stupid, you'll take that in: "Well, I must be stupid"—when you're not. So being labeled a sex offender, you know, I carried that badge. If I got on a train and it was time for school to let out and the car filled up with kids, I just sat there like, "Well, they know I'm a sex offender, I'm not going to look to the left or to the right." And I never really paid them any attention at all. Like they might be making too much noise, you want to tell them to shut up. . . . So like I said, that state of paranoia. I just felt paranoid, you know. If you're under age get away from me. Don't ask me the time; you're going to get me in trouble.

A trivial experience like riding the subway had become fraught with danger. Reggie began to look at people differently, believing that they knew he was a sex offender, and feeling ashamed and vigilant. Reggie became acutely aware of himself in situations with young people and children. He was more alive to the situation, and more aware of himself as someone marked as a dangerous "other." He was conscious of his status as an outsider who did not truly, or officially, belong.

Although his family supported him and did not view him as dangerous, he felt different about himself among them: "It didn't change them.

It just changed me. Like I said, it just made me very paranoid thinking someone's thinking something about me. If my family came to visit and my niece was there. You know, she would run up to me . . . I would get up and go in the bedroom. Because I felt like, don't pick her up. What kind of person are you? But they never felt like that about me." The experience of being labeled literally made him doubt the "kind of person" he was. He reframed his encounters in light of the new label, and modified his behavior accordingly. Although he had asserted himself with the woman at the employment agency who called him a "rapist," her words stung him and made him question himself: "I already feel like paranoid and down about myself. Once she said that, you feel [like a rapist]. It's just how I felt. I didn't feel like I needed to run outside and just grab someone and rape them. But I felt like, maybe I am [a rapist]. I'm not even human anymore. Keep my head down." The label, expressed in the horrified words of the interviewer, took on so much power over Reggie that he doubted that he was not in fact a rapist. This idea was so disturbing to him that he questioned his own humanity and began to truly see himself as a dangerous other. His orientation to the world was so altered that he felt he could not look up at it, but must keep his head down in front of others ("I used to always have my head down when I saw my probation officer"). His physical posture reflected and communicated the transformation in his sense of self from someone who belonged to the community to someone who had transgressed against it.

Karl

Karl's vision of his life altered greatly after being convicted and learning the restrictions that would be imposed on him as part of his probation and his status as a registered sex offender. His sense of future possibilities was truncated and constrained, and this was most evident in his imaginative projection of opportunities. He considered all aspects of his life as dependent on the whims of his probation officer, and his loss of autonomy was a source of great anxiety. He viewed himself as marked and could not take his freedom or his sense of belonging for granted. In his inner world he saw himself as an outsider within the community.

Living under the conditions of probation for two years reinforced Karl's awareness of the insecurity of his future: "And after two years of adjusting to it and after a time of starting to realize, still, there could be a lot of policy changes that could really have a negative effect on me. And at any point my probation officer could, when I go in there to say look I need to . . . see my parents for Christmas; they can say, 'you can't travel.' And I wouldn't be able to go." He could not fully adjust to his situation because he lived at the discretion of the PO. This figure emerged in his narrative as a looming embodiment of the constant uncertainty under which he lived. Any potential mundane contingency would have to be addressed through the bureaucracy. This meant that many opportunities that Karl might consider would involve this apparatus. For instance, just like his concern about explaining surprise PO visits to his boyfriend, the idea of visiting his parents was actually an imagined scenario; it existed only in his mind, yet it inhabited his present. Even though a request had not yet been rejected, the possibility was experienced as real. For Karl, uncertainty about the future created a sense powerlessness and anxiety. His fears were focused on the arbitrary nature of decisions about events that were important to him: "So if I write a letter to somebody [for permission to travel], who's to say that person's just not going to be an asshole and look at my file and decide you're traveling a little more than you should? You know? You never know when they're just going to decide to be an ass to you. And you don't have any recourse for that." The probation officer was presented as a character who could just "be an ass" and decide to make life difficult for Karl for no particular reason. Power and control over minor and major decisions in his life resided in the hands of agents of the social control apparatus, and he felt he had few ways of directing the course of events in his life.

Karl was aware of his anxiety and did not want worries about the future to overwhelm his present: "I try not to live in fear of what could happen. With the system or what laws could change or how my freedoms could be even more restricted or because I realize my probation could change at any time and I could be dealing with a whole new probation officer that doesn't know me. . . . That could take a way a lot of my freedoms and wait until I build up to them again." Although Karl asserted that he tried not to live with this fear, clearly the fear of what could happen in the future was very present to him. As we have seen, the system, embodied in the PO, loomed over him as an ever-present constraint over which he had no control. He needed his PO to trust him, to view him "as a person" rather than a rap sheet. Starting at square one with a new officer would require time and effort in establishing a positive rapport all over again. It would require renewed efforts toward a successful performance of a trustworthy, nondeviant identity.

Convicted sex offenders are knowledgeable about laws and policies that affect them and others in their situation. They hear about changes through others in their programs and through state agents. These pieces of information make individuals alive to potentially more stigmatizing measures of social control. Karl kept abreast of these policies and discussed some of the more alarming possibilities: "But there are places that want sex offenders to have neon green license plates so that everybody knows that that's a sex offender driving that car. I think it was Ohio that was doing that. And if I had an ankle bracelet or some GPS, if all of a sudden they decided I needed to have one of those because I'm a sex offender, and I have to wear that around. That's something I would have to deal with in a very different way. So those are things I realize are all possibilities." Knowledge about other legislative initiatives generated fear, taking on a reality in the present situation, regardless of whether they would ever actually impact Karl. The neon green plates represented a modern-day scarlet letter intended to let everyone know a sex offender's status. It is an imposed "stigma symbol" (Goffman, 1986, p. 92) that hovers over experience as a frightening form of potential exposure. Karl also knew offenders in his program who had to wear tracking devices, and expressed that he felt so powerless regarding decisions affecting his freedom that stigmatizing mechanisms of social control such as these felt real. His fears were reinforced by members of the system who warned him that laws may become even more constraining in the future: "And I try not to listen to the people who are like, it's only going to get worse for you. The laws are going to get worse. A lot of people, my probation officer says it; the therapist says it. They're like, it doesn't look good." Thus the future was a landscape wherein he would be even more restricted and controlled, and more indelibly marked as an outsider.

Karl voiced concerns that were similar to Reggie's about being in public places with children. Being labeled a sex offender and having to live with specific conditions of his probation impacted Karl's thoughts in such a way that he could not take normal routines for granted: "I realize I'm in situations, you know, I have to think twice. If I get in an elevator, if there's a kid in the elevator, I shouldn't get in the elevator. I should wait, let that elevator go, and then get in the next. Because technically I'm not supposed to be alone with somebody that's under the age of eighteen." Simply being in a building and needing to use the elevator could turn into a potential violation of the terms of his probation. Having committed a crime against a minor, he was restricted to not being alone with members of that cohort. And yet each day there are many innocuous situations where one cannot control the people in one's surroundings, such as, in this case, in an elevator. This restriction generated a constant tension in routine life and was another source of anxiety.

Karl was more alive to these situations because of the stigma he carried, which affected his thought process to the point that he doubted his own normalcy. "The whole situation I'm in makes me think twice about a lot of things I would never think twice about. And not in a good way. It makes me think twice when I'm sitting on the subway and there's this adorable little baby playing with her mother and I—we're all naturally drawn to watch and think how cute and smile and wave. And there's that part of me that feels very self-conscious when I smile and wave, because oh, but if they knew I was a sex offender smiling and waving, then that wouldn't be so great." Karl's status as sex offender was always present in his mind, reframing his definition of the situation. Karl saw himself through the lens of his stigma, imagining how others would define his behavior if they knew the discrediting information. He described enjoying the common and seemingly harmless interaction that adults engage in when they encounter babies. Yet friendly interaction with anyone under eighteen, particularly a very young person, was grounds for suspicion if the adult in question had committed a sex offense against a minor. The same action assumed a loaded, perhaps sinister, meaning. Connotations surrounding "pedophiles" entered the situation, and he imagined that his actions would be interpreted in light of those stereotypes.

Furthermore, here Karl was describing a particular consciousness of self—he was aware that people in the general public did not regard him on sight as a sex offender; they saw him as a normal citizen. He was simultaneously aware of how he was seen and how he could be seen. His self-consciousness was in part related to his awareness of the fact that discrediting information about him existed, and reflected the fact that he was not comfortable with managing this aspect of his personal identity. Thinking twice about minor and routine interactions, Karl was never at ease, but always vigilantly aware of his stigma.

This awareness included fears about possibly and inadvertently incriminating himself.

> Or if there's a kid sitting next to me even with their mother, brushing up against me and I think what if I my DNA gets on their clothes and then something happened to them and then they found my DNA and then they said I did it. I mean, those things go through my head. And I'm like, "why do I have to think like that?"—but it's because I know they have my DNA. At the same time I know I'm not doing anything that that would be a problem. Like, just, I want to make sure my trash is in the chute and not left there. [These thoughts] pop into my head. I don't obsess over them, but they pop in and I have to be like, it's okay, you're just a person.

Much information about Karl's personal identity, including his DNA and fingerprints, was on file and could be easily accessed during investigations of any crime. Because of this, he was more vulnerable to false accusations and could more easily incriminate himself than someone who has never been processed by the criminal justice system.

He tried to stop himself from this train of thought, but implied that the thoughts have a life of their own ("they pop in"). In other words, the thoughts were part of his internal landscape, and he had to make active efforts to resist them. The fact that he saw his own thoughts as intrusive or problematic indicated a consciousness of how his status as sex offender was affecting his inner world. When he said he tries to tell himself that he is "just a person," he expressed the fact that he needed to make efforts to see himself as normal and belonging to the social world. This was a new cognitive process, a transformation in his internal processing of experience. It indicated a dialectical relationship between his sense of self as a stigmatized other and his sense of self as a normal member of society. Both identities needed to be managed, and ways of resisting the stigmatized label are explored in the next chapter.

Sex Offenders and Social Control

This chapter has presented the numerous ways sanctions against sex offenders affected the men in this study in such a way that their social bonds and ability to perform important roles were compromised. Each of these men experienced the policies in ways unique to them.

The section on social control highlighted how extensively their autonomy was undermined and the degree to which laws created a form of civil death, a state in which the offenders lived with limited rights and numerous restrictions.

The impact of their sex offense convictions was keenly felt in the area of employment. Although only one participant had an offense that related to his job (Karl), half lost their job as a direct result of their conviction. The loss of their job meant a loss of careers in which they had invested years of their lives, and this was experienced as a loss of meaningful social identity. The specter of background checks loomed large for all participants, who recognized themselves as essentially barred from legitimate employment. In addition they recognized the fact that as sex offenders they bore a double stigma—as felons and as sexual deviants. This would make the job search even more frustrating and fruitless. Some reported additional frustration with the fact that probation officers could offer little help in their efforts to find work. Their status as convicted sex offenders severely impacted their ability to find employment and left all these men in a financially vulnerable position with little hope for future opportunities.

Stigma was experienced intimately and internally as the men in this study struggled with their new social identity and what that meant for them as individuals. Reorienting themselves to their label brought up shame and self doubt as they attempted to regain a stable sense of identity. In the following chapter I address this issue in greater detail, looking at the ways these men worked to create viable social selves worthy of social inclusion.

CHAPTER 5

Strategies to Reestablish Social Bonds

IN ADJUSTING TO LIFE as labeled sex offenders, all participants developed strategies that enabled them to maintain a sense of social connection. As we have seen, each had endured significant damage to important social bonds as a result of their conviction. Some of these consequences were largely irreparable, particularly those that involved employment. Some of the damage was experienced deeply, manifesting in experiences of anxiety and shame and affecting their inner states and sense of self, as connections to community are entwined with the experience selfhood. However, the narratives also included approaches for constructing their situation and orienting themselves to their label that resisted acceptance or integration of their outsider status—in spite of exclusionary policies. Living with stigma and managing a discredited identity, participants strove to articulate their own normalcy. Residing in the community at the same time that they have been labeled outsiders, these men worked to maintain external and internal connections that could reinforce their sense of belonging. In doing so they retained a sense of their own humanity.

I identified four intertwined motifs employed in these efforts. Participants asserted the primacy of a "real" self, which they constructed as distinct from their official label as sex offenders. All of the participants maintained some relationships with family members who continued to affirm this self. Second, to some degree all the offenders voiced mainstream opinions regarding sex offender policies. In so doing they aligned themselves with the larger community that embraces Megan's Law; at the same time they differentiated themselves from those whom they perceived as legitimate outsiders and put forth the idea of the dangerous other. Importantly, most did not include themselves in that category, and used it to contrast and highlight their own normality. The third motif involved critiques of sex offender policies; participants argued that they are overinclusive and ineffective. Finally, in expressing frustration with unjust and irrational criminal justice policies, some of the men were able to construct themselves as victimized by the processes of labeling. I have interpreted these motifs as personal strategies designed to reestablish a sense of belonging to community, and I do not see them as "techniques of neutralization." For one, the following excerpts from the narratives were not intended to explain how or why they engaged in deviant behavior. Rather, they were elicited in the context of discussing stigma and policy. This chapter is organized around these themes, looking at ways each offender's narrative illuminated these issues. In this chapter I present some interview responses that have been examined in previous chapters so that it becomes clear how they illustrate some of these strategies.

The Real Self

These men all referenced a "real" self—an aspect of their identity that they privileged over their deviant and criminal sexual behavior. It is important to keep in mind that of course "there is no objectively, but only a subjectively, true self" (Turner, 1976, p. 1012). In these sections of the narratives the offenders argue that their authentic self did not commit the sexual offense (although this is more complicated in the case of Terry). Sociologist Ralph Turner (1976) has suggested that there are two self-orientations—institutional and impulsive. An individual or culture can regard an individual's formal social roles (including familial ones) as more true, with wild desires and urges representing something other. In contrast, the "true" self can be seen as inhabiting these more unacceptable drives and the institutional self is masking these (Turner acknowledges a similarity between this idea and Freud's "id" and "superego") (p. 992). From the institutional framework "the real self is revealed only when the individual is in full control of his faculties and behaviors.... When control is impaired by fatigue, stress, alcohol or drugs, an alien self displaces the true self" (p. 993). In the following sections we can hear the men favoring the institutional self as more real than the impulsive self that engaged in the sanctioned behavior. When Terry describes his "double life," there is a more complicated articulation of a tension between these two self-orientations.

Karl

Karl's creditable self was expressed through his insistence that if people knew him—as opposed to his label—they would accept him and his presence in their community. Elaborating his opinions about the angry villagers, he explained, "The frustrating thing for me is they don't know me. If they would just take a second to meet me and ask me questions that they need to ask. Ask me questions about what happened, and hear me be able to talk about it and then if they would know everything that I have gone through in order to get to where I am now, then, they probably wouldn't have had an issue with it at all." Karl did not see his sex offense as indicative of a separate self in the way we have seen in previous chapters that Terry did. Instead he saw his offenses as part of what seemed like an *explainable* self. Karl maintained that if people heard his construction of the offense and knew the specific nature of his relationship with the student, they would see him as he saw himself: "just a person." The sex offense conviction did not threaten Karl's sense of his own normalcy. Yet in order for others to see this normal and worthy self they would have to interact with him. Karl believed that through face-to-face interaction he could establish a legitimate, nonthreatening social identity. He must be given a chance to actively work at impression management to reveal the true self. The problem with the angry villagers was that they didn't know his true self: "The people that were trying to drive me out . . . they didn't know me. You know, they just saw that I'm a sex offender. So they don't want me there. But it's like, you don't know me. I'm not interested in children. At all." Knowledge of the circumstances around the offense could have offset the spoiling of his identity. To "know" Karl would be to understand that he did not conform to the stereotype of a sex offender. He was not a pedophile. He was not a threat to their community. He was an understandable, accessible, and safe person.

Karl asserted that the people who knew him, such as one of his employers, recognized that he was truly a valued member of the community: "And [my boss] was just astounded, because these people, they didn't know me; they didn't know how much I'd done for the [organization] in the past. . . . But every single one of the board members wrote recommendations for me that are now in my file with my probation officer. And they all know . . . I had already established myself with them." He invoked past accomplishments and contributions to emphasize the support he received from people who really knew him. He asserted the legitimacy of his creditability by referring to recommendations that are now part of his official record, or what Goffman refers to as one's "dossier" (Goffman, 1986, p. 57). In this way Karl asserted that he was officially worthy of inclusion in the community.

Karl distanced his self from the stigma of being a sex offender by refusing to internalize the stigma. Instead he constructed it as an external imposition on his identity: "It's a label put on to me by our justice system. It's not a label that I identify with. Because I don't think it's in my best interest and my well-being to label myself a sex offender. What other people choose to label me is one thing, and what I identify with I think is totally different. Because I think people respond to those labels when they take them on for themselves. And, that's not what I choose to identify with." Karl's self-definition overrode his stigma. He presented his refusal to self-label as a choice he was personally empowered to make. Resistance to the official definition of the situation was an available option. Distancing himself from his ascribed deviant role, he asserted his ability to make choices about his own identity. Through this role distance he constructed a self that truly belonged in the community, even if the community itself did not recognize this. Furthermore, he presented the idea that internalizing the deviant label would reinforce external social ostracism. In his worldview there existed a dynamic between self and others, and an identity could not simply be imposed by others—it needed be accepted as well.

Reggie

Reggie found the experience of being labeled a sex offender deeply shattering to his sense of self. This manifested in what he described as "depression." His shame led to "paranoia" and "doubt." His way of overcoming stigma involved reasserting his real self, a process he described as a returning. For instance, as we have seen, after his arrest he initially felt like he was a "monster" himself when watching television programs about sex offenders. Over time, however, this experience became less upsetting for him: "Well, right now after two years it doesn't bother me so much because I really got back in contact with *who I am*." It took Reggie two years to see himself as a person separate from the label, and he described this as returning to the self-image he maintained prior to conviction. Who he really was had gotten lost in the aftermath of the conviction, but that real self remained intact, there for him to get back into contact with.

For Reggie, "getting back in touch with *who I am*" meant reasserting his sexual identity as someone attracted to consenting adults. As discussed in the previous chapter, his conviction led him to doubt the nature of his sexuality. He had become uncomfortable around young girls as a result of the label. But over time Reggie was able to assure himself that "who I am" is someone that is not interested in sex with children. He stated that "getting back in touch" meant "knowing I don't like young girls. I'm not attracted to younger children at all." He asserted a number of times that the incident with the minor was not part of a pattern of behavior (not a "problem"), and that "getting back in contact" with himself involved reminding himself that "I've never been in a chat room. I don't log on to my computer and look for children's porn or anything with a young child in it. Like, even when my nieces would come by, I was never like, let me give them a bath. It just wasn't in me." He asserted that he never had a sexual interest in children or any particular curiosity about their bodies. There was no history, no recurring pattern of desire or behavior that he could identify with or incorporate into his personality. It just wasn't "in" him—it was not part of his real self. Reminding himself of this fact allowed him to resist the self-stigmatization attendant with his label. He continued to assert, "My wife is only a year younger than me. So there's never been a thing with me with younger women. I've always dated older women, actually." Recalling his past romantic relationships allowed him to reassure himself that the real Reggie did not fit the stereotype of a sex offender and that his sexuality was in fact directed toward female age-mates.

Reggie's probation officer helped him come to understand that he did not necessarily need to be ashamed of himself: "I used to always have my head down when I saw my probation officer and she used to ask me, why do I have my head down? And I told her that I feel embarrassed for what I did. It's very embarrassing and very hard, and she's always telling me 'don't put your head down, put your head up.' Once she said that it maybe put me back." The weight of the negative sanction against his behavior was felt so deeply that it affected how Reggie carried his physical person. His shame was manifest in his presentation of self. The words of another person—one who knew what he had done—allowed him to begin to see himself as the same person he was before the conviction. Perhaps because his probation officer, who was aware of his actions, was able to see him as deserving dignity, he could begin to see himself in a more positive light. Recognizing that other members of the community saw him as deserving of dignity enabled him to restructure his internalized version of himself.

Part of reclaiming his sense of his true self meant using his new experiences as opportunities to better himself, something that Reggie proclaimed he always strove for, and which was apparent when he discussed how he took his negative experiences as a sex offender and used them to provide lessons for his children. He asserted that although he did not need group therapy in order to prevent him from committing another sex offense (which he stated would never happen again), the experience was still valuable: "Honestly, I can't use this as a negative because I'm learning a lot. And there's a lot of things with this criteria that I didn't even know. Like there's a lot of things you may say online—like I used to go online and play poker. There's a lot of things you're not supposed to say online to another person, like inviting someone to your private parts, telling them to kiss this when you're having an argument. You really don't know who you're speaking to, who's on the other end." Reggie looked to his group for education about him appropriate online conduct and regarded any new information as useful knowledge. He claimed "there's always knowledge to know." He absorbed the new material earnestly and modified his behavior accordingly. Using the experience to improve himself and learn more allowed Reggie to resist the negative impact of his label.

In addition, Reggie used his experiences to reinforce his role as father, and to provide his children with important life lessons.

> Also, my eighteen-year-old and seventeen-year-old know what happened. So I also explained every time I go to my group I basically explain to them what I'm going through so they don't go down that road . . . basically get on the computer saying the wrong thing in a chat room. That'll get you in trouble. My eighteen-year-old, you know, if he's in a chat room and there's a girl with a three year age difference . . . and he's like saying the wrong things. . . . It's going to get him in trouble. So I say watch what you say online, don't click on any websites, ask a girl her age, meet her parents, don't be so fast. And they respond.

By transforming his difficult experiences as a registered sex offender into a potential learning experience not only for himself but for his sons as well, Reggie's ordeal became an opportunity for him to improve, assert his role as father, and impart what he considered important life lessons to his children.

Aaron

Aaron emphasized the consensual aspect of his offense against the sixteen-year-old girl with whom he had the brief affair. As we have seen, he insisted that had he known her real age, he would not have gotten involved with her. In highlighting the fact that he did not know that she was a minor, Aaron asserted an aspect of self that was constructed around the idea of what he *would have* done had he known: "Had I known the young lady—the young girl—was sixteen years old, I would not have participated in anything. 'Cause there's nothing that someone of that age could do for me.... Sixteen, I wouldn't do that." He declared that had he known the reality of the situation, he would have been able to act according to his true self. The event that took place was "a mistake" because he wasn't able to behave as he truly would have. His behavior reflected not who he was but rather the fact that he was operating under false pretenses.

Aaron asserted that the bonds he was able to maintain with family and friends were based on his real self: "People who know me know that that's not my character. They know that's not who I am. A mistake happened. You know. A mistake happened. Those who know me are supportive to that." Thus, his real self was affirmed by those around him who did not alter their view of him once they had discrediting information. In fact, they supported him in discrediting the validity of the information itself. Being a "mistake," the offense was not indicative of his character. He further elaborated that he had "no history" of any kind of sexual misconduct, attraction to children, or incestuous relationships and asserted "that's not my makeup."

Similar to the way that Reggie distinguished a "mistake" from a "problem," Aaron distinguished a "mistake" from "rape," an act he asserted that he would never commit. "When people hear the [charge], they read R-A-P-E.... You know what I'm saying? But the people that know me know that that's not my character, that's not me. I would not, I would not willingly put myself into a position to force myself on someone, to encourage someone to do something. *That's not me.* If I knew that person was too young, I would not engage myself. So my people who know me, like my family, and my kids, my friends, like my true honest friends. They know this was a mistake." Aaron articulated that his true self is absolutely not a rapist. The friends who supported this view are "true" friends, friends who recognized and reaffirmed his true self. He believed that the friends who were "distant" were not responding to his real self. Instead, they reconstructed their image of him through the lens of his label, discrediting him and reinforcing stigma.

Raoul

For Raoul, the real self was articulated through recourse to his masculine identity, which he contrasted to his status as sex offender, as we saw in an earlier chapter: "I'm a sex offender, right? But you know what, before I was a sex offender I was a father, a brother, an uncle, a son." He invoked these kinship roles to mitigate his deviant status and distance himself from the label. He was highly identified with these roles, and they enabled him to see himself as belonging within a larger social framework. He gave these greater weight and more significance in terms of his social situation. The male kinship roles stood in contrast to the outsider status enforced on sex offenders through public policy, cultural stereotypes, and media hyperbole. Traditional masculinity provided a buttress against an internalized deviant identity and allowed him to construct a socially viable selfhood deserving of recognition.

In addition to articulating his real self in terms of his familial roles, Raoul asserted a real self based on behavioral boundaries. Raoul stated that he was originally charged with rape—sexual assault. However, like Aaron, he was very clear that his violation was not legally rape, vehemently resisting the first official label his offense was given: "I didn't rape nobody. But they also took my stepdaughter to the hospital and they did all kinds of exams and they came back with the results and actually they had to reduce the charge and they gave me a lewd act.... Her hymen, all that internal stuff, was intact, so how could you do sexual battery rape?" The definition of the situation was very important to him, as rape represented a line that he would not cross. It was important that the listener understand that the offense was not physically invasive, a distinction he associated with his principles. "And just my reasoning, my logic, my family-orientated values that I had. Although I was out of control, I still had some principles . . . I still had some things that I would not do. This was one of the things that I wouldn't do was have sex with one of my kids . . . I wouldn't have sex with [my stepkids]. . . . But I can honestly say that I wouldn't have tried to have sex with her or penetrate her, you know, me get nude and try to have sex with her. That's one of the things that I say I would never have done." Sex with one of the children he cared for would violate his "family-oriented values"—what he did not do was just as important in his construction of the offense as what he did do, because it enabled him to demarcate clear boundaries of self and assert a less deviant identity.

Terry

In the previous five narratives a tension exists between the new official label—or a new aspect to the institutional identity (to use Turner's framework)—and the offender's sense of authenticity. Other formal roles in the community are given weight and credence and are seen as reflecting the true self. But the stigma attached to the deviant status is alien and outside the offender. In Terry's case, he expressed contradictions and confusion regarding the extent to which the institutional or the impulsive self was more "real."

Terry's articulation of his real self was particularly complex, as it involved the construction of a dual existence. As we have seen, Terry relegated his sex offenses to a "completely separate life," which allowed him to affirm a normative identity. The boundary he strove to demarcate between deviance and normalcy helped him carve out a legitimate social identity while disavowing the deviant behavior. His offenses existed within their own separate realm, and he said they did not affect his interaction with people in his other, legitimate, social world. He could present a socially acceptable and "normal" self in the majority of his interactions with others.

However, at the same time that he constructed the acceptable self as the real self, he also presented this self as tenuous and contingent: "Until it hit the papers, no one, completely no one, knew about it, including family. So you could pursue your life normally, *as if you were a normal person.*" Although he felt able to maintain the duality between the two realms, his master identity—that is, the primary social self that maintained his bond to the community—was based on concealing crucial facts. "As if" he were normal signifies a falsehood, a misrecognition. He did not posit his normalcy as unequivocally authentic; instead he described his ability to effectively engage in impression management and to effectively present an intended version of self. Because of his discreditable status, his performance was always dependent on his ability to keep his deviant behavior private.

As long as his secret remained hidden, his deviance did not divide him from the community, and to some extent he was able to maintain an internal sense of his own normalcy: "I considered myself a normal person. I didn't consider myself a normal person, but I considered myself someone who was acting normal, who was able to conform to society's demands." The narrative swings back and forth between a genuine normalcy and a contingent, performative one. He could not definitively affirm the public social identity as completely separate from his deviant behavior. Actually being normal and merely acting or performing normal became confused. He defined a normal person as "someone who conforms to society's demands" and was capable of doing so in virtually all realms of his life. Yet his deviant behavior prevented him from fully identifying with the performance. He claimed dual identities and attempted to ascribe authentic primacy to the performative or institutional one. However, his commitment to it was undermined by the other life wherein he engaged in sexually deviant acts. There loomed the threatening possibility that the deviant behavior represented the true self that needed to be masked.

In contrast, at other times in his narrative, the conforming self *was* the real self. He asserted that once the community learned of his crimes, "They didn't see me for who I *am*. They saw me for that separate life." Here he really was the normal law-abiding citizen who participated in church activities and played on community sports teams. The deviant self was the false self. The people who "shunned" him were shunning the wrong person. They misidentified him. Once they did so, the deviant label subsumed his prior social identity and became a master identity. However, while the community may have revised its impression of him, he maintained that he was still the same person, the one worthy of inclusion.

In explaining his history of not "always feeling normal," Terry ascribed generalized deviant behavior to another person within him: "I had a temper and lashed out at my brother and sister, but I was always so loving, they realized that wasn't me, that was *someone else* lashing out."

It is worth nothing that while his "temper" may refer to unsocial, difficult, or unpleasant behavior, lashing out on occasion is not generally "deviant" in the same sense that sexual misconduct is. In most circumstances lashing out verbally is not criminal but a form of socially unacceptable behavior that is tolerated to different degrees in various social settings. Yet Terry disavowed not only his sexually deviant activities but his anger and aggression toward others. Significantly, these are impulses that, like sexual offending, have potential to damage social connections. Terry constructed the self that acts in ways that threaten social bonds as the one that is relegated to the unreal. The deviance was performed by "someone else." The behavior that didn't fit his sense of who he "always" was got cordoned off. On the other hand, he iterated a real self that was "loving" and benevolently social. He continued, "Overall I'm just a very honest and caring person and a good listener and sensitive." The true self was presented as not only nonthreatening, but also particularly mild and in possession of constructive sociable traits.

In the construction of his real self, Terry seemed to conflate normalcy and goodness. I observed that the characteristics he listed reflected a two-dimensional ideal person that stood in stark contrast to the clinical picture of many sex offenders. For example, where Terry affirmed his honesty, clinicians assert that sex offenders are manipulative and highly invested in self-serving cognitive distortions (Marshall et al., 1999, p. 59). Terry cared about others, whereas sex offenders are believed to have considerable empathy deficits (ibid., p. 62). Terry stated that he was sensitive and a good listener, but typical sex offenders are often unaware of others' feelings and often minimize their own impact on them (ibid., p. 80). Terry's narrative strategy was to affirm the good self, rather than a complex self. He thus cast himself as belonging to the community by establishing an ideal identity worthy of inclusion, unthreatening, and capable of connecting to others.

The Dangerous Other

All six men created an image of the dangerous other—the type of person that is an actual and concerning threat to the community, someone who inflicts great harm and is deserving of punishment and severe methods of social control, someone for whom the stigma of a sex offense conviction is appropriate. They constructed this other in order to demarcate themselves as safe. They affirmed their allegiance to the dominant community by asserting the legitimacy of the community's concern about the threat and the reasonableness of taking action to protect the community from harm. The dangerous other was characterized as particularly threatening to children, and offenders upheld the mainstream sentiment that children deserve special protection. In addition this figure was one who commits heinous crimes—crimes for which all sex offenders bear the stigma. Finally, some participants aligned themselves with populist zero-tolerance policies toward this menace, further asserting their ideological commitment to mainstream values regarding protecting children from dangerous predators.

Protecting Children

All the participants articulated some belief about the nature of children and supported the idea that they need special protection. Child abuse is what Katherine Beckett has described as a "valence issue"—a topic "seen as immune from contestation." She points to the fact, for example, that no "pro child abuse" lobby can exist in the current cultural climate (Beckett, 1996). Given the uncontested sanctity of children, it is not too surprising that the sex offenders in this study shared mainstream indignation about violations against them. They particularly expressed indignation at the idea of sexually abusing children, echoing sentiments of the current cultural milieu in which fears about child molesters have increased. In articulating their belief in the sanctity of the child, these men distanced themselves from truly dangerous others and asserted their rightful place within the community.

When Tim expressed his intolerance for sex offenders, he explained, "I've got three nephews of my own. And I got a lot of second cousins that are young." Constructing himself as someone woven into the social fabric through kinship ties, he claimed that his familial connections with children particularly sensitized him to the need for harsh policies regarding sex offenders. He then articulated his idea of a "truly sick" person, invoking one of his uncles: "He's got a sick, twisted mind. 'Cause he had done things in his past. Some of my aunts, he had raped them when they were young." Here he described the real dangerous other as one who engages in incest and rapes children. The "sick, twisted mind" is indicative of a true deviant.

Similarly, when Raoul asserted his status as a grandfather, he invoked his kinship relationships to affirm his alliance with mainstream community values: "Children are the future. Children are innocent. I mean, you know, I love children. I have four grandchildren now." Not only did he express popular sentiments regarding the innocence and social importance of children, indicating that he thought and felt like most members of society, Raoul also asserted that he particularly loved children. In this way he distanced himself from the dangerous other, while positing himself as a protector and caregiver.

Raoul encountered other sex offenders in group therapy whose acts he distanced himself from because of, among other things, the ages of their victims: "Because everyone in the group is a convicted felon, sex offender. Somebody might have done something that was more severe, more worse than you. Raped an eleven-year-old or had sex. . . . Even convicted sex offenders look down on each other too." Group is an environment where sex offenders can evaluate each other and their respective crimes, and they begin to develop a hierarchy of deviance. The real deviant he pointed to was one who commits forcible intercourse on a child. Force, penetration, and the age of the victim were factors in his construction of the dangerous other. Sex offenders, he argued, do not fully accept their label, but look at each other and critically assess who is worthy of stigma and who, in contrast, is less deviant and implicitly more worthy of inclusion in normative society. He explained that sex offenders share the values of the larger society.

Terry also maintained that children need special protection and that this should manifest itself in different forms of social control for those who offend against them: "I really do believe there should be different policies [for people who offend against minors]. I truly believe it's easier to influence a minor. They're more susceptible to what happens when they're young. It's how you think of yourself when you get older; it's how you grow up." He explained that children are more seriously harmed by sex offenses, that the consequences of an offense are greater on a minor victim than an adult. Because of the harm they inflict, these offenders should be more severely sanctioned. In fact, the assessments in most states do take into account the age of the victim when assigning a risk level.

Reggie argued that in today's society children are more vulnerable to strangers.

> I think now in this generation we put too much responsibility on our children. They don't even teach the concept of don't talk to

strangers. I see a lot of kids on the street now, maybe eight years old, going home by themselves from school. And kids don't know, "oh, I'm a good friend of your mom's, I'll drop you off...." They see a nice fancy car, they see jewelry. And even the kids that play basketball in the park, you know, "Let me show you a move" or whatever, "put you on my basketball team; oh, you like Michael Jordan?" The kids go right up to them.... So I feel [Megan's Law] is definitely a good law.

He articulated a belief that children need special protection, and that potentially dangerous adults may prey on their vulnerabilities and naïveté. Megan's Law was presented as a valuable policy because it was seen as offering help to unsupervised children who bear undo responsibility for judging the safety of strangers. Presumably Megan's Law would allow parents to alert their children to the presence of dangerous others in the community and the children would then be less likely to "go right up to them."

Heinous Crimes and the Truly Sick

In addition to casting the offender against children as the dangerous other, all participants in the study at some point enumerated the types of heinous acts and dangerous criminals who share their stigma but who, unlike themselves, really are deserving of social excommunication. Tim's disgust for his "sick" uncle was similarly expressed as resentment about being grouped in treatment settings with those who have committed worse acts than he had: "And we have people in my group that have different sexual offense. Let's say for instance, for computer Internet sting operations, rape of a minor, sexual contact with a minor, and family members in sexual contexts. And then you have man to man action with an older man and young boy. You know, giving oral pleasures and all that. I hear that kind of sick stuff." As someone who was involved in a "sting operation" where there was no physical contact or actual victim, Tim argued that he did not belong among people who have committed these more dangerous and harmful acts. He defined the "sick stuff" as forcible rape, sexual contact with a minor, incest, and male homosexual activity.

Karl also found himself in group therapy with people he considered more legitimately threatening to society. The experience was initially difficult for him, and he explicitly distanced himself from the dangerous others.

I had a hard time when I started in my group therapy. Because I was like, "wow . . . this is not where I belong, like, why am I am in this group?" These are rapists and pedophiles, and there were people that murdered their baby's mama and then had sex with their corpse. I remember hearing these stories, and I'm sitting here going, like, "wow, what am I doing here?" I had consensual sex with a fourteen-year-old and it was not even sex and then it never happened again. I've never done anything like that in my life. And now, well especially now, would never imagine doing that again. But I felt like I was not in a place where I should have been. I thought, "oh those are the sex offenders: the rapists and the pedophiles and the child pornography people. Those are the people that are the danger to society, not me."

Rape and pedophilia, child pornography and necrophilia: these are the crimes Karl identified as real dangers, and those that perpetrate these acts are the people for whom sex offender policies should apply. He argued that his encounter with the student was far removed from those acts. Asserting that his situation was consensual, he indicated that force is a necessary element of heinousness. When he pointed out that his victim was fourteen, he indicated that teenagers are less vulnerable victims than younger children. He argued that it "was not even sex," making a qualitative distinction between intercourse and oral sex, where intercourse constitutes a more serious violation. He reiterated that it happened once, distinguishing between a pattern of behavior and an isolated incident, the former being more threatening to society. Because his acts involved comparatively less harm, he did not belong in the same category as the real offenders.

Invoking "the sexual predator," Karl argued that the level of social control he was under was not necessary in his situation, but that there are people for whom that level of surveillance is appropriate. He argued that "I also didn't seek out; I'm not a predator. And I think there are predators. There are sexual predators. And I think that is something that is very different. And I think people that do go and seek out victims and victimize people and prey on people might need a little more monitoring because of the nature of what they did." Karl reinforced the validity of the now commonly used, but legally imprecise, term "predator," defining it according to intentionality. People who plan crimes, who are on the lookout for potential victims, and who "prey" on them are the real danger. Employing vernacular that casts the offender in animalistic terms, Karl relied on stereotypical associations and popular fears to align himself with community values and delineate himself as safe.

Karl contrasted his own situation with the predator/innocent prey scenario, arguing that he was not looking for sex and the victim was not wholly innocent. "If I was looking for a student to have sex with, because I really needed to have sex, and I really needed some deviant behavior in my life, and was looking for okay, who can I pick out of my class that I can do this with? That is a very different mindset than someone who keeps coming up to me and flirting with me and establishing a relationship. To me they're very different mentally and they're two types of individuals and those two types of crimes would be very different people." Karl produced these two mirror-like scenarios, with actors in the same age and relationship to each other respectively. While the alternative scenario was characterized by structural similarities to his own situation, the motives of the actors were different, which was highly significant to Karl. The real dangerous other has a sexual agenda and is "looking" for a victim. However, if anyone had an agenda in Karl's construction of the offense, it was the student. In this way, Karl demarcated the dangerous other as someone who may commit the same act, but does so consciously with possibly harmful intentions. The dangerous other was also presented as having compulsions that drive his behavior: someone who "really needed some deviant behavior in my life." Importantly, this other is cast as a "very different" person from Karl.

As we have seen, the concept of the "mistake" was a recurring motif for Reggie. Explaining the difference between himself and someone who his "sick," Reggie relied on his distinction between a "mistake" and a "problem." He argued that what he did was a mistake—he knew it was wrong and he stopped. Speaking of people in group, Reggie said, "Some of them I know when they speak, use the word 'mistake.' And I don't see it as a mistake; I see it as a problem. Because a mistake is, if there's a young girl and you may touch her in the wrong manner, then you made a mistake. But if you sit there and you log on to a computer, and you've been chatting for a month, two months, that's not a mistake you're making." He emphasized the prolonged contact and the agency on the part of the person with a "problem," and presented the mistake as something that happened just once. Explaining his notion of people with problems, he described those in his group therapy who had lengthy email or chat room exchanges with people who disclosed that they were fourteen. He argued that this was "a problem" and that one way of determining the extent of the problem is that "if a child is young enough to be your child, then I feel it's a problem," and a problem that signified a legitimate danger. His construction of the danger rested on the extent of the age difference between the sexual actors, and on a construction of the child. These motifs allowed Reggie to demarcate the dangerous other.

The most severe form of a problem for Reggie involved a contact crime with a biological child.

> Well, a lot of guys in the group have the Internet crimes. Only a couple of us, maybe three or four of us, have contact crimes. You know, one guy that was in the group, the contact crime was with his own daughter. I feel like he's kind of sick. Because he was convicted of a crime, and then he had a violation for the same thing. Now she's older, she's twelve. He said they were getting ready for church, and he was like, "before we leave can you please show me your breasts." So I feel like he really has a problem. He has a bad problem . . . for your daughter! Your biological daughter! . . . He should have been incarcerated, no probation, not programs. Because he has a problem. . . . He has an attraction to very young girls, to his own daughter.

He emphasized the repeated nature of the violation, the fact that it was incestuous, and the girl's youth. Repeated, incestuous contact crimes with young victims constituted a "very bad problem." Distinguishing this type of dangerous, "sick" behavior from his own "mistake," Reggie argued that this dangerous other is someone from whom society needs protection. He asserted that this type of person should be incarcerated and his bonds to society completely severed. He implied that in this case the punishment was not severe enough for the crime.

Aaron also identified incestuous transgressions as the worst type of sex crime, and, as we have seen, also distinguished them from the "mistake" he made in unknowingly having sex with a minor. Like others in the study, Aaron referred to situations he learned about in his group as examples of people who had committed worse acts, "much worse": "They sit there and they say, 'I'm here because I had sex with my niece, with my nephew, and they were eleven years old.' . . . I'm sitting next to people that talk about they're molesting young boys." Aaron presented these cases in order to contrast his own act with theirs, and emphasized that he couldn't "relate" to what they had done. He stated that he had "no identification" with their actions because they were so far removed from anything he had done or would consider doing. Articulating his inability to relate to this type of offender, Aaron affirmed his difference from people that are truly dangerous to society.

In the previous chapter we saw that Raoul invoked media images of offenders to explain his sense of stigma. He also did so to distinguish himself from active threats to the community: "I was reading on the Internet the other day that sex offenders are likely to offend like a 117 kids. I'm like, yeah right. That's a damn lie. That's a sick person. I know I'm not sick . . . because I have a conscience." As we have seen, Raoul argued that his offense was an "isolated incident," not a pattern of behavior. The repeat offender, with alarmingly high numbers of victims, is not typical of sex offenders in general, nor does he have anything in common with Raoul. Such a person may exist, but he would be an exception. He asserted that they are true deviants, "sick," but in presenting such a person, he confidently affirmed his own normalcy and mental health. Raoul knew he was not sick.

Defining sickness, Raoul invoked the concept "conscience." He further elaborated its significance and its relationship to social danger: "Sickness is a person that repeatedly offends without regard to other people's feelings, or consequences. . . . A person with a sickness would do something and try to justify it, rationalize it, and want to believe that it was okay in his mind." Here the word "repeatedly" again iterated Raoul's distinction between isolated incidents and patterns of behavior. Raoul asserted his moral compass as he presented a theory about the relationship between conscience and deviance. Defining himself in opposition to the sick, he articulated his own regard for others' feelings and the fact he does not justify the infliction of harm. An important distinction for Raoul was that between what a person *did* and how a person *felt* about what he did. While the deviant other is self-righteous, uncaring and self-justified, Raoul presented himself as recognizing his offense as a moral lapse: "I mean I know I was wrong." He qualified this statement by comparing what he did to what a truly dangerous person might have done: "But you know what? Thank god I didn't go further. I could have gone further, meaning having sex with her and really violating her. I mean, I did violate her, but, taking pictures of her private parts it's a violation, okay? ... But, I've been around guys that have actually done. ... If I compare it, it's actually nothing to what they've done. I'm not trying to minimize, because I know I was wrong." He expressed the belief that there are gradations of harm, and that his actions should be viewed in light of more heinous ones. That he did not have intercourse with his victim mitigated the extent of his deviance, and this fact was used in the delineation of the true deviant and dangerous other.

Providing another example of someone who poses a true threat to society, Raoul stated, "I was reading a case of a guy who had AIDS and raped three kids. To me, that guy, they should give him the chair. 'Cause he just ruined three lives. And he knew he had it and he still did it." He described someone who committed multiple crimes (part of a pattern of behavior), whose victims were children, and whose actions involved force and intercourse. In addition, that this man had AIDS meant that he potentially transmitted a deadly disease ("he passed a death sentence"), and that his actions might therefore have even greater consequences. For Raoul, this was the dangerous other par excellence against whom he could construct his own normative identity. Stating that "they should give him the chair," Raoul espoused populist zero-tolerance punitive ideology. In so doing, Raoul aligned himself with a segment of the mainstream. He reinforced this point, asserting "that for certain crimes" the death penalty "is mandated." He believed that society should absolutely not tolerate certain heinous threats, and that in cases of true danger, the ultimate form of social exclusion is appropriate.

Tim also aligned himself with populist punitiveness. We heard him state that some of his neighbors think sex offenders "should be taken out back and shot." He continued to explain, "People don't like the idea that sex offenders are walking free. And I actually agree with them. ... I would feel the same way." Articulating the same intolerance toward sex offenders that he attributed to his community, Tim was asserting his membership within that community. In agreeing that there are those who should not be "walking free," he reaffirmed his own sense of deserving to participate unencumbered in ordinary community life like any other member.

Critiquing Policies

All the sex offenders interviewed articulated a need to protect society from those who truly threaten society. They also criticized current policies for being irrational and casting too wide a net. They qualified the meaning attached to their official social label through a critique of the labeling process. Thus they managed their outsider status by intellectually engaging with policy.

These men took issue with the fact that the phrase "sex offenders" encapsulates men who committed a variety of offenses. People outside the criminal justice system tend to assume the term refers to the worst and most dangerous. Thus, in articulating a need for policies to encompass more nuanced categories and sentencing responses than currently exist, offenders were still aligning themselves with those who do think there should be laws in place for sex offenders. But they were critiquing the implementation of the policies from the stance of knowledgeable agents, specially privileged because of their lived experience with the label. They addressed the ways the current system is unfair, creates undue stress for offenders, and unnecessarily stigmatizes those who do not conform to the stereotypical predatory menace.

Although Terry believed that he was the type of offender from whom society *does* need protection, he argued that current policies are overly inclusive. He presented his theory from the position of someone more knowledgeable than the layperson, locating himself within professional discourse through the use of facts and generalizations espoused by the "wise" ("persons who are normal but whose special situation has made them intimately privy to the secret life of the stigmatized individual") (Goffman, 1986, p. 28)—such as professionals who work with the population.

> I am one of the people who probably should be under Megan's Law to some extent. It goes over and above what it needs to for me and most sex offenders, I'm sure. But ninety-nine out of one hundred people who are in group therapy with me, both this group and my previous group, were sex offenders and should not have been under Megan's Law. Ninety-nine percent did not have crimes against minors or hands-on crimes. They attempted to meet a minor or watched pornography on the Internet. Instead of actual hands-on crime.... It's a real fallacy, as far as I know, that people who watch pornography on the Internet or TV are going to have a hands-on crime. It just doesn't happen very often. Same thing with people who molested a family member. It just doesn't happen that the public is in danger. And they're still under Megan's Law although they shouldn't be.

Unlike the participants who asserted that they are in group therapy with people more dangerous than themselves, Terry argued that most of the people he meets in group do *not* present a danger to society. Although he stipulated that the degree to which he himself was monitored is extreme, he also viewed himself as in need of some form of supervision and believed that it was reasonable for particular laws to apply to him. However, he argued that he is atypical: *most* offenders have not committed acts that have caused harm or would conform to stereotypical sex crimes. Speaking with a sense of authority and providing statistics, he indicated that many offenders he encountered have not had physical contact with a victim or inflicted harm. Furthermore, he stated that their behavior is unlikely to escalate to the extent that the public needs to be concerned with them. He did not see most convicted sex offenders as a risk to the community.

For this reason he believed the current system should be reevaluated: "The legal system I feel needs to be looked at a little more. Not that sex offenders shouldn't be singled out as someone to be monitored more carefully." He aligned himself with the community by conceding that sex offenders present a particular kind of social problem and require greater levels of social control than other types of criminals. By identifying "monitoring" as the necessary form of social control, he indicated that punishment *as punishment* is not enough for those he considered "true" sex offenders. Sexual criminals need to be managed within the community in addition to their formal punishment because of the presumed special danger they pose. Punitive measures themselves will not prevent crimes. In this way he suggested that sexual offenders present a special class of criminal.

Karl, Raoul, Tim, and Aaron also expressed frustration with grouping sex offenders under three categories and one general label. Karl believed "it should be on a case-by-case basis." Raoul argued that the stigma of the label itself is a reason to fine-tune the existing system: "They need to like, put categories. They need to make some type of system, coding system for the offenders and put them in perspective, because it does effect anybody that's labeled a sex offender. When he's trying to find a job, it becomes very, very difficult. Not only, as it is you're already a convicted felon. But then you have the sex offender label on top of that which makes it even worse." Raoul brought attention to the problems created by the double stigmatization that sex offenders face, and specifically focused on the ways it prevents reintegration into the community through employment. He felt that offenders who do not conform to the public's view of sex offenders should be distinguished more clearly from those who are truly dangerous. Were this the case, deserving people in Raoul's position would be in a better position to reenter society.

Aaron argued that in his case the "statutory" nature of the "rape" charge gets subsumed under the stigma attached to rape, and that he suffered from the effects of that label. He expressed frustration that the levels assigned to sex offenders do not come with "fine print" addressed to the public explaining "mitigating circumstances." Aaron argued that this "cookie-cutter approach" needed to be "looked into" and reflected that this may happen only when someone in power gets caught in a similar situation to his.

In addition to critiques about the way offenders are categorized and labeled, some participants maintained that even if sentences are appropriate, the social control measures that are used can be counterproductive. Terry in particular believed that the stress caused by certain punishments renders offenders more likely to recidivate. House arrest is one example: "It's pretty much three hours out a week. That is extremely difficult. Because myself and many sex offenders are very people-friendly, people-oriented people, like social environments, that sort of thing." He argued that house arrest punishes and curtails offenders' socially acceptable, normative aspects of self. Here he championed sex offenders as good, prosocial people. Aligning his normative identity with the less threatening sides of other sex offenders, Terry challenged the underlying intent to exclude them. His critique of the isolating aspect of the punishment included an assertion about the extent to which he and others like him are worthy of inclusion. To the extent that he agreed that sex offenses need to be prevented by the criminal justice system, he supported some of the goals of current policies. However, he objected to the exclusionary means that unnecessarily constrain many offenders' prosocial traits.

Furthermore, he argued that house arrest creates a situation wherein some offenders may be more driven to commit another crime. He addressed this concern at length:

> Why house arrest is punishment: I've never figured that out. Because almost all sex offenders that I know, myself included were isolated or lonely when they committed their crime; it was a contributing

factor in their crime. And putting people on house arrest where they can't have interaction with people seems counterproductive. But the reason they do it, I've been told, is to keep you away from society to protect society.

The monitoring situation does in itself exacerbate the problem, because like I said before, most of the sex offenders, a contributing factor was their loneliness or aloneness, and monitoring and a lot of the other things that are in place force you to be isolated and apart from humanity. Which you know just cause you to commit another crime. So their solution is causing the problem, or increasing the problem.

The exclusion itself, meant to protect society, could result in more harm by further isolating people who offend out of loneliness. In order to critique the policies, he constructed a theory of motivation and invoked knowledge about sex offenders to make his point. He argued the nature of policies aimed at sex offenders in general, and house arrest in particular, segregate the offender in such a counterproductive way that the contributing factors are exacerbated.

Echoing some researchers' critiques (which will be discussed in the next chapter), Terry also argued that the community notification aspect of Megan's Law is unnecessary as in many cases it would not be effective in preventing crimes: "I don't think my neighbors need to know about me. . . . I don't think people at work needed to know either. Like I said, it was a separate life and sex offenders try to keep it away from the people they interact with every day. True sex offenders like myself don't know their victims, so the people in the neighborhood have no reason to know because you deal with them every day and you're not going to commit a crime against friends, family, neighbors." Terry relied on his knowledge of "true sex offenders" to critique existing policies for not achieving their putative aims. He was not arguing against the need for sex offender policies, but pointing to the fact that they are essentially flawed. He stated that they do not seem to be based on an awareness of the situations within which offenses take place; nor do they address the real relationships of the social actors in most situations of sexual offense. Terry maintained that since his neighbors and friends were never at risk they did not need to know about his deviant behavior.

His sense of the community had altered in recent years with media attention surrounding Megan's Law and the "problem" of sex offenders:

"There's a fear in the public, growing concern and fanaticism, against, you know, sex offenders. It's somewhat warranted, but it's really gone beyond the bounds of normalcy." His description of the "fear" and "fanaticism" indicated a menacing level of concern. Abnormality was being ascribed not to the behavior of the offender, but to the community's focus on the issue. Experiencing himself outside the community, he did not participate in its fanaticism but rather felt himself to be the object of it and a potential target.

Raoul also complained that sex offender policies place people under undue stress and social control and that this has a number of social consequences.

> I just think they need to come up with some kind of system that could alleviate the stress on sex offenders because sex offenders do go through a lot. Especially when they're getting released from prison, they make the whole neighborhood aware. You have to go to programs. They check on you. You have to register. It's a lot of stuff. Sometimes, if you're not strong minded, you'll do something stupid just to end up back in prison because in prison you don't have to deal with all that. You don't have to deal with the people. Because people always stereotype and people always label you. And there are some mean people out there.

Like Terry, Raoul claimed that the policies that apply strictly to sex offenders, such as registration, notification, treatment, specific probation demands, and types of surveillance, create a stress that is constantly experienced. Like Terry, Raoul asserted that these differing conditions may place the subject in a position that exacerbates the situations and makes him more, not less, likely to commit a crime. In this way Raoul articulated his opinion that the policies are counterproductive to their stated purpose—preventing recidivism. By "strong-minded" Raoul might have meant a capacity to resist internalizing stigma and to affirm a nondeviant identity.

Reggie argued that the "twenty-year registry is too steep in most cases" and that the current policies "need to be looked into." His own experience, as well as those of others whom he had encountered in group—most of whom were convicted for noncontact crimes—indicated to him that "some of the guidelines and laws are kind of strong." When he elaborated, he recalled the cases of people in group who were convicted of statutory violations with their girlfriends. He mentioned a person who "might have been twenty, they had a loving relationship, but the age difference, fifteen, sixteen years old"—indicating that the "loving relationship" and the relative proximity in age should be considered mitigating factors. These more benign and common situations were seen as less of a violation of social and sexual mores. He did not think they should be regarded as serious offenses. Reggie provided another example of a case that was punished too severely, this one concerning interaction on the Internet: "You know, there was another guy. He had wrote a love letter, an explicit love song, put it on the Internet. But he didn't put a parental advisory on it, so one of the girls that downloaded it was fourteen, and she wrote on the fan blog about 'how much I love you and how much just experiencing your song . . . ,' and the parent got a hold of it and now he's a registered sex offender!" When Reggie relayed this story he was clearly outraged by a sense of injustice. The person who posted explicit lyrics on the Internet should not be grouped in the same category as the man who attempted to fondle his own daughter's breasts.

Reggie also felt that the specific punishment and Megan's Law were unnecessary in his case because of his certainty that he would never make the same mistake again ("This is something I'll never do again, so it's something they don't have to worry about me"). That is, Megan's Law is meant to prevent further offenses, and in cases such as his there would be no recurrence.

Reggie asserted that the current climate surrounding sex offender laws and the overzealous legislation of the past decades has created an environment of mistrust that affects innocent people. He stated that the laws place the community "in a state of paranoia" and told the story of a couple he and his wife knew from church that sponsored a number of children's activities. Although this couple had never been officially accused or convicted of any misconduct, members of the community viewed their interest in children with mistrust. Reggie felt that this was "not right" and stated that he would feel confident sending his children to their programs because "they do a lot of good." He argued that this type of "paranoia" was a negative consequence of the general public's heightened concern about sex offenders.

Frustrations with Unjust or Irrational Policies

While critiquing the policies affecting sex offenders and discussing life under their constraints, a number of the men at some point expressed a sense of powerlessness, constructing themselves as passive objects within an unjust system. In so doing they positioned themselves as members of the community who have been unfairly treated and subtly reinforced a righteous sense of a normal real self—they were just regular people. Specifically, the irrationality of the system placed unfair burdens on an otherwise normative identity and rendered them powerless. In addition, powerlessness (and hopelessness) can be seen as a way of framing or coping with the stigmatizing label. It provided a means by which the person could distance himself from the labeling process. If the process is out of his hands, it is not a reflection of him.

Tim's narrative included many descriptions of life's unfairness. Suffering a host of illnesses and watching his mother die as a result of what he characterized as malpractice, Tim presented a worldview wherein he had little control over significant events in his life. Positioning himself as a victim of irrational sex offender policies, he aligned himself with the powerless little guy who can't beat the system, who is always getting screwed. He saw the policies as another instance of this. He threw up his hands against his excommunication and aligned himself with the "average guy." When he critiqued the system, he emphasized the unpredictability of the laws. "Because they keep changing the laws every single day and it keeps affecting us every day. Been putting stress on me and other people that attend this program. And they don't know what the law covers on their behalf and our behalf and so forth. They keep changing it every day and we don't know what's going to happen tomorrow. One day it's five years, and then the ten-year registry and the twenty-year registration, and now it's going to be a lifetime registration no matter what level you are, and it's ridiculous." Tim attributed personal stress to the fact that the rules that applied to him were continually being changed for reasons that had nothing to do with his behavior or individual conduct. Rather, these decisions were made in the legislature and passed down to him through state agents. He characterized them as confused and unhelpful ("My lawyer is a joke") and who themselves were barely abreast of new policies: "I had conflicting probation papers. 'Cause my lawyer got a piece of paper from the probation officer giving me a set of rules. Then I get one from probation and they're completely different . . . such as telling me I have a curfew. I have to be in by nine PM. And the other one says I have no curfew, only on Halloween, which I understand.... I went to my PO. He took it to his boss, the head honcho of probation, and we sat down and discussed it." Tim also critiqued current policies for being inconsistently implemented: "But you know, one of the guys who's in my group therapy session has an identical case to mine and he's got access to the Internet. He's got his own computer and laptop. His case is identical to mine. Same judge, same lawyer, same district, same DA. He's got an identical case, but he's got a computer, the access, and I don't." Because he saw no logic to the way sex offenders are punished and managed, it was not easy for him to view himself as having the ability to rationally make changes through his own actions. He indicated that the system, not he, is deviant.

Portraying sex offenders as regular people, Tim presented the system as persecutory. As we have seen, he was particularly upset by the experiences of someone in his group who he felt was targeted by a local politician. Tim used this story to illustrate his conviction that sex offenders are powerless against a larger system.

> I don't think anyone should be above the law. And this borough president, or councilman, came to his house with all the probation officers and lined them up to measure exactly how far it was from his bedroom to the nearest school. They lined him up and they measured it with a tape measure. It was supposed to be like a thousand feet and he was like nine hundred and eighty-five feet. And they said he was too close to the school. Fifteen feet. What do you want the guy to do? Move upstairs to the roof, to make it an even thousand? I mean, this guy should not be above the law. This guy went there and he wanted this guy gone and he didn't care what it took.
>
> He served twelve years in jail, and he was doing lifetime probation and lifetime registry. What more do you want him to do? And this guy, he was a very nice guy. I was with him for the first year that I was out and talking to him and from what I understand from him, he was very nice, very pleasant to talk to. And they just totally turned his life upside down. I mean, I don't think that's right.

Tim recounted this story at relative length, and referred to it a few times—the injustice clearly made an impression on him. He characterized the sex offender in question as a regular guy—a particularly nice guy. This man was the victim of an overzealous display of political power.

Asking "What more do you want him to do?" Tim expressed frustration with the unfairness of the system and the helplessness of the little guy.

Aaron and Reggie voiced similar frustrations with legal inconsistencies and expressed a sense that they themselves were unfairly punished. Reggie expressed confused outrage over the fact that the man who attempted to molest his own daughter was only a Level I like Reggie himself. He stated, "He's a Level I like me, and his level is too low. I mean he really needs to be watched." In addition, Reggie felt that it was frustrating that the laws vary from state to state and that there is little consistency: "Each state you have to re-register. In certain states, like Florida, even Level I they put them right out there." Aaron also felt that it was unfair that the laws varied from state to state and was dismayed at the fact that because the age of consent varies in some states, had his encounter with the sixteen-year-old girl taken place elsewhere it would not even have been defined as a crime.

Like Tim, Karl was exasperated with ever-changing laws: "It's frustrating. I also feel totally powerless over it. I mean, you never know. I was reporting every other week to probation and now I have to report every week and it's not because of me or anything I did." For Karl, the changing laws contributed to a sense of chronic uncertainty, an inability to feel secure about the future and his daily life. However, this powerlessness helped him disidentify with the label because he argued the laws did not reflect his actions.

Karl argued that because he was on probation and a labeled sex offender, he had no power to address the system on its own terms: "And I'm on probation and I don't have any rights in that way. And, even if I wanted to try to get the rights, I would have to have a lot of money to get a lawyer to be able to do that, and I don't have that money to put into that. So I don't even feel like there's any way for me to even stand up for myself in that sense." He stated that the system does not allow offenders to act as active participants in the framing of policies that affect them. The injustice is in part economic, as he lacked the necessary financial resources to advocate on their behalf. Thus Karl felt like his hands were tied, that there was nothing he could do to improve his situation.

Furthermore, like others, Karl observed that because punishment is not administered on "a case-by-case basis," there was no logic or justification in the ways policies were implemented: "There's this one guy in our group, he walks around with his ankle bracelet all the time. And he's one of the most well-adjusted guys in the group, and it's just something that he has to walk around with. And we live in that kind of society where people are afraid." The punishments meted out and the applied methods of social control did not seem to reflect the real danger posed by any individual in question. Instead, Karl attributed punishment to a general fear pervading society. He argued the system expresses the irrational, emotional sentiments of the society, rather than legitimate needs for punishment and social control. Referencing the public's fear, Karl invoked the idea of a society that is vulnerable to policy makers who posit heavy-handed solutions to social problems.

Raoul also expressed exasperation with the criminal justice system:

> Okay, I did it to myself, but when does it end? When does the closure come? Nine years in prison for taking two photographs! I worked in the law library and had guys tell me they spent a weekend with thirteen-year-olds. They screwed them through the ears and they had less time than me. And I tell them, "you just better get out of my face with that, you got eight counts, and you had sex, you had sex, and you're over here and they gave you five years for eight counts and you're over here crying. And I got nine years for two photographs and I'm eating it. Get out of here man." Sometimes I don't know how they dispense the justice. I really don't know how they do it.

Here we see the anger he felt when he compared others' sentences to his own. Looking at crimes on a continuum of harm, Raoul was enraged at the length of his sentence and expressed powerlessness in the face of irrational justice. The policies placed him in a position of not being able to find "closure"—that is, move on and pursue a life free from stigmatization and social control. His sense of frustration was fueled by the way the system overly punishes sex offenders in comparison to other types of crimes. "But I know something has to change, because you have sex offenders. But what about people that kill and are released from prison? What about people that commit armed robberies? You're telling me somebody who does a lewd act, for example somebody that solicits a prostitute, that's a sex offense. And somebody that does armed robbery, so the guy that's soliciting a prostitute is labeled a sex offender, that right there is going to destroy him for life. Now, the armed robber, it's not emphasized that much." For Raoul there was a hierarchy of harm, and current policies defied what he considered to be a commonsense notion of fairness. He saw criminal justice policies as overzealous in labeling as sex offenders many people who are not harmful, at the same time that they are more lenient with people who have committed more serious acts.

These men strove to carve out narrative space wherein they could assert their own humanity and resist the label "monster." Such a label marked them as outsiders, stripping them of a sense of social belonging, and undercutting their essential humanity. Through articulating an authentic self, participants asserted that their actions were understandable and that their human essence remained intact. They were still the same people they were before they committed their offense. These men repeatedly asserted that they were primarily attracted to adults and were not pedophiles—from whom society should protect itself. Invoking the same stereotypes and connotations mainstream society associated with their label allowed them to reestablish their own humanity in contrast to them. This provides a way for aligning with community, resisting stigma, and defying outsider status.

In spite of the fact that being labeled as sex offenders severed many of their significant social bonds, none fully and unequivocally saw themselves as monstrous. Even Terry, who very much felt that he was someone from whom society should be protected, articulated an idea of a real self that was in some ways normal. Sharing society's values about sex offenses enabled offenders to maintain their own socially viable sense of self and helped them adjust to the conditions of stigma. More than just easing an adjustment to a difficult situation, these strategies allowed offenders to view themselves as fully human and worthy of social inclusion.

CHAPTER 6

Personal Stories and Public Policy

IN HIS ARTICLE "SEX Offender as Homo Sacer" (2009), Dale Spencer argues that sex offender policies have resulted in a "camp" that is diffused throughout society. This is a space of lawlessness where subjects do not have rights accorded regular members of a democracy. It is a state of "inclusive exclusion" (p. 223). The stories presented here detail the experiences of life in this state; they reveal the ways individual actors make meaning out of structural conditions and find humanity when legal wholeness has been stripped. The six men considered here have committed crimes that are typical of those committed by the large numbers of people who must register as sex offenders. Using an approach grounded in the sociology of deviance has helped me recognize and highlight some of the ways public policy and social control impact identity. The generalizability of this small sample can be seen in the overall patterns and similarities between these unique individual experiences. The different accounts of their offenses included elements of rationalization that seemed intended to place their behavior in a context where it could be understood (although not necessarily excused). These men had substantial and meaningful ties to the communities, and their families stood by them after they were convicted. However their less intimate ties tended to be disrupted, enhancing the sense of stigma attached to the label "sex offender." In making sense of these life events, the men in this sample offered various accounts and strategies to repair their spoiled identities. This micro-analysis of their texts allows the readers to hear and perhaps empathize with the men in a way that is particularly significant given the extent to which they are marked as outcast and living in a lawless "camp." In the context of the "moral panic" surrounding this group, attempts to humanize them are particularly valuable.

Across the country versions of Megan's Law were passed in response to brutally horrific and violent events in which children were murdered by strangers. Yet the offenders who are subject to these policies have committed a range of offenses that vary in harmfulness. Research has shown that generally these offenders pose little, if any, risk of reoffending. This appears to be the case with the sample in this study. Like the general population of sex offenders on probation/parole, five of the six men I interviewed demonstrated little likelihood that they would reoffend. For them the conviction was for a first offense. At least from their accounts, the behavior in question represented and isolated instance, and their stories do not lend themselves to interpreting the speakers as dangerous menaces. But public policy concerning sex offenses is based on the assumption that perpetrators of sex offenses have high rates of recidivism—in spite of ample evidence to the contrary. While the public maintains a belief that sex offenders are incurable recidivists, "people with prior sex offender convictions pose the smallest risk of all" (Janus, 2006, p. 43). The majority of sex crimes that result in a conviction are not committed by people who have been labeled by the criminal justice system. Those who have committed a repeat offense represent a small minority of the population of convicted sex offenders.

Megan's Law is designed to protect society from the "stranger predator," and there is little reason to think that community notification will have much impact on preventing most sex crimes—those that occur between people who already know each other (Winick, 2003; Zilney & Zilney, 2009, p. 83). Based on a stranger danger mentality, these laws do not address the most common instances of sexual transgression. Instead they wind up targeting people who pose little safety risk to the community (Meloy, 2006, p. 41), affecting the majority of offenders who are least at risk for recidivating (ibid., p. 43). In addition, Megan's Law has been critiqued for numerous other reasons, including draining local law enforcement's resources (Finn, 1997); serious logistical difficulties with implementation (ibid.); relying on "static" diagnostic and clinical tools to classify offenders (Hanson, 2003, p. 71) and assuming experts can predict future behavior (ibid.); inappropriate application to people who have not committed an offense against a person (e.g., visiting a child pornography website, consensual homosexual encounters, homosexual "cruising" in public places, public urination) (Jones, 1999); increasing public anxiety (Jones, 1999; Lotke, 1997; Winick, 2003); promoting vigilantism (Jenkins, 1998; Mcalinden, 2006; McGuicken & Brown, 2001; Meloy, 2006); unjust application to juvenile offenders (Zimring, 2004); and generating a host of "collateral" consequences for offenders (Levenson et al., 2007;

Tewksbury & Lees, 2006). Finally, there is little evidence that community notification actually helps community members protect themselves from sex offenders. Studies to date have not shown any demonstrable effects in reducing sex offenses (Zgoba & Bachar, 2009). A survey study on the actual impact of community notification in Wisconsin found a number of problems with the community notification meetings held by local law enforcement (Zevitz & Farkas, 2000). The public was unclear as to the purpose of the meetings and thought they were gathering to discuss how to remove the offender from the neighborhood or how to prevent him from moving in. Rather than empowering the community, information about the presence of sex offenders only increased public anxieties (Winick, 2003; Zevitz & Farkas, 2000; Zilney & Zilney, 2009, p. 122). Thus, even if one does not question the premise of community notification, little research demonstrates that it has accomplished what it is intended to do. Importantly, these policies have not been shown to help victims (Bandy, 2009, p. 503).

This project emerged from sociological questions about the moral panic surrounding sex offenders. Interested in how the subjects of the panic make sense of their stigmatization and civil death, I saw the problem as existing within a particular culture of punishment practices. Megan's Law and other sex offender policies are part of the expansion of the criminal justice system, which is increasingly spreading formal social control into the community. The more than eight hundred thousand currently registered sex offenders contend not only with these mandates, but with connotations surrounding their label. Ideas about who and what a sex offender is are deeply entrenched, tapping into fears of violation, sexual aggression, and dangerous strangers. This became clear to me when I started planning my project. Colleagues and other scholars expressed serious concern about what I would be getting myself into. Friends, family, and acquaintances were disturbed by my focus on sex offenders, seeing the entire topic as disconcerting and worrisome. Few people were interested in developing an analytic distance and exploring the myriad deep-seated assumptions we have about deviant sexual behavior. This was an early indication of the extent of stigma faced by convicted sex offenders. It also alerted me to the difficulty of initiating a debate about existing policies.

Victims' Perspective

In Chapter 2 I observed that in listening to these men's stories, I was aware of various counternarratives. Other possible versions of truths that were not explicit in their narrative were in some ways implicated by their absence. One version that was notably absent from the texts was the victims' perspectives. Many researchers report that the consequences of sexual abuse can be "devastating" (Meloy, 2006, p. 19; Schultz, 2005, p. 12). While many victims of sex crimes suffer a range of reactions, that *range* is often overlooked. Various responses to victimization tend to be lumped into the same "devastating" category. This erases the possibility that harms may vary in their severity. In this study we cannot know how the participants' victims were affected. We do not know how the women Terry rubbed against or fondled dealt with these incidents, or how the teens who engaged in activity with Karl, Reggie, and Aaron felt afterward. Though Raoul stated his stepdaughter held nothing against him, we can only surmise how the violation affected her. Of course, in Tim's case there was no "actual" victim, and an important criticism of the Internet sex sting is that it focuses on what "might" have happened but in fact did not (Wright, 2009). Their constructions of the victim challenges prevailing notions about abuse, harm, and victimizations. And it is difficult to hear their stories without recourse to these.

Rationalizing Behavior

Many of the stories presented here include aspects of rationalization—making the deviant act understandable to a presumably nondeviant listener. In the second chapter I highlighted the ways in which their narratives employed some techniques of neutralization that included denial of responsibility and denial of victim and injury. All sexualized their victims to some extent. Few articulated that they saw their behavior in terms of abuse. Some presented the deviant incidents as events over which they had little control either because of a sexual momentum within the relationship (Karl and Tim) or because of compulsive illness (Terry). Although at times they reflected on the impact of their actions on others, their stories were primarily vehicles for asserting their own fundamental social and sexual normalcy. Wrongdoing on one side and harm on the other were not always neatly distinguishable. For instance, Aaron felt deceived by his victim, who had control of the situation; Karl argued his victim was not harmed; Tim did not in fact have an actual person as a victim. These men brought meaning to the situation that complicated and undermined the clear-cut offender/victim paradigm. Sexualizing their victims, all the men subtly or overtly brought this distinction into question. We can see this in the way Terry emphasized that the women he offended against were highly "feminine"; Raoul described becoming aware of the sexuality of young teens in his household, and emphasized that his victim had "planted the seed" by showing him pictures of her friend; in Tim's account, the person on the other end of the chat room exchanges showed great interest in sexual banter; Karl described his student as particularly sexually precocious; Reggie highlighted the mature physical appearance of the girl he became involved with; and Aaron met the girl he had an affair with in a sexually charged situation in which she was an exotic dancer. With the exception of Terry, they all presented their victims as playing a role in the unfolding of events that led to the offense; Karl, Tim, Aaron, and Reggie all presented their victims as having independent sexual agency. Doing so may be seen as an attempt to mitigate their own responsibility in the events.

Constructing the "Minor"

What are we to make of this? These texts question the validity of "statutory" criminal charges, and challenge us to consider the sexuality of teenagers independent of the concept of the child. Many of the offenders invoked the age of consent to explain why sexual activity with young people is considered wrong and illegal, and drew on the idea that young people are not mature enough to make decisions. In addition Karl, Terry, and Raoul speculated somewhat about the harm their actions caused their victims. Karl stated that his victim was precocious and probably not damaged by the experience. He also reflected on peers' accounts of positive experiences they had with adults when they were teens. Although he implied that some adult/young person sexual interactions might be damaging to the youth, he asserted that they should be viewed on a case-by-case basis and not assumed to always be harmful. Terry articulated that sexual molestation causes harm to victims, but that some people are less affected by it. He also said that violating minors had greater consequences. Neither Karl nor Terry espoused the view that sexual violation is always and clearly harmful and both articulated a belief that not all victims are equal. Raoul specifically invoked the concept of abuse of power from someone in a custodial position, and was the only person who used the word "violation." He stated that abusing trust is inherently wrong. Although on the other hand he presented the fact that his victim was not angry as him as evidence that she was not harmed. According to him, the extent to which someone is harmed by sexual transgression is contingent on aspects of the situation and characteristics of the social actors involved. Reggie did not reflect on the impact his behavior had on the teen girl, but he did acknowledge that he was taking advantage of her youth and that he had power in the situation.

It is easier in some of these stories than in others to see the situation from the offender's point of view. For instance, Reggie and Aaron, who were involved with teenage girls, presented narratives that are already familiar to us. We are accustomed to seeing sexualized images of young people in popular culture, and in many movies and TV shows young people are sexually active and sexually desiring subjects. Research suggests that half of all teens are sexually active (Levine, 2002, p. xxv), and an adult male who is attracted to adolescent girls is not necessarily considered sexually deviant (ibid., pp. 28–29). There is even a motif in popular culture that depicts the sexually predatory teenage girl seeking to destroy the lives of adult men (*Poison Ivy*, etc.). Listening to Reggie and Aaron's narratives, it is not difficult to grant some veracity to their version of events and to question the appropriateness of the punishments meted against them. Some of the stories presented in this research beg a question: are people who engage in consensual sex with teenagers sexually deviant or normative males in a culture that eroticizes teen sexuality? This is a difficult question not only to answer but to simply raise in a culture currently influenced by the victims' rights and child protection movements. These have led to important and meaningful changes in law and society, but their unintended consequences—which include sanctifying the child and victim in such a way that these definitions cannot, as well as zero tolerance of different types of transgressions—cannot be off-limits. An examination of the tropes used to describe what are considered abusing situations can only lead to a better understanding of them.

Truths or Distortions?

For many researchers, aspects of the accounts presented in this study might read like examples of the cognitive distortions, minimizations of harm, and rape myths routinely employed by sex offenders (Marshall et al., 1999; Scully, 1994; Terry, 2006). Such discourses cumulatively posit an explanation of the situations in which sexual transgression occurs and reject the validity of offenders' stories that do not conform to it. Labeling theory allows us to look beyond the question of what "really" happened. We can see that "victim" and "offender" (or "perpetrator") are entwined labels. Once someone is labeled a sex offender, the person he "offended" against is labeled a victim. While dominant discourses cast the offender as dishonest and tending to minimize harm, the participants in this study can be heard as speaking against these, offering alternative definitions. In listening to these stories, we are able to hear some of these alternatives and understand how they ascribed meaning to their stigma—something absent in the political and criminal justice landscape where victims' rights and subjectivity are granted ever greater prominence in legislative decision making (see Simon, 2007).

The criminal justice system includes legal processes that are designed to help actors determine the "facts" of the case—what really happened. This generally is supposed to occur as part of a trial—our theory of how justice is achieved assumes this critical aspect of trials as establishing truth. However, the majority of cases are plea-bargained—as were all the cases in this study. This leaves the definition of the situation to attorneys in a system where the prosecutor's office holds most of the cards. The object of this analysis is not to privilege the accounts of offenders over others in these negotiations for truths. Having shown how stigmatized individuals give meaning to their deviant identity, I now argue that these voices must be given some sort of valid space in both individual-level case management and public policy debates. Otherwise the situation is determined by emotional reactions to atypical high-profile crimes that generate public outrage but are not conducive to rational legislation and punishment practices. Granting any amount of validity to offenders' versions of truth, acknowledging a range of responses to sexual transgression, and questioning the meaning of victimhood may be intellectually, socially, and emotionally repugnant to many people. Yet doing so may lead to more rational, less costly, and safer criminal justice practices.

Policy

Megan's Law is known to stigmatize sex offenders (Tewksbury, 2012). A critique of Megan's Law particularly worth noting in the context of this study is the impact of registration and community notification on offenders themselves. Some scholars have pointed to the significant antitherapeutic effects of these policies on sex offenders in the community (Zilney & Zilney, 2009, p. 123). Although it may not be effective in preventing further sexual assaults on children, Megan's Law may be very effective in expressing the community's hostility. It ensures that the released offender is returned to "a rejecting community that often has been influenced by the media" (Jones, 1999), and expresses retributive justice at the expense of reintegration (Mcalinden, 2006). Sex offender policies are counterproductive to rehabilitation (Winick, 2003), and their dehumanizing nature may undermine possible benefits of treatment (Schultz, 2005). The likelihood that neighbors will avoid or distance themselves from known offenders and that prospective employers will not hire them can have negative social and psychological consequences (ibid.). The "continued shaming and stigmatization" inherent in registration/notification characterize offenders as deviants to be "ostracized by the community in ways that may seem impossible to overcome. By denying them a variety of employment, social, and educational opportunities, the sex offender label may prevent these individuals from starting a new life and making new acquaintances, with the result that it may be extremely difficult for them to discard their criminal patterns. Furthermore . . . [these laws] may produce anger in the discharged offender, further norm deviance, and, in extreme cases, even physical violence" (ibid., pp. 219–220). Establishing and stigmatizing the individual as truly and essentially "a sex offender," these policies reinforce a notion that offenders are unchangeable (Williams, 2003). In so doing they may produce more conditions in which the offender might commit another sex crime. Megan's Law "may potentially exacerbate risk factors for recidivism such as lifestyle instability, negative moods, and lack of positive social support" (Levenson et al., 2007, p. 590). Proponents of cognitive-behavioral treatments for sex offenders have raised specific concerns about the antitherapeutic effects of Megan's Law and heavy reliance on static risk assessment measures that may reinforce the belief that offenders cannot change and may make it easier for them to absolve themselves from personal responsibility (Williams, 2003; Winick, 2003). As researchers such as Marshall et al. (1999) and some of the offenders in this study have noted, increased social alienation and personal isolation can play a role in offenders' likelihood to recidivate. Marking individuals as outsiders may lower their stakes in conformity and create extreme stress that might lead to antisocial and inappropriate ways of releasing tension and seeking intimacy, such as sex offending.

Many aspects of these critiques were expressed by the offenders in my study. Interestingly, none of the participants argued that registration/notification should be completely repealed. They all supported a need for special civil policies aimed at managing sex offenders in the community, and shared assumptions about the dangerousness of some types of offenders. None questioned the justice or logic of civil management of portions of the population. Instead, they advocated for modifying the implementation of the laws. They argued that policy makers need to further refine the risk levels and the methods of categorizing offenders so that people like themselves would not be unnecessarily overcontrolled. They did not question the stereotypes of the predatory monster and shared mainstream views about how to handle this dangerous other.

My policy recommendations are somewhat more radical than theirs. There is little evidence to suggest a need for any type of registration/notification policy at all. We know that most sex offenders are first-time offenders. The rate of recidivism is so low that the assumption that this population of offenders needs special management is unfounded and illogical. To reiterate, registration/notification laws have not been shown to be effective at reducing sexual offenses; they make burdensome demands on local law enforcement, reinforce stigma, and could possibly have a counterproductive effect on recidivism. This means that registration/notification policies not only have little ability to protect society from repeat offenders, but they may put communities at greater risk by alienating individuals who were not going to recidivate in the first place. Furthermore, by imposing civil social controls on individuals who have already been punished by the criminal justice system through incarceration, parole, or probation, these policies extol emotionally driven populist punitiveness at the expense of a democracy that upholds civil liberties and freedom of citizens. These policies amplify stigma, damage important social bonds, and make communities less safe.

The emotionally driven outrage that led to the passing of these laws in the mid-1990s seems to still exist, making it unlikely that these laws will be completely repealed. I would support some of the modifications posed by the participants in this study, although I would go further than they in some respects. In order to reduce the additional stigma endured by being labeled a sexual offender, it is worth considering categorizing some "statutory" offenses as nonsexual misdemeanors. That is, for first-time offenders who have been involved in what are likely consensual acts with teenagers, such as Karl, Reggie, and Aaron, arrest and probation are severe enough sanctions that such offenders are unlikely to make the same "mistake" again. The label "sex offender" only deepens and broadens their sense of stigma and pushes them to the margins of society. In addition, in revising risk levels, I would propose for some offenders a new category of "not applicable risk," which would not include civil management such as registration/notification. This would mean that some first-time sex offenders, with certain sex-related violations, such as Raoul's transgression, would still be convicted of sex-related charges, but would not be subject to sanctions that endure beyond their criminal justice sentence, such as registering with law enforcement for decades. They would not be defined at all in terms of risk. In *Sex Panic and the Punitive State*, Roger Lancaster cautions us to "be wary of the construction of the monster and monstrosity" (2011, p. 244)—we need to see humans who commit crimes as exactly that, and recognize that "the monster is a distorted mirror image or screen projection of collective fears and desires" (ibid., p. 244).

Of course, offenders such as Terry pose a particular problem. He too is a human being. Yet his actions are more concerning than those of the other five men I interviewed. From his account of multiple sex crimes, and his own admission that he is someone Megan's Law should apply to, it is reasonable to suggest he might offend again. His crimes are certainly the sort that harass, demean, and violate women. Yet registration/notification is not necessarily the answer. Perhaps if he hadn't received so many "slaps on the wrists" and his jail time hadn't been catered to his work schedule, his first public offense might have been his last. Stronger initial sanctions against sexual harassment might be more effective than civil monitoring in the community. On the other hand, perhaps there is only so much we can expect of the criminal justice system in addressing social and psychological problems. Perhaps it is possible to recognize that life involves some risks that the punitive state cannot fully control or prevent (Lancaster, 2011, p. 245). Historically formal punishment has not been successful in this regard, and it may be a misplaced expectation to hope it can resolve complex issues of gender and power.

Philip Jenkins argues that the moral panic around sex offenders that began in the early 1990s is here to stay, that it has a "durable quality" linked to many structural and cultural facets of modern life (Jenkins, 1998, p. 232). These include "the institutionalization of the child-protection movement" (ibid., p. 233), the politically infeasible option of appearing "soft on child molestation" (ibid., p. 233), the expansion of the therapeutic health care industry (ibid., p. 233), and the growing victims' rights movement (ibid., p. 234). Although the 2006 Federal Adam Walsh Act, which provides for a federal registry of sex offenders, expanded its jurisdiction over increasing types of crimes and establishing new and stricter penalties, it is important to note that the moral panic around sex offenders began prior to the September 11 attacks on New York and Washington in 2001. These events have perhaps heralded a new era of social control that is no longer so strongly directed against the sex offender but instead focused on the foreign terrorist. After nearly two decades since the passing of New Jersey's Megan's Law, there is some hope that the conversations I have argued are unlikely to occur may in fact become possible. This is evidenced in recent newspaper and magazine articles that criticize these policies for being too stringently applied to minor offenses (Harlem, 2009), or that are critical of the unintended consequences of residency restriction laws (Cave, 2009; Skipp & Campo-Flores, 2009). A "Room for Debate" section of the *New York Times* asked "Too Many Restrictions on Sex Offenders, or Too Few?" and included a multiplicity of perspectives that questioned the assumptions and efficacy of these policies (Lancaster et al., 2013). Although monstrous stereotypes of sex offenders may still be deeply rooted, it is also possible that the wave of panic is abating and we are on the cusp of an era when the recommendations I have presented can be seriously considered. Mass incarceration and the numerous untenable restrictions on felons are reaching a critical moment when some scholars, journalists, activists, and policy makers are trying to make an impact. This critique has somewhat recently been voiced in popular culture by the comedian John Oliver in a segment on his news satire program, *Last Week Tonight*, that focused on the absurdities and indignities of the problem (HBO, 2014). There may be a limit to how much tolerance exists for managing citizens as human waste. At the same time, it is hard to imagine any person in the public eye risk being perceived as an advocate for sex offenders.

In constructing their identity, the offenders in this study needed to address problematic aspects of self that had been "spoiled" by their label. They told stories in which their humanity was repeatedly asserted. The consequences of social policy on the individuals most affected are too often neglected, particularly when those individuals are thought to be monstrous and deserving of expulsion. This study has hopefully provided the reader with an opportunity to get to know people who live with these experiences, and in so doing has the potential to shape how they understand contemporary public policy toward sex offenders. Identifying and managing "social problems" are areas of civic contest wherein multiple interest groups participate. Because of the high degree of stigma assigned to "sex offenders," their voices are generally excluded. Perhaps this study will help make room for them, and this "social problem" will become less of a one-sided valence issue. Public debate on the subject may become one in which complexities are acknowledged and a multiplicity of perspectives are engaged.

Appendix

Doing the Research

To FIND PARTICIPANTS, I researched local sex offender treatment centers. Only three were listed as such. One had closed and another would not return phone calls. I met with the director of the third center, who showed great interest in my project and was willing to distribute fliers to clients of his organization. It is worth noting that the difficulty I encountered researching treatment facilities is an indication of the level of stigma attached to sex offenders. Providers do not want neighbors to know that sex offenders are frequenting the area, nor do they want to contribute to public labeling of their clients, further stigmatizing them.

In addition, I was able to meet with the director of the city's Department of Probation, who agreed to distribute fliers to probation officers who would then distribute them to their probationers.

The fliers announced a life history project for which participants would be paid fifty dollars for two interviews (twenty-five paid at each session). It specified that participants should be convicted sex offenders who had offended against a minor.

Phone calls began trickling in after the first set of fliers was sent to treatment centers. During the first three months after distribution I was contacted by thirteen men. However, many of these callers would not return my calls. I also made appointments with several men who did not show up for their interviews or return further calls. During a period of six months I interviewed four men. I continued to send fliers to the treatment center and the Department of Probation, but calls stopped coming in. During this time, the director at one of the treatment centers had left the organization, and her replacement was not interested in the project. I decided to raise the amount of the stipend from twenty-five to forty dollars per interview, and sent more flyers to my two remaining contacts. When I still received no calls, I arranged to go to one of the treatment centers and distribute fliers in person at the beginning of the groups. This way I was able to introduce myself, explain the project, and answer any questions. Within a week I had seven more interested offenders and was able to interview two of them.

The participants' first interview session was devoted to their life history. I asked questions about their biography, establishing where they grew up, what their families were like, what career goals they had pursued, and what their significant relationships were like. Although intended to elicit a narrative, this style of questioning helped establish a comfortable rapport. Asking relatively nonthreatening or confrontational questions early on provided an opportunity for each of us to become familiar with the other's presence and adjust to the interview situation. As the interview progressed I asked follow-up questions to gain clarity and allow them to elaborate. The second session specifically focused on the nature of their offense. It included questions asking them to describe what they were charged with and what led up to the incident(s). They were asked some general questions about criminal proceedings and conditions of their probation/parole. Questions also pertained to how others in their life reacted when they found out about the conviction, and how their lives had changed since that event. Finally, participants were asked to voice their opinions on current sex offender policies and how sex offenders are portrayed in the media.

Each interview with participants lasted between sixty and ninety minutes. The second interview was always scheduled within the following two or three weeks. The interview questions were designed to allow participants to speak as much as possible about themselves, and to create opportunities for them to direct their own narratives. For this reason, not all questions were necessarily asked of every person (although most were), and very many questions arose spontaneously. In order to explore how meaning is made of events in their lives, I needed to conduct interviews in such a way that they could generate narratives unique to them. For this reason, imposing a structure to the interviews would risk dictating meaning and structure on the narratives.

When researchers study "human subjects," they must receive institutional approval, usually through an Institutional Review Board (IRB) that examines the research design to determine if there might be any negative effects on participants. Because criminal populations in general, and sex offenders in particular, are highly stigmatized and subject to supervision by the social control apparatus, they are a particularly vulnerable population. Participating in research poses special risks to this group, which include but are not limited to (a) exposure, which could have negative social consequences if their status were discovered; (b) imprisonment, as people on probation or parole who might inadvertently disclose any innocuous violation of their status could be incarcerated for the remainder of their sentence; and (c) possibilities of social retribution. Among issues raised for this project was the fact that recent legislation in New York State was seeking to impose retroactive requirements on those who were released prior to the state's 1996 sex offender act, indicating that "the state is not respectful of the basic legal rights of sex offender" and thus elevating the risks involved in research participation. Also of concern were recent incidents of vigilantism in Maine that resulted in the murder of two released sex offenders. Precautions, including anonymity, were taken to protect the participants in this project.

In examining the process of IRB approval, I became aware of the imaginative work in which researchers engage in pre-anticipating risks to participants. There is a narrative embedded in the preconstruction of the researcher and subject, where the researcher is cast as an authoritative figure who powerfully dominates the situation. In contrast the subject is vulnerable and endangered by the researcher's privileged position. Latent in concerns about the possible psychological harms to subjects who might be distressed during interviews pertaining to their offence is a judgmental expectation that they *should* be distressed. Although I adopted a theoretical perspective intended to create analytic distance, I entered the situation with preconceptions regarding the extent to which they would be ashamed of their actions. That is, I held beliefs about the nature of their wrongdoing that led me to assume they too would have negative feelings about their actions.

While the IRB process framed the participants as endangered and vulnerable, during this stage of research I had conversations with colleagues that generated scenarios where *I* was the one cast as at risk. People with whom I consulted relied on many of the claims in mainstream media about sex offenders. They were concerned about my safety working with this population, often referring to me as "brave." A forensic psychologist I spoke with became alarmed, presenting fantastic scenarios in which I was the one in need of protection and anonymity. From his perspective, I would be vulnerable to stalking and harassment. That I intended to be a relatively compassionate, nonjudgmental listener, as opposed to a confrontational one, would make me a gullible target for lies and self-justifications. Being a woman, I would be vulnerable to sexual assault. His concerns were framed largely in terms of who sex offenders are. Like other psychologists, he argued that they are particularly manipulative and accustomed to either concealing their deviance or having others confront them with it. Without challenging their "cognitive distortions" I might be in a position where they would capitalize on my naïveté in some unspecified, self-serving way. While some of these concerns informed my research design (for instance my last name and that of the IRB administrator were removed from the consent form), these conversations with colleagues illuminated the landscape of shared beliefs surrounding sex offenders—the cultural landscape the interviewed men inhabit.

Bibliography

Abel, G., Osborn, C., & Gardos, P. (1992). Current Treatments of Paraphiliacs. *Annual Review of Sex Research, 3,* 225–290.

Abel, G., & Rouleau, J. L. (1990). The Nature and Extent of Sexual Assault. In W. Marshall, D. Laws, & H. Barbaree (Eds.), *Handbook of Sexual Assault: Issues, Theories, and Treatment of the Offender* (pp. 9–21). New York: Plenum Press.

Angelides, S. (2004). Paedophilia and the Misrecognition of Desire. *Transformations,* 8. http://www.transformationsjournal.org/journal/issue_08/article_01.shtml

Bandy, R. K. (2009). The Impacts of Sex Offender Policies on Victims. In R. Wright (Ed.), *Sex Offender Laws: Failed Policies, New Directions* (pp. 471–508). New York: Springer.

Becker, H. (1973). *Outsiders: Studies in the Sociology of Deviance.* New York: Free Press.

———. (1963/1997). *Outsiders: Studies in the Sociology of Deviance.* New York: Free Press.

Beckett, K. (1996). Culture and Politics of Signification: The Case of Child Sexual Abuse. *Social Problems, 43*(1), 57–76.

———. (1997). *Making Crime Pay: Law and Order in Contemporary American Politics.* New York: Oxford University Press.

Bedarf, A. R. (1995). "Examining Sex Offender Community Notification Laws." *California Law Review, 83,* 885–937.

Bickley, J., & Beech, A. (2001). Classifying Child Abusers: Its Relevance to Theory and Clinical Practice. *Journal of Offender Therapy and Comparative Criminology, 45*(1), 51–69.

Blinder, A. (2013, July 28). Double Murder Seen as Part of Man's Quest to Kill Sex Offender. *New York Times.*

Blumer, H. (1969). *Symbolic Interactionism: Perspective and Method.* Berkeley: University of California Press.

Bradford, J. (1990). The Antiandrogen and Hormonal Treatment of Sex Offenders. In W. Marshall, D. Laws, & H. Barbaree (Eds.), *Handbook of Sexual Assault: Issues, Theories, and Treatment of the Offender* (pp. 297–310). New York: Plenum Press.

Burn, M. F. (2006). A Review of the Cognitive Distortions in Child Sex Offenders: An Examination of the Motivations and Mechanisms That Underlie the Justifications for Abuse. *Aggression and Violent Behavior, 11*(3), 225–236.

Callero, P. L. (2003). The Sociology of the Self. *Annual Review of Sociology, 29,* 115–33.

Cave, D. (2009, July 10). Roadside Camp for Miami Sex Offenders Leads to Lawsuit. *New York Times.*

Center for Sex Offender Management. Retrieved December 15, 2009, from http://www.csom.org/

Chin, G. (2012). The New Civil Death: Rethinking Punishment in the Era of Mass Conviction. *University of Pennsylvania Law Review, 169,* 1789–1833.

Christensen, T. (2010). Presumed Guilty: Constructing Deviance and Deviants through Techniques of Neutralization. *Deviant Behavior, 31*(6), 552–577.

Cohen, S. (2002). *Folk Devils and Moral Panics: The Creation of Mods and Rockers* (3rd ed.). London: Routledge.

Davey, M., & Goodenough, A. (2007, March 4). Doubts Rise as States Hold Sex Offenders After Prison. *New York Times.*

Denzin, N. K. (1990). Harold and Agnes: A Feminist Narrative Undoing. *Sociological Theory, 8*(2), 198–216.

———. (1992). *Symbolic Interaction and Cultural Studies: The Politics of Interpretation.* Cambridge, MA: Blackwell.

———. (2001). *Interpretive Interactionism.* Thousand Oaks, CA: Sage.

Durkheim, E. (1984). *The Division of Labor in Society.* New York: Free Press.

———. (2001). *The Elementary Forms of Religious Life* (C. Cosman, Trans.). Oxford: Oxford University Press.

Duwe, G., & Donnay, W. (2008). The Impact of Megan's Law on Sex Offender Recidivism: The Minnesota Experience. *Criminology, 46*(2), 411–446.

Erikson, K. T. (1966). *Wayward Puritans: A Study in the Sociology of Deviance.* New York: Macmillan.

Feeley, M., & Simon, J. (1992). The New Penology: Notes on the Emerging Strategy of Corrections and Its Implications. *Criminology, 30,* 449–474.

Finkelhor, D. (1984). *Child Sexual Abuse: New Theory and Research.* New York: Free Press.

Finn, P. (1997). *Sex Offender Community Notification.* Research in Action. Washington, DC: National Institute of Justice.

Fitch, L. W., & Hammen, D. A. (2003). The New Generation of Sex Offender Commitment Laws: Which States Have Them and How Do They Work? In B. Winick & J. Q. LaFond (Eds.), *Protecting Society from Sexually Dangerous Offenders: Law, Justice, and Therapy* (pp. 27–39). Washington, DC: American Psychological Association.

Furby, L., Weinrott, M., & Blackshaw, L. (1989). Sex Offender Recidivism: A Review. *Psychological Bulletin, 105,* 3–30.

Garfinkel, H. (1956). Conditions of Successful Degradation Ceremonies. *American Journal of Sociology, 61*(5), 420–424.

Garland, D. (2001a). *The Culture of Control: Crime and Social Order in Contemporary Society.* Chicago: University of Chicago Press.

———. (Ed.). (2001b). *Mass Imprisonment: Social Causes and Consequences.* London: Sage.

Gecas, V., & Libby, R. (1976). Sexual Behavior as Symbolic Interaction. *Journal of Sex Research, 12*(1), 33–49.

Giddens, A. (1984). *The Constitution of Society.* Berkeley: University of California Press.

———. (1991). *Modernity and Self-Identity: Self and Society in the Late Modern Age.* Stanford: Stanford University Press.

Goffman, E. (1959). *The Presentation of Self in Everyday Life.* New York: Anchor Books.

———. (1961/1990). *Asylums: Essays on the Social Situation of Mental Patients and Other Inmates*. New York: Anchor Books.

———. (1963/1986). *Stigma: Notes on the Management of Spoiled Identity*. New York: Simon & Schuster.

Goode, E., & Ben-Yehuda, N. (1994). *Moral Panics: The Social Construction of Deviance*. Oxford: Blackwell.

Greenfeld, L. A. (2003). *Sex Offenses and Offenders*. Washington, DC: Bureau of Justice Statistics, US Department of Justice.

Groth, N., & Birnbaum, H. (1979). *Men Who Rape: The Psychology of the Offender*. New York: Plenum Press.

Grubin, D. (2000). Complementing Relapse Prevention with Medical Intervention. In D. Laws (Ed.), *Remaking Relapse Prevention with Sex Offenders* (pp. 201–212). Thousand Oaks, CA: Sage.

Hall, G. (1995). Sexual Offender Recidivism Revisited: A Meta-Analysis of Recent Treatment Studies. *Journal of Consulting and Clinical Psychology, 53*(5), 802–809.

Hammel-Zabin, A. (2003). *Conversations with a Pedophile: In the Interest of Our Children*. Fort Lee, NJ: Barricade Books.

Hanson, K. R. (1996). *Predictors of Sexual Offender Recidivism: A Meta-Analysis*. Ottawa: Public Works and Government Services of Canada.

———. (2003). Who Is Dangerous and When Are They Safe? Risk Assessment with Sexual Offenders. In B. Winick & J. Q. LaFond (Eds.), *Protecting Society from Sexually Dangerous Offenders: Law, Justice, and Therapy* (pp. 63–74). Washington, DC: American Psychological Association.

Hanson, K. R., & Harris, A. (2000). Where Should We Intervene? Dynamic Predictors of Sexual Offense and Recidivism. *Criminal Justice and Behavior, 27*, 6–35.

Hanson, K. R., Scott, H., & Steffy, R. (1995). A Comparison of Child Molesters and Nonsexual Criminals: Risk Predictors and Long-Term Recidivism. *Journal of Research in Crime and Delinquency, 32*(3), 325–337.

Harlem, G. (2009, August 6). Sex Laws: Unjust and Ineffective. *Economist*.

Holmes, S. T., & Holmes, R. M. (2002). *Sex Crimes: Patterns and Behavior* (2nd ed.). Thousand Oaks, CA: Sage.

Jacobson, M. (2005). *Downsizing Prisons: How to Reduce Crime and End Mass Incarceration*. New York: New York University Press.

Janus, E. S. (2006). *Failure to Protect: America's Sexual Predator Laws and the Rise of the Preventive State*. Ithaca, NY: Cornell University Press.

Jenkins, P. (1998). *Moral Panic: Changing Concepts of the Child Molester in Modern America*. New Haven, CT: Yale University Press.

Jones, K. D. (1999). The Media and Megan's Law: Is Community Notification the Answer? *Journal of Humanistic Counseling, Education and Development, 38*(2), 80–88.

Kamoie, B., Teitelbaum, J., & Rosenbaum, S. (2003). "Megan's Law" and the US Constitution: Implications for Public Health Policy and Practice. *Public Health Reports, 118*(4), 379–381.

Kincaid, J. (1998). *Erotic Innocence: The Culture of Child Molesting*. Durham, NC: Duke University Press.

KlaasKids. (2009). KlaasKids Foundation for Children. Retrieved December 15, 2009, from http://www.klaaskids.org/

Knight, R. A., & Prentky, R. A. (1990). Classifying Sexual Offenders: The Development and Corroboration of Taxonomic Models. In W. Marshall, D. Laws, & H. Barbaree (Eds.), *Handbook of Sexual Assault: Issues, Theories, and Treatment of the Offender* (pp. 23–52). New York: Plenum Press.

Kohm, S. A. (2009). Naming, Shaming and Criminal Justice: Mass-Mediated Humiliation as Entertainment and Punishment. *Crime Media Culture, 5*, 188–205.

Lacoursier, R. B. (2003). Evaluating Offenders under a Sexually Violent Predator Law: The Practical Practice. In B. Winick & J. Q. LaFond (Eds.), *Protecting Society from Sexually Dangerous Offenders: Law, Justice, and Therapy* (pp. 75–97). Washington, DC: American Psychological Association.

LaFond, J. Q. (2003). The Costs of Enacting a Sexual Predator Law and Recommendations for Keeping Them from Skyrocketing. In B. Winick & J. Q. LaFond (Eds.), *Protecting Society from Sexually Dangerous Offenders: Law, Justice, and Therapy* (pp. 283–300). Washington, DC: American Psychological Association.

Lancaster, R. (2011). *Sex Panic and the Punitive State*. Berkeley: University of California Press.

Lancaster, R. N., Coughlin, K., Leguizamo, A., Hislop, J., Tallian, K., & Jennings, W. G. (2013, February 20). Too Many Restrictions on Sex Offenders, or Too Few? *New York Times*.

Laws, Acts, and Legislation 128th General Assembly of the State of Ohio. (n.d.). Retrieved December 15, 2009, from http://www.legislature.state.oh.us/bills.cfm?ID=126_HB_217

Lea, S., & Auburn, T. (2001). The Social Construction of Rape in the Talk of a Convicted Rapist. *Feminism & Psychology, 11*(1), 11–33.

Leon, C. (2011). *Sex Fiends, Perverts, and Pedophiles: Understanding Sex Crime Policy in America*. New York: New York University Press.

Levenson, J. S. (2009). Sex Offender Residence Restrictions. In R. Wright (Ed.), *Sex Offender Laws: Failed Policies, New Directions* (pp. 267–290). New York: Springer.

Levenson, J. S., D'Amora, D. A., & Hern, A. L. (2007). Megan's Law and Its Impact on Community Re-entry for Sex Offenders. *Behavioral Sciences and the Law, 25*, 587–602.

Levine, J. (2002). *Harmful to Minors: The Perils of Protecting Children from Sex*. New York: Thunder's Mouth Press.

Lieb, R. (2003). State Policy Perspectives on Sexual Predator Laws. In B. Winick & J. Q. LaFond (Eds.), *Protecting Society from Sexually Dangerous Offenders: Law, Justice, and Therapy* (pp. 41–59). Washington, DC: American Psychological Association.

Lotke, E. (1997). Politics and Irrelevance: Community Notification Statutes. *Federal Sentencing Reporter, 10*(2), 64–68.

Lovett, K. (2009, December 1). More Than 3,500 Sex Fiends from Facebook, MySpace Get Boot in Crackdown of Internet Predators. *New York Daily News*.

Marshall, W. (1989). Intimacy, Loneliness and Sexual Offenders. *Behavior Research Therapy, 27*(5), 491–504.

Marshall, W., Anderson, D., & Fernandez, Y. (1999). *Cognitive Behavioral Treatment of Sexual Offenders*. New York: John Wiley.

Marshall, W., & Barbaree, H. (1990). An Integrated Theory of the Etiology of Sexual Offending. In W. Marshall, D. Laws, & H. Barbaree (Eds.), *Handbook of Sexual Assault: Issues, Theories, and Treatment of the Offender* (pp. 257–275). New York: Plenum Press.

Mcalinden, A. (2006). Managing Risk: From Regulation to the Reintegration of Sexual Offenders. *Criminology and Criminal Justice, 6*(2), 197–218.

Meloy, M. L. (2005). The Sex Offender Next Door: An Analysis of Recidivism, Risk Factors, and Deterrence of Sex Offenders on Probation. *Criminal Justice Policy Review, 16*(2), 211–236.

———. (2006). *Sex Offenses and the Men Who Commit Them: An Assessment of Sex Offenders on Probation.* Boston: Northeastern University Press.

Meloy, M. L., & Coleman, S. (2009). GPS Monitoring of Sex Offenders. In R. Wright (Ed.), *Sex Offender Laws: Failed Policies, New Directions* (pp. 243–266). New York: Springer.

Mills, C. W. (1940). Situated Actions and Vocabularies of Motive. *American Sociological Review, 5*(6), 904–913.

Misiano, C. (1997). Mad Dog. *Law & Order.* NBC.

New York State Division of Criminal Justice Services. Retrieved December 15, 2009, from http://criminaljustice.state.ny.us/

Ohio Public Safety Office of Criminal Justice Services. (2006). *Report to the Ohio Criminal Sentencing Commission: Sex Offenders.* Columbus: Author.

Oliver, J. (2014, July 20). *Last Week Tonight with John Oliver.* HBO.

Orbuch, T. (1997). People's Accounts Count: The Sociology of Accounts. *Annual Review of Sociology, 23*, 455–478.

Petrosino, A. J., & Petrosino, C. (1999). The Public Safety Potential of Megan's Law in Massachusetts: An Assessment from a Sample of Criminal Sexual Psychopaths. *Crime and Delinquency, 45*(1), 140–158.

Pithers, W. D. (1990). Relapse Prevention with Sexual Aggressors: A Method for Maintaining Therapeutic Gain and Enhancing External Supervision. In W. Marshall, D. Laws, & H. Barbaree (Eds.), *Handbook of Sexual Assault: Issues, Theories, and Treatment of the Offender* (pp. 243–261). New York: Plenum Press.

Pryor, D. (1996). *Unspeakable Acts: Why Men Sexually Abuse Children.* New York: New York University Press.

Putnam, R. D. (2000). *Bowling Alone: The Collapse and Revival of American Community.* New York: Simon & Schuster.

Radford, B. (2006, May 16). Predator Panic: A Closer Look. Retrieved from http://www.livescience.com/776-predator-panic-reality-check-sex-offenders.html

Reiman, J. (2001). *The Rich Get Richer and the Poor Get Prison: Ideology, Class, and Criminal Justice* (6th ed.). Boston: Allyn & Bacon.

Reissman, C. K. (2002). Analysis of Personal Narratives. In J. Holstein & J. Gubrium (Eds.), *Handbook of Interview Research* (pp. 695–710). Thousand Oaks, CA: Sage.

Rice, M., & Harris, G. T. (2003). What We Know and Don't Know about Treating Adult Sex Offenders. In B. Winick & J. Q. LaFond (Eds.), *Protecting Society from Sexually Dangerous Offenders: Law, Justice, and Therapy* (pp. 101–118). Washington, DC: American Psychological Association.

Rosler, A., & Witzum, E. (2000). Pharmacotherapy of Paraphilias in the Next Millennium. *Behavioral Sciences and the Law, 18*, 43–56.

Salter, A. (2004). *Predators: Pedophiles, Rapists, and Other Sex Offenders: Who They Are, How They Operate, and How We Can Protect Ourselves and Our Children.* New York: Basic Books.

Sample, L. L., & Bray, T. M. (2003). Are Sex Offenders Dangerous? *Criminology and Public Policy, 3*(1), 59–83.

Sample, L. L., & Evans, M. K. (2009). Sex Offender Registration and Community Notification. In R. Wright (Ed.), *Sex Offender Laws: Failed Policies, New Directions* (pp. 211–242). New York: Springer.

Schopp, R. F. (2003). "Even a Dog . . .": Culpability, Condemnation, and Respect for Persons. In B. Winick & J. Q. LaFond (Eds.), *Protecting Society from Sexually Dangerous Offenders: Law, Justice, and Therapy* (pp. 183–196). Washington, DC: American Psychological Association.

Schultz, P. D. (2005). *Not Monsters: Analyzing the Stories of Child Molesters.* Lanham, MD: Rowman & Littlefield.

Scott, C., & del Busto, E. (2009). Chemical and Surgical Castration. In R. Wright (Ed.), *Sex Offender Laws: Failed Policies, New Directions* (pp. 291–338). New York: Springer.

Scott, M. B., & Lyman, S. M. (1968). Accounts. *Sociological Review, 33*(1), 46–62.

Scully, D. (1994). *Understanding Sexual Violence: A Study of Convicted Rapists.* New York: Routledge.

Records and Access Unit, National Center for Missing & Exploited Children. (2015, June 1). RSO Data: State or Territory Sex Offender Registries Population Range: 2010 U.S. Census BureauMapping Software Donated to NCMEC by Esri, Redlands, Calif. Retrieved from http://www.missingkids.com/en_US/documents/sex-offender-map.pdf

Simon, J. (1998). Managing the Monstrous: Sex Offenders and the New Penology. *Psychology, Public Policy, and Law, 4*(1–2), 452–467.

———. (2000). Megan's Law: Crime and Democracy in Late Modern America. *Law & Social Inquiry, 25*(4), 1111–1150.

———. (2007). *Governing through Crime: How the War on Crime Transformed American Democracy and Created a Culture of Fear.* Oxford: Oxford University Press.

Skipp, C., & Campo-Flores, A. (2009, July 25). A Bridge Too Far. *Newsweek.*

Snyder, H. N. (2003). *Sexual Assault of Young Children as Reported to Law Enforcement: Victim, Incident and Other Characteristics.* Washington, DC: Bureau of Justice Statistics, US Department of Justice.

Spencer, D. (2009). Sex Offender as Homo Sacer. *Punishment and Society, 11*(2), 219–240.

Sykes, G. M., & Matza, D. (1957). Techniques of Neutralization: A Theory of Delinquency. *American Sociological Review, 22*(6), 664–670.

Terry, K. J. (2006). *Sexual Offenses and Offenders: Theory, Practice, and Policy.* Belmont, CA: Thomson Wadsworth.

Tewksbury, R. (2012). Stigmatization of Sex Offenders. *Deviant Behavior, 33*(8), 606–623.

Tewksbury, R., & Lees, M. (2006). Perceptions of Sex Offender Registration: Collateral Consequences and Community Experiences. *Sociological Spectrum, 26*, 309–334.

Travis, J. (2002). Invisible Punishment: An Instrument of Social Exclusion. In M. Mauer & M. Chesney-Lind (Eds.), *Invisible Punishment: The Collateral Consequences of Mass Imprisonment* (pp. 15–36). New York: New Press.

Turner, R. (1976). The Real Self: From Institution to Impulse. *American Journal of Sociology, 81*(5), 989–1016.

Wacquant, L. (2001). Deadly Symbiosis: When Ghetto and Prison Meet and Mesh. In D. Garland (Ed.), *Mass Imprisonment: Social Causes and Consequences* (pp. 82–120). London: Sage.

Waldram, J. (2007). Everybody Has a Story: Listening to Imprisoned Sexual Offenders. *Qualitative Health Research, 17*(7), 963–970.

Weeks, J. (1985). *Sexuality and Its Discontents: Meanings, Myths and Modern Sexualities.* London: Routledge.

Welchans, S. (2005). Megan's Law: Evaluations of Sexual Offender Registries. *Criminal Justice Policy Review, 16,* 123–149.

Williams, D. (2003). "Quality of Life" as Perceived by Sex Offenders on Early Release in a Halfway House: Implications for Treatment. *Journal of Offender Rehabilitation, 38*(2), 77–93.

Winick, B. (2003). A Therapeutic Jurisprudence Analysis of Sex Offender Registration and Community Notification Laws. In B. Winick & J. Q. LaFond (Eds.), *Protecting Society from Sexually Dangerous Offenders: Law, Justice, and Therapy* (pp. 317–331). Washington, DC: American Psychological Association.

Wirth, L. (1938). Urbanism as a Way of Life. *American Journal of Sociology, 44*(1), 1–24.

Wright, R. (2009). Internet Sex Stings. In R. Wright (Ed.), *Sex Offender Laws: Failed Policies, New Directions* (pp. 115–158). New York: Springer.

Young, J. (1999). *The Exclusive Society: Social Exclusion, Crime and Difference in Late Modernity.* London: Sage.

Zanini, J. P. (1997). Symposium: The Treatment of Sex Offenders: Considering *Hencricks v. Kansas* for Massachusetts: Can the Commonwealth Constitutionally Detain Dangerous Persons Who Are Not Mentally Ill? *New England Journal on Criminal and Civil Confinement, 23,* 427–462.

Zevitz, R. G., & Farkas, M. A. (2000). *Sex Offender Community Notification: Assessing the Impact in Wisconsin.* Washington, DC: National Institute of Justice.

Zgoba, K. M., & Bachar, K. (2009). Sex Offender Registration and Notification: Limited Effects in New Jersey. In Short. Washington, DC: US Department of Justice, Office of Justice Programs, National Institute of Justice.

Zilney, L. J., & Zilney, L. A. (2009). *Perverts and Predators: The Making of Sexual Offending Laws.* Lanham, MD: Rowman & Littlefield.

Zimring, F. E. (1996, August 16). Crying Wolf over Teen Demons. *Los Angeles Times.*

———. (2001). Imprisonment Rates and the New Politics of Criminal Punishment. In D. Garland (Ed.), *Mass Imprisonment: Social Causes and Consequences* (pp. 145–149). London: Sage.

———. (2004). *American Travesty: Legal Responses to Adolescent Sexual Offending.* Chicago: University of Chicago Press.

Zonana, H. V., Bonnie, R. J., & Hoge, S. K. (2003). In the Wake of *Hendricks*: The Treatment and Restraint of Sexually Dangerous Offenders Viewed from the Perspective of American Psychiatry. In B. Winick & J. Q. LaFond (Eds.), *Protecting Society from Sexually Dangerous Offenders: Law, Justice, and Therapy* (pp. 131–145). Washington, DC: American Psychological Association.

Index

abandonment, fear of, 79
accounts: defined, 21; of entrapmemt, 35; of intrafamilial offender, 23–24; of seductivity, 49–50; of study participants, 21. *See also* narratives; stories
acquaintances, sexual assaults among, 13
Adam Walsh Child Protection and Safety Act (2006), 9–10, 173
addiction: medical model of, 64; of serial offenders, 61–62, 63
adolescent sexuality, and intrafamilial offenses, 27
adult/child dichotomy, for statutory offenders, 40
adult-minor relations, mainstream sanctions against, 55
adult/young person sexual interactions, 167
age: of consent, 36, 167; relationships and, 157
aggression, of serial offender, 143
alcoholism, and sex offenses, 61
alienation: of convicted sex offenders, 19; of sex offenders, 7. *See also* isolation
American society, activities valued in, 66
anger: of serial offender, 143; of study participants, 30, 32
angry villagers episode, 117–118, 135
ankle bracelet, 129
arrest, as "wake-up call," 83
athletics, for convicted offenders, 113

attorneys, deference of, 68
autonomy, individual: in house arrest, 98–99; and sex offender policies, 91
avoidance tactic, of study participant, 69

background checks, 90; for civil servant jobs, 105; disqualification with, 102; specter of, 132
banishment: possibility of, 119; sense of, 18
Becker, Howard, 14
Beckett, Katherine, 144
behavior, rationalizing, 166–167
behavioral boundaries: with dual existence, 141–143; self based on, 1
belonging, sense of, 133; and church membership, 74; and community bonds, 66; in neighborhood, 79; with relative anonymity, 78
Bush, Pres. George W., 9

camera, job using, 106
"carceral state," 1. *See also* incarceration
careers: ending of, 104, 111; loss of, 107, 109
caregiver, offender's role as, 26–27, 30
case studies, in social sciences, 16
castration: "chemical," 62; physical, 62
celebrities, on child molesters, 12
Center for Sex Offender Management, 13
chemical castration bill, 12
child abuse, as "valence issue," 144

child care abuse, 8
child molesters: concept of, 11; construction of, 12; denial of identification as, 36; fears about, 144; stigma of, 2; study participants' views of, 149–150; use of term, 16. *See also* sex offenders
child pornography, 5, 8; as heinous crime, 145; intrafamilial, 24–25
Child Protection and Safety Act, Adam Walsh (2006), 9–10, 173
child protection movement: institutionalization of, 173; rise of, 8; unintended consequences of, 168
children: of intrafamilial offender, 141; of sex offenders, 38, 79–80, 81–82, 84, 138–139; of statutory offenders, 38, 42; vulnerability of, 145–146
child sexual abuse, as valence issue, 2
Christianity, for statutory offenders, 74–75
churches: acceptance by, 124; in community structure, 79; excommunication from, 112–113, 158; gay-friendly, 75–76; as social support, 86
"civil death": consequences of, 88; experienced, 18; felony conviction as, 6
civil liberties, constraints on, 18
Clinton, Pres. Bill, 9
cognitive distortion, in offenders' stories, 168–169
colleagues: and probation, 107; support of, 135–136
communication: mediated, 40, 71. *See also* media
communities: and housing, 114–115; and sex offender policies, 171
community: loss of subjective bonds with, 120–131; offenders positioned outside of, 156; offenders' relationship to, 88; and serial offender, 121–124, 141–142; social self and, 86–87; workplace, 100–101. *See also* notification
community, loss of, 112–114; for intrafamilial offender, 124–125; for statutory offenders, 125–127, 127–131
community bonds: career and, 82; employment in, 67; extended family, 71–72; family in, 69–70, 78–82, 82, 84; friendships, 70–71, 72; for homosexuals, 75–76; for Internet offender, 70–74; for intrafamilial offender, 84–86; neighborhood, 65–66, 71; professional, 66; and serial offenders, 65–70; for statutory offenders, 74–84
community notification, 15; impact of, 165, 169–170; implementation of, 10–11; and Megan's Law, 10, 114, 155; popularity of, 11. *See also* notification
community notification meetings, 165
community notification policies, 18
compulsion, medical model of, 64
computer, access to, 159
conscience, and deviance, 150
consensuality, offenders' evocation of, 54
consent, age of: and construction of minor, 167; wrongdoing associated with, 36
control, lack of, for intrafamilal offender, 24–25
conversation, online sexually explicit, 33–34. *See also* Internet
"cordon sanitaire," 2
courts, sex offenders' sanctions of, 6
courtship drama, narrative of, 49
Crime Bill (1994), 9
crimes: on continuum of harm, 161–162; in electoral politics, 1;

emotional reactions to high-profile, 169; governance through, 2; heinous, 146–151; incestuous contact, 149; Internet *vs.* contact, 149
criminal justice policies, 14
criminal justice system: and community bonds, 67; house arrest in, 99; Internet offender in, 73; middle-class whites in, 67–68; and noninstitutional world, 1; offenders' critique of, 176; plea-bargaining in, 169; sex offender policies in, 165; sex offenders in, 88–89, 119; socialization process in, 73. *See also* sex offender policies
crowded places, sexual offenses in, 57
culture, popular, sexualized teenagers in, 168
curfew: arbitrary nature of, 159; constraint of, 92

dangerous other. *See* other, dangerous
database, national sex offender, 9
Dateline (television program), 125
dating websites, 33
death penalty, justification for, 151
deception, offender's complaints of, 41
"degradation ceremonies," 6
denial of responsibility, of Internet offender, 32–33. *See also* responsibility
Denzin, Norman, 20
depression: of convicted sex offenders, 126; of sex offenders, 6
deviance: and conscience, 150; and convicted sexual offenders, 2; self-diagnosis of, 63–65; self-serving elements in, 17; of serial offender, 143; sociology of, 14, 16–17, 163; as technicality, 53
deviant conduct, reaction of family to, 70

deviant label, internalization of, 136
deviant self, 6
dialogue, sexually explicit, 31. *See also* Internet
disclosure: of discrediting information, 96–97; to family, 72–73, 73, 77; to potential partner, 97; rejection of, 119; and shame, 125
disdain, of study participant, 33
"distinctive garb," for sex offenders, 11
divorce, and statutory offenders, 38–39
DNA, on file, 131
double life, 121
dressing, sexual way of, 48
drug screening, 90
drug treatment programs, long-term impact of, 86
dual existence, construction of, 141–143
duality, offenders' sense of, 122, 123
Durkheim, E., 88

electoral politics, crime in, 1
Electronic Security and Targeting of Online Predators Act (2008), 89
elevator use, as potential violation, 130
embarrassment: for serial offenders, 58–59; for sex offenders, 121, 124
employment: for convicted sex offenders, 4; course on seeking, 103–104; and house arrest, 100; impact of sex offense convictions on, 132; for Internet offenders, 101–102; for intrafamilial offenders, 108; and probation officer's role, 105–106; and registration conditions, 92; reintegration into community through, 154; restrictions on, 90; for serial offender, 110–112; for sex offenders, 89; and social status, 100; for statutory offenders, 102, 104–107, 109–110. *See also* work

entrapment, accusation of, 35
epidemic, child sexual abuse as, 8
Erikson, K. T., 88
exclusion: "inclusive," 99, 163; possibility of, 119
exposure: fear of, 97; feeling of, 115; possibilities of, 96–98; protection from, 123; sense of, 125
eye contact, with study participants, 22, 30, 56

family, 71–72; and coming-out process, 77; extended, 71, 72, 73; reaction to offenders' behavior of, 69–70, 72; social bonds with, 18; support of, 71, 78–82, 85, 87, 114, 126, 139
family life, for intrafamilial offender, 29
family members, sexual assaults among, 13
father role: for intrafamilial offender, 29, 84–85; for statutory offenders, 138–139
felons: sex offenders as, 6; untenable restrictions on, 173
felony conviction, as "civil death," 6. *See also* civil death
feminine, serial offender's definition of, 59–60
feminist movement, 8
financial provider, offender's role as, 26–27, 30
fingerprints, 90, 131
flashing, 4
friendships: and probation, 107; of sex offenders, 113; in workplace, 100–101
frottage, 4, 57
frustration, of study participants, 23
fulfillment, sense of, 67

gambling, and sex offenses, 61
Garfield, D., 88
gay offenders, coming-out process for, 75
Giddens, Anthony, 90–91, 97
Goffman, Erving, 6, 15, 65, 73, 88, 96, 118, 120, 136
GPS monitoring: arbitrary nature of, 129; with probation, 99–100
GPS monitoring devices, 90, 98
grandfather role, for intrafamilial offender, 144–145
groping strangers, 4
group therapy: for offenders, 118–119, 120; offenders' view of others in, 145, 146–147, 149–150, 152–153. *See also* treatment groups

harassment: of convicted sex offenders, 18; neighborhood, 115, 116; of sex offenders, 7
harm: hierarchy of, 19, 161–162; minimization of, 168–169; *vs.* wrongdoing, 166–167
health care industry, expansion of therapeutic, 173
heinousness, defining, 147
"homo sacer," 99
homosexuality: coming-out process, 47; *vs.* religion, 75
homosexuals: community bonds for, 75–76; as statutory offenders, 47–56
hopelessness, of sex offenders, 7
hotline, toll-free sex offender, 89–90
house arrest, 4, 98, 99; offenders' view of, 154–155; as social control, 99
housing: for convicted sex offenders, 114–120; for Internet offender, 119–120; for statutory offenders, 115–119
human resources: interviewers in, 102–103. *See also* employment

husband role, for intrafamilial offender, 29–30, 84–85

ice cream truck prohibition, 90
identity: and conditions of probation, 96; deviant, 64; gay, 75; institutional, 141; of labeled sex offender, 97; managing discredited, 133; and offender convictions, 89; professional, 66, 76; reasserting sexual, 137; for sex offenders, 14–15, 98; split in, 122; spoiled, 15; stigmatized, 65, 125
identity maintenance, for convicted sexual offenders, 2
identity-reinforcing bonds, 64
ideologies, in participant accounts, 21–22
"ill-fame," 118
impression management: for serial offender, 142; for sex offenders, 15
incarceration: mass, 6; rate of, 1; as social problem, 14
incest, 117; and dangerous other, 144; offenders' view of, 149
incest taboo, in offenders' narratives, 30
incriminating self, fears about, 131
indecency, public, 5
indignation, of study participants, 32, 35
infidelity: and intrafamilial offenders, 22, 23, 25; of statutory offenders, 45
institutional framework, "real" self in, 134
Institutional Review Board (IRB), 176–177
intentionality, of sexual predator, 147–148
interests groups, punishment practices supported by, 13
Internet: appropriate online conduct on, 138; and isolation, 74; posting explicit lyrics on, 157; sex offenders' pictures on, 115–116; and social identity, 71
Internet accounts, offenders', 89
Internet sex sting, 31, 166
Internet stalking, 8
interview questions: design of, 176; follow-up, 176
intimacy, online, 31
isolation: feelings of, 123; of house arrest, 98; imposed on sex offenders, 93; nondeviant identity reinforced by, 112; respite from, 99; of sex offenders, 3, 7, 18, 19

Jacob Wetterling Act (1994), 9
Janus, E. S., 13
Jenkins, Philip, 7, 8, 173
jobs: "off-the-books," 101; and sense of belonging, 66. *See also* work
job satisfaction, 87
job seeking, 103–104; for intrafamilial offender, 108
judges, deference of, 68
juvenile facilities, long-term impact of, 86

Kanka, Megan, 10. *See also* Megan's Law
kinship relationships, for intrafamilial offender, 144–145
kinship roles, male, 140

label: internalization of, 126, 127; "monster," 162; "sex offender," 172
labeling process, 14; assumptions in, 124; cookie-cutter approach to, 154; coping with, 158; critique of, 152; resistance to, 32–33; for statutory offenders, 135–136; victims of, 134
labeling theory, 17, 169
Lancaster, Roger, 172

language, in participant accounts, 21–22
Last Week Tonight (news satire program), 173
law, sex offender, arbitrary changes in, 160
law enforcement, and neighborhood harassment, 116–117
lawlessness, for convicted sex offenders, 163
Law & Order (television series), 8, 12, 125–126
legal status, of sex offenders, 11
legal system: need for change in, 153. *See also* criminal justice system
legislation: overzealous, 157; sex offender, 1; victims' rights and, 169; in Washington State, 9
legislators, on recidivism, 13
license plates, for convicted sex offenders, 10–11, 129
life history project, 175
Lock Up (television series), 82

Maine, vigilantism in, 177
mainstream media, sex offenders in, 177. *See also* media
maladaptation, psychological, of serial offender, 59
manipulation factor, for statutory offenders, 45
marriage, for statutory offenders, 42
Marshall, W., 170
masculine, serial offender's definition of, 59–60
masturbation, public, 4, 57
Matza, D., 20
meaning, making: for convicted sex offenders, 163; with offender/victim paradigm, 167; of participant narratives, 21–22; with work, 82–83

media: child molesters in, 11, 12; and public's perception of sex offenders, 124; punishment practices supported by, 13; on recidivism, 13; sex offenders portrayed in, 12–13, 177; sex offenders' sanctions of, 6; sexualized teenagers in, 168
Megan's Law, New Jersey's, 2; antitherapeutic effects of, 170; community notification in, 114, 155; critique of, 5, 19, 164–165, 169–170; impact on sex offenders of, 6, 115; implementation of, 10; long-term effects of, 163–164, 170; and media attention, 155–156; offenders covered under, 152; offenders' views of, 133, 157; purpose of, 164; residence in, 89; significance of, 10; unintended consequences of, 117–118; and unsupervised children, 146
Meloy, M. L., 5
middle-class life, for convicted sex offenders, 101
Miller, Dennis, 12
Mills, C. W., 21
minor, constructing, 167–168
minors: consensual sex with, 38; Internet solicitation of, 5; offenses against, 5; sex abuse forcible touching of, 43
monitoring: beyond criminal sentence, 8; and offender's loneliness, 155; for social control, 153
monitoring devices, GPS, 4
monitoring system, national, 9
monster: construction of, 172; label of, 162; predatory, 171. *See also* other, dangerous
morality, of sex offenders, 122
moral panic, 7; "durable quality" of, 173; sociological questions about, 165

Moral Panic: Changing Concepts of Child Molester in Modern America (Jenkins), 8
motives, vocabularies of, 21
movies, sexualized teenagers in, 168
murderers, 13

"naming and shaming campaign," 12
narrative analysis: counternarratives in, 19; generalizability of, 16; role of gender in, 16; technique, 15–16
narratives: analytic, 47; counternarratives, 20, 21, 166; financial stress in, 31; of Internet offender, 30–37; self-reflective, 47; of serial offender, 69, 142; of sex offenders, 14; socially empathic, 30; of statutory offenders, 37–56, 110; stories, 20; techniques of neutralizations in, 64. *See also* accounts; stories
necrophilia, as heinous crime, 145
neighborhoods: harassment in, 116; middle-class, 114; negative impact of, 85–86; sense of belonging in, 78; and sex offenders' residency, 115
neutralizations, techniques of, 20–21
new penology, 1, 14, 88
New York State: retroactive requirements proposed in, 177; sex offenders registered in, 89–90
New York State Division of Criminal Justice Services, 89
New York State Sex Offender Registration Act. *See* SORA
notification: critique of, 171; impact of, 170; offenders' views of, 171; stress of, 156; unintended consequences of, 170

obsessive compulsive disorder (OCD), and serial offending, 61–62
offender, defined, 19

offenders: with AIDS, 151; community-dwelling, 5; cultural landscape of, 178; lived experience of, 5–6; policy impacts on, 6–7; recidivism of, 13; versions of truth of, 169. *See also* sex offenders
offenders, Internet, 30–37; community bonds for, 70–74; on dangerous other, 144–145; employment for, 101–102; housing for, 119–120; justification of, 33–35; passivity of, 33; probation for, 92–93
offenders, intrafamilial, 5, 22–30; and adolescent sexuality, 28; charges against, 24; community bonds for, 84–86; on dangerous other, 144–145; drug use of, 22, 23, 24–25; effects of social control on, 91–92; employment and, 108; justifications of, 42; loss of authority of, 24; loss of community for, 124–125; narratives of, 22–30; need for retaliation of, 25–26; probation for, 91–92; "real" self of, 140–141; religious conversion of, 22; roles threatened for, 27; sense of self of, 140–141; stepdaughter assaulted by, 22–23; victims seen by, 42; violation acknowledged by, 30
offenders, online, self-identified as victims, 37
offenders, registered, access to information about, 122
offenders, serial, 56–64; addiction of, 61–62, 63; community bonds of, 65; on dangerous other, 145; deferential treatment given to, 68–69; "double life" of, 134; employment for, 110–112; loss of community for, 112, 121–124; narratives of, 56–64, 69, 112, 142; OCD of, 61–62; probation for, 98–100; "real" self of,

offenders, serial (*continued*)
141–143; recidivism of, 172; sense of self of, 141–143; social identity of, 142; view of other group members of, 152–153

offenders, statutory, 127–131; adult/child dichotomy for, 40; blaming victim of, 45; boundary-threatening behavior of, 52–53; charges against, 38, 43; children of, 38, 42, 79–80, 81–82, 84; community bonds for, 74–78, 78–82, 82–84; on consensuality, 54; on dangerous other, 145–146; drug use of, 37–38; employment for, 102, 104–107, 109–110; fear of social recriminations of, 55; homosexual, 47–56; housing for, 115–119; justification of, 39; and loss of community, 125–131; marriage of, 42, 79; narratives of, 37–56; passive role of, 50, 51–53, 52; probation for, 93–97; "real" self of, 135–140; self-recrimination of, 44; sense of guilt of, 55; sense of self for, 135–140; social control of, 95

offense, construction of, 20–21; age awareness in, 40; definitions and meanings in, 47; with denial of responsibility, 41–42; as illness, 70; as imposition on identity, 136; for intrafamilial offender, 140; as lewd act, 140; as mistake, 46, 56, 80, 81, 139–140, 148; mistake *vs.* problem, 148–149; with offender as passive target, 32, 51–53; rationalizing, 166; situational approach, 48; and techniques of neutralization, 21; traveling in, 48; "wrongness" in, 54, 55

offenses: categorizing "statutory," 172; "hands off," 5; social ramifications from, 122; statutory, 4

Oliver, John (comedian), 173
ontological security, 91, 92, 93, 119
oral sex, arrest for, 52
other, dangerous: construction of, 149; critiquing sex offender policies for, 151–158; defining, 148; heinous crimes of, 146–151; offenders' construction of, 143–145, 171; protecting children from, 144–146; truly sick, 146–151
otherness, sense of, of offenders, 123–124
outcasts, sexual offenders as, 6
outsiders: adjusting to life as, 133; convicted sex offenders as, 170–171; in deviance studies, 64; serial offenders as, 58; sex offenders as, 6, 88, 120–121

paranoia, of convicted sex offenders, 3
parole, restrictions with, 90
partner role, for intrafamilial offender, 29
pedophiles: denial of identification as, 36; stereotype of, 130, 135
pedophilia, 117; criteria for, 13; as heinous crime, 145
penis, as deviant, 62
plea-bargaining, 169
police, insensitivity of, 104
politicians: and concept of child molester, 11–12; punishment practices supported by, 13; on recidivism, 13; and sexual abuse of children, 8
pornography, and study participants, 5. *See also* child pornography
power dynamic, for statutory offenders, 45, 46
powerlessness, sense of, 128; of convicted sex offenders, 158; of probation, 93, 94; of sex offenders, 159–160; of study participants, 32

predatory monster, offenders' views of, 171
prison, religious conversion in, 86
probation: arbitrariness of, 93–94, 159–160; conditions of, 4, 127–128; and feelings of powerlessness, 160; financial costs of, 93; for Internet offender, 92–93; for intrafamilial offender, 91–92; and job seeking, 106–107; lifetime, 159; restraints of, 92–93; restrictions with, 90; for serial offender, 98–100; for statutory offenders, 81, 93–95, 95–97; stress of, 156, 158–159; travel restrictions during, 97; unintended consequences of, 92
probation officers: assistance of, 132; home visits of, 3; and job seeking, 105–106; and neighborhood harassment, 116; random checks by, 94; relationship with, 128–129; research role of, 175; supportive, 38, 83, 137–138; unannounced inspections by, 96–97; unscheduled visits of, 96, 128
profession, and probation, 107
property values, concern about, 117
provider role, for intrafamilial offender, 29
public menace, sexual offenders as, 58
public opinion, on child molesters, 12. *See also* media; sex offender policies
public policies, concerning sex offenders, 164; and deviant selfhood, 16; impact on offenders of, 6–7; and lived experience, 5; sociological perspective on, 7. *See also* sex offender policies
punishment: arbitrary nature of, 160–161; and current policies, 156–157; house arrest as, 154–155; "invisible," 6; isolating aspect of, 154; lived experience of, 18; for middle-class whites, 68; in new penology, 2; and recidivism, 172; rituals of, 88
punitive measures: with community management, 153; offenders' support for, 151
Putnam, R. D., 100

rape: and dangerous other, 144; as heinous crime, 145; label of, 154
rape myths, in offenders' stories, 168–169
rape shield laws, national, 8
rationalizing behavior, 166–167
"real" self, of serial offenders, 141–143
recidivism, 12–14; of convicted sex offenders, 19; and house arrest, 154; likelihood of, 170; prevention of, 156; rate of, 171; risk for, 164
reciprocity, norms of, 66
recognition, for intrafamilial offender, 29
"reduced-rights zone," 11
registration laws: purpose of, 9; requirements of, 9
registration of sex offenders, 15; constraints of, 92; critique of, 171; impact of, 169–170; for intrafamilial offenders, 91; lifetime, 159; offenders' views of, 171; requirements of, 89; restrictions of, 91; sanctions associated with, 172; as "state of exception," 88; stress of, 156, 158; unintended consequences of, 117–118, 170
reintegration, barriers to, 7
rejection, of convicted sex offenders, 18
relationships: and age, 157; difficulties with, 7; managing tensions in, 84; serial offender's view of, 60; support of, 76–77

religion, sexuality and, 75
reoffending: likelihood of, 164. *See also* recidivism
research: finding participants, 175–176; interview sessions in, 176; and IRB, 176–177. *See also* study participants
researcher, role of, 177–178
residency restriction laws, 7, 115, 173
respectability: and community bonds, 67; for intrafamilial offender, 29
responsibility, acceptance of, of statutory offenders, 44–45
responsibility, denial of: of Internet offender, 32–33; of statutory offenders, 41
retaliation, need of offender for, 25
revenge, offender's need for, 27

sadness, of study participants, 42
salary, and probation, 107
sanctions against sex offenders, 6; impact of, 131; negative impacts of, 16; as social control, 88
sanctions against sexual harassment, 172
schools, and housing restrictions, 118
scientific perspectives, and public policy, 11
Scully, Diana, 17
seductivity, accounts of, 49–50
self: and community, 86–87; definition of, 122
self, sense of: for intrafamilial offender, 140–141; and labels for offenders, 6; "real" self, 134; role of community in, 133; for serial offender, 141–143; for statutory offenders, 135–140
self-acceptance, and spiritual community, 76
self-definition, 136
self-esteem: of convicted sex offenders, 3; of sex offenders, 7; source of, 83

self-hate, 75
selfhood, deviant, 14
self-orientations, 134
sentencing: and community bonds, 67; and current policies, 156–157; for middle-class whites, 68
sex crime, media representation of, 11
sex offender, label of, 105
sex offender policies, 6; consequences of, 88, 91; critique of, 134, 151–158, 171; current, 9–11; debate about, 165; evolution of, 1–2; frustrations with, 158–162; impact of, 6–7; mainstream opinions regarding, 133; offenders' views of, 171; overinclusiveness of, 152; recidivism and, 164; rehabilitation and, 170; in 1990s, 7; social consequences of, 156; state variations in, 160; study participants' views of, 134
Sex Offender Registration Act, New York State. *See* SORA
sex offenders: abandoned by law, 88; adjusting to life as, 133; categories of, 152, 153; collective experience of, 120; defined, 10; as felons, 6; and growing public concern, 156, 157; identity for, 14–15; labels for, 32–33, 169; legal status of, 11; Level I, 125; Level III, 120; loneliness of, 155; low recidivism rates of, 164; mainstream attitudes toward, 19; in media, 12–13; narratives of, 14; number of registered, 165; as outsiders, 64; powerlessness of, 15–160; public policy toward, 174; self-diagnosis of, 63; self-serving cognitive distortions of, 143; shared beliefs of, 178; social construction of, 7–8; and social control, 131–132; and society's values, 145; sociological perspective on, 16; stereotype of,

135; stigma of, 163; use of term, 5; vulnerability of, 7
sex offenders, convicted: constructing identity of, 174; coping strategies of, 162; employment for, 4; financial difficulties of, 101–102, 106; housing for, 114–120; laws and policies for, 129; lived experience of, 2; social stigma of, 15
sex offender treatment, mandated, 95. *See also* treatment
sex offenses: legislation cycles around, 8; society's values about, 162; therapy for, 60–61
Sex Panic and the Punitive State (Lancaster), 172
sex roles, stereotypes of, 60
sexual abuse: consequences of, 166; national concern about, 8
sexual aggressor, construction of victim as, 50–51
sexual assault, commonplace instances of, 13
sexuality, adolescent, and intrafamilal offenses, 27
"sexual predator," defining, 148
shame, sense of, 125, 126; of convicted sex offenders, 3; of sexual offenders, 6; of statutory offenders, 136, 137–138
shopping malls, sexual offenses in, 57
Shriner, Earl, 9
siblings of sex offenders: relationships with, 113–114; support of, 84
sickness, role of "conscience" in, 150
"sick stuff," offenders' view of, 146
Simon, Jonathan, 88
"situational withdrawal," 97
social bonds: and offender convictions, 89; severance of, 18; and sex offender policies, 171; for study participants, 17–18. *See also* community bonds
"social capital," 66
social control: apparatus for, 89; of convicted sex offenders, 18; house arrest as, 99; "monitoring" for, 153; power of, 120; role of punishment in, 161; and sense of powerlessness, 128; after September 11, 2001 attacks, 173; of sex offenders, 131–132, 162; of statutory offenders, 95
socialization process, in criminal justice system, 73
social rejection, possibility of, 119
social sciences, case studies in, 16
social self, and community, 86–87
social stigma, 65
social values, in offenders' narratives, 30
"social waste," 88
sociology, of deviance, 14, 16–17, 163
SORA (Sex Offender Registration Act), New York State, 89–90; employment and, 111; information available with, 90
Spencer, Dale, 99, 163
sports, for convicted offenders, 113
statutory charges, 5. *See also* offenders, statutory
stereotypes: offenders' views of, 171; of pedophiles, 130, 135; and public policy, 11; of sex offenders, 13, 135; of sex roles, 60
stigma: of convicted sex offenders, 165; "courtesy," 111; defined, 15; of double life, 111; dual, 110; effects of, 3–4; internalization of, 125, 130; and job seeking, 106; lived experience of, 15, 133; meaning ascribed to, 169; of new social identity, 132; self-stigmatization, 137–138;

stigma (*continued*)
  of sex offender, 163; and sex offender policies, 171; study participants' views of, 134
Stigma: Notes on the Management of Spoiled Identity (Goffman), 15
"sting operation," Internet, 31, 33, 35, 37
"stinking thinking," 25, 26, 29
stores, large, sexual offenses in, 57
stories: of convicted sex offenders, 174; defined, 20
stories, personal: sex offender policies in, 169–173; teenagers in, 167–168; truth *vs.* distortions in, 168–169; victims' perspective in, 166. *See also* narratives
stranger danger mentality, and law, 164. *See also* other
study participants: backgrounds of, 17; description of, 3–6; eye contact with, 22, 30, 56; finding, 175–176; Internet offenders, 30–37; intrafamilial offenders, 22–30; preanticipating risks to, 177; "real" self of, 133; serial offenders, 56–64; social bonds for, 17–18; statutory offenders, 37–56
surveillance: routine, 1; stress of, 156
surveillance videos, 69
Sykes, G. M., 20
symbolic interactionist perspective, 17

teacher, as statutory offender, 51–52
teacher-student relations, mainstream sanction against, 55
teenagers: and intrafamilial offenders, 28; in personal stories, 167–168; sexualized, 168
telephone: and isolation, 74; and social identity, 71. *See also* Internet
television: programs about sex offenders on, 8, 12, 125–126, 136; sexualized teenagers on, 168
threat to community, serial offenders as, 58
Timmendequas, Jesse, 10
To Catch a Predator (investigative reporting program), 12
"total institutions," 6
tracking devices, 129
travel, probation restrictions on, 97
treatment facilities, researching, 15
treatment groups: variety of offenders in, 146; weekly, 94
treatment programs: for statutory offenders, 81; stress of, 156
trust, abusing, in personal stories, 168
trustworthiness: imputation of, 67; norms of, 66
Turner, Ralph, 134

uncertainty, for convicted sex offenders, 128
unemployed, on house arrest, 100
unemployment, 18

values, in offenders' narratives, 30
victimization, responses to, 166
victims: and community notification, 165; construction of, 166; defined, 19; identification of offenders as, 37; labeling of, 169; role playing of, 167; sexualizing, 167; as sexually and socially knowledgeable, 49
victims' rights movement, 168, 173
video surveillance monitors, increased use of, 57–58
vigilantism: angry villagers episode, 117–118; in Maine, 177; neighborhood, 115
vigilantism justice, 7

violation, sexual, offenders' view of, 167–168
Violent Crime Control and Enforcement Act (1994), 9
violent offenders, 5
vulnerability, of sex offenders, 7

Washington State: Community Protection Act (1990) in, 9; sex offender legislation in, 9
waste: managing citizens as, 173; "social," 88
website, for New York State sex offenders, 90
Wilson, Gov. Pete, 12
wives of sex offenders, support of, 80–81, 85
women: negative feelings toward, 59; as researchers, 178

work: and community bonds, 71; and house arrest, 100; making meaning with, 82–83; and registration conditions, 92; and sense of belonging, 66; and sense of fulfillment, 67; social benefit from, 83; social identity expressed with, 18; and social status, 100; tolerance at, 71–72; white-collar, 68
working-class status, moving from middle-class to, 110
workplace, 100
wrongdoing, *vs.* harm, 166–167

"zero risk," 10
zero tolerance, 168
zero-tolerance punitive ideology, 151
Zilney, L. A., 13
Zilney, L. J., 13

About the Author

DIANA RICKARD received her PhD in sociology from the Graduate Center of the City University of New York. She is an assistant professor in the Criminal Justice Program at Borough of Manhattan Community College, CUNY.

AVAILABLE TITLES IN THE CRITICAL ISSUES IN CRIME AND SOCIETY SERIES:

Tammy L. Anderson, ed., *Neither Villain nor Victim: Empowerment and Agency among Women Substance Abusers*

Scott A. Bonn, *Mass Deception: Moral Panic and the U.S. War on Iraq*

Mary Bosworth and Jeanne Flavin, eds., *Race, Gender, and Punishment: From Colonialism to the War on Terror*

Loretta Capeheart and Dragan Milovanovic, *Social Justice: Theories, Issues, and Movements*

Walter S. DeKeseredy and Martin D. Schwartz, *Dangerous Exits: Escaping Abusive Relationships in Rural America*

Patricia E. Erickson and Steven K. Erickson, *Crime, Punishment, and Mental Illness: Law and the Behavioral Sciences in Conflict*

Luis A. Fernandez, *Policing Dissent: Social Control and the Anti-Globalization Movement*

Timothy R. Lauger, *Real Gangstas: Legitimacy, Reputation, and Violence in the Intergang Environment*

Michael J. Lynch, *Big Prisons, Big Dreams: Crime and the Failure of America's Penal System*

Raymond J. Michalowski and Ronald C. Kramer, eds., *State-Corporate Crime: Wrongdoing at the Intersection of Business and Government*

Susan L. Miller, *Victims as Offenders: The Paradox of Women's Violence in Relationships*

Torin Monahan, *Surveillance in the Time of Insecurity*

Torin Monahan and Rodolfo D. Torres, eds., *Schools under Surveillance: Cultures of Control in Public Education*

Leslie Paik, *Discretionary Justice: Looking Inside a Juvenile Drug Court*

Anthony M. Platt, *The Child Savers: The Invention of Delinquency*, 40th anniversary edition with an introduction and critical commentaries compiled by Miroslava Chávez-García

Joshua M. Price, *Prison and Social Death*

Diana Rickard, *Sex Offenders, Stigma, and Social Control*

Jeffrey Ian Ross, ed., *The Globalization of Supermax Prisons*

Dawn L. Rothe and Christopher W. Mullins, eds., *State Crime, Current Perspectives*

Susan F. Sharp, *Hidden Victims: The Effects of the Death Penalty on Families of the Accused*

Robert H. Tillman and Michael L. Indergaard, *Pump and Dump: The Rancid Rules of the New Economy*

Mariana Valverde, *Law and Order: Images, Meanings, Myths*

Michael Welch, *Crimes of Power and States of Impunity: The U.S. Response to Terror*

Michael Welch, *Scapegoats of September 11th: Hate Crimes and State Crimes in the War on Terror*

Saundra D. Westervelt and Kimberly J. Cook, *Life after Death Row: Exonerees' Search for Community and Identity*

CPSIA information can be obtained at www.ICGtesting.com
Printed in the USA
BVOW08*1053170716

455865BV00005B/7/P

9 780813 578293